STREETWISE

MOTIVATING & REWARDING EMPLOYEES

New and Better Ways to Inspire Your People

by Alexander Hiam

Adams Media Corporation
Avon, Massachusetts

Published by Adams Media Corporation
57 Littlefield Street, Avon, MA 02322. U.S.A.
www.adamsmedia.com

ISBN: 1-58062-130-9

Printed in the United States of America.

J I H G F E D

Library of Congress Cataloging-in-Publication Data
Hiam, Alexander.
Streetwise motivating and rewarding employees / by Alex Hiam.
p. cm.
Includes index.
ISBN 1-58062-130-9
1. Employee Motivation. I. Title.
HF5549.5.M63H5 1999
658.314–dc21 98-49361
CIP

DILBERT reprinted on page 130 by permission of United Feature Syndicate, Inc.
Photograph used on page 20, courtesy of ©1998 Ken Kipen Photography.
All other charts reproduced by permission of Alexander Hiam & Associates.
All other cartoons reproduced by permission of Alexander Hiam & Associates.

Illustration by Eric Mueller.

Contents

Contents

ACKNOWLEDGMENTS

I'm especially grateful to the many people and firms within the incentive and reward industry who have permitted me to question them and examine their products, services and philosophies. I learned a great deal from them. There are so many I cannot mention them all here, but any list would certainly include Joe Lethert of Performark, Inc., Bill Sims, Jr. of The Bill Sims Company, the researchers at Towers Perrin, BI Performance Services, Russell L. Campbell of Search Resources, and Anya Weisbrod and her associates at The Jack Morton Company. And others have shared their enthusiasm for the subject over the years too, including Bob Nelson, whose work has drawn much-deserved attention to employee rewards and incentives, and Ken Blanchard, who has been generous with his ideas. You will find some of his teachings on feedback and goal-setting are reflected in this book.

Richard Petronio of Surcon International made a major contribution to the project.

I'm also grateful to the many audiences who have encouraged me as I tested and refined my ideas, such as the members of the Polyurethane Manufacturers Association, who have stuck with me through an evolving series of presentations, to the U. Mass Family Business Center, whose members took a lively and helpful interest in my thesis that the manager's interpersonal style has hidden but powerful linkages to bottom-line financial performance, and to the many other audiences of managers and employees who have lent me their ears or participated in events, including the sales managers at GMAC.

This book was made possible by the commitment of Robert Linsenman, my literary agent, and Jere Calmes, my editor, and the "Streetwise" vision of Bob Adams. Thanks, guys.

I also am grateful to the many youth soccer teams who have honored me with the opportunity to coach them. I don't think the players have any idea how much I learned about motivation and management from them over the years. And I owe the biggest thanks to my family, who encouraged and motivated me through the most intense and challenging writing project of my life. Thanks!

Executive Summary

How to Motivate Employees

If you are impatient (and why not? there's lots to do in a day!), you may appreciate the following diagram. It is a visual summary of everything the book contains. It shows you in the most simplistic form what you must do to obtain sustained peak performances from your people. It is based on feedback–the scoreboards by which we all judge our own and others' performances. It shows your tasks in the left-hand set of boxes, and it shows the impact they have on employees in the right-hand set of boxes.

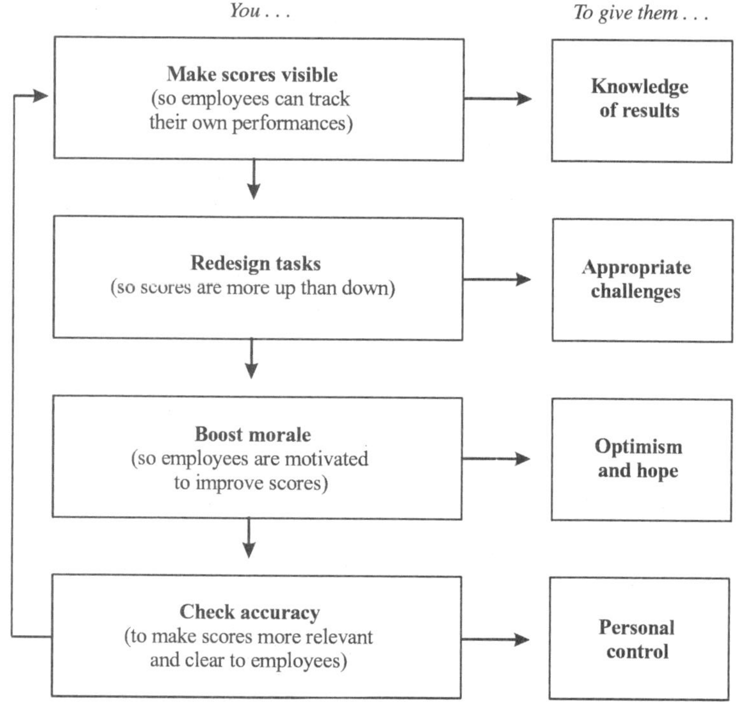

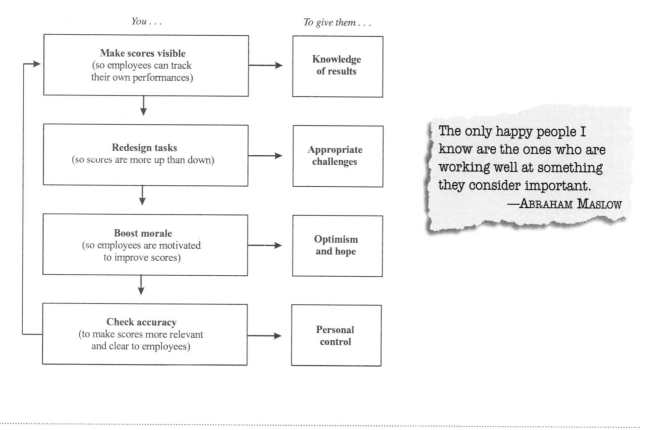

> The only happy people I know are the ones who are working well at something they consider important.
>
> —ABRAHAM MASLOW

He is well paid that is well satisfied.
—WILLIAM SHAKESPEARE

That's all you need do: make sure they have knowledge of the results of their work, appropriate challenges to pursue, optimism and hope to keep them enthusiastic about those challenges, and enough personal control to feel that they can rise to the challenges on their own initiative. See, motivation isn't that hard after all, is it?

How to Motivate a Problem Employee

Someone messing up? Giving you trouble? Try this! Instead of focusing on all their mess-ups, talk to them about what psychologists call exceptions–times when they did the job well or came in early instead of late. Mention and praise the *exceptions.* Ask them to just do whatever worked to create these exceptons again. "Problem" employees are viewed, and view themsleves, as the problem, when the problem is really the result of specific behaviors. They can and do get it right at least some of the time. Build on that!

Introduction

However good your people are, they could be a lot better. That's the gist of this book, and my goal in writing it is to show you how to achieve dramatically better performances from those you supervise or manage.

There is a great opportunity on the table, whether you run a huge multinational, a small department, or a tiny business, and whether you are profit oriented or pursue some social benefit. People are people, and the principles of motivating and rewarding great performances are universal.

Which leaves me deeply puzzled by the fact that most organizations do not manage their people in ways that bring out the best in them. Motivation is a problem in most organizations if you consider that the employees are capable of much more than they currently give.

Most organizations do not manage their people in ways that bring out the best in them.

Why? The answers are many and varied, and it takes the rest of this book for me to explore the subject fully. But there is a simple answer, too. It is that we manage in a command-and-control style that we have inherited through generations of tradition. Our standard approaches to managing others are oriented to compliance, not inspiration. And they've worked adequately for so long that most people never give those traditional methods much thought. Most people do not really examine the ways they relate to their employees or consider all the alternatives.

Which is fine, as long as you are happy with the current levels of performance. We get a decent level of performance out of people quite reliably. Even when our organizations downsize, replace benefited positions with temps, reengineer in ways that increase workloads, and require more time and effort from employees, we still get acceptable performances from our people. People have a strong desire to perform well, and do not feel good about themselves or their jobs when they don't. Nobody comes to work with the goal of doing a bad job (well, hardly anybody).

And there has been gradual progress in employee performance over the years. Average weekly hours worked by employees in the United States have risen about 3 percent in the last two decades, according to U.S. Bureau of Labor statistics, so people are working a little more than they used to. And if you look at productivity trends, you find that companies are getting more value out of an hour of work than they used to. In fact, when I plotted representative productivity and earnings data for the last few decades in the United States, I found that productivity is growing considerably faster than pay (when pay is measured on a "real" basis, which adjusts for inflation). The figure entitled Productivity and Compensation Trends illustrates this triumph of management quite clearly.

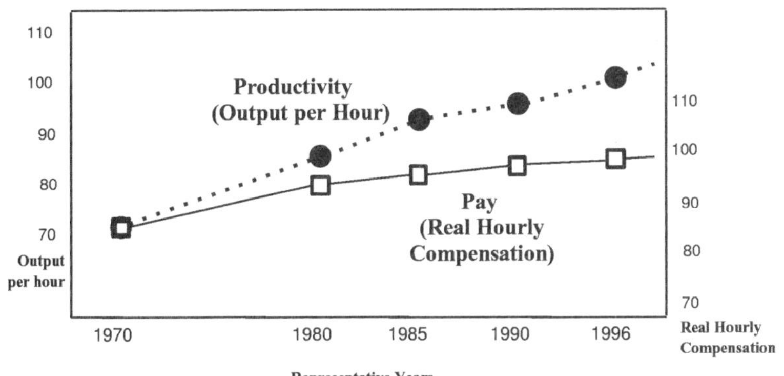

The vast majority of managers feel strongly that the people they supervise could be doing much better than they are.

But such statistics should not blind us to the possibility of achieving higher motivation and better performances in our organizations. The vast majority of managers feel strongly that the people they supervise could be doing much better than they are. They sense that employees are often just "putting in their time" but not "powered up" to their full level of intelligence or commitment. Managers see much more potential in their employees, and believe they should be able to achieve far more rapid and impressive performance than the gradual upward slope that graph represents. What's wrong?

We make slow progress because we are reaching the upper limits of our potential to motivate people *the way we currently do it.*

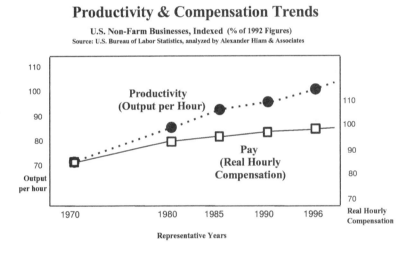

Balancing Work and Life at Amazon.com

There is a very real side to the virtual bookstore Amazon.com operates on the Web. At gigantic warehouses in Seattle and Delaware, scores of employees wrestle books off of trucks, into temporary storage on metal shelves, then into packages for shipment to customers. It takes a high level of organization and productivity to turn around orders as quickly as Amazon.com does, and each employee is well aware of the daily quota of books to be moved. This makes these distribution centers high-productivity workplaces in which employees need to be motivated and enthusiastic. So at first it might strike visitors as incongruous to see most of the employees wearing headphones. Why are they tuned in to their portable CD players instead of their work? Many managers would order those headphones removed except during breaks. But that would be a big mistake.

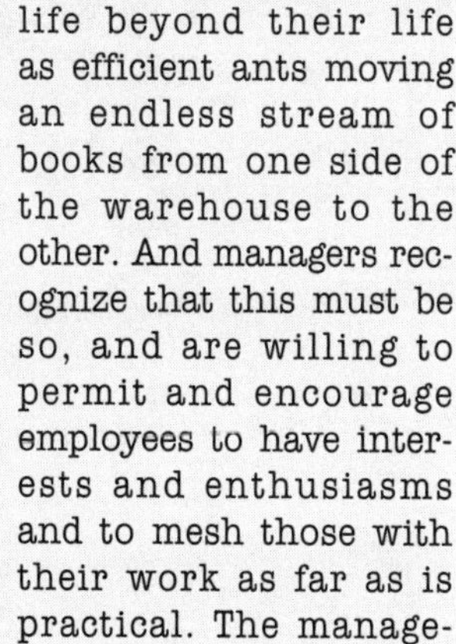

The headphones represent a considerate approach to the twenty-something workers who handle inventory. The work for Amazon.com is often just one part of their busy lives. In the Seattle distribution center, many work late or early shifts so as to leave time for a life in the arts. Many are enthusiastic musicians, actors, painters, or writers, and almost all are enthusiastic readers. They have a life beyond their life as efficient ants moving an endless stream of books from one side of the warehouse to the other. And managers recognize that this must be so, and are willing to permit and encourage employees to have interests and enthusiasms and to mesh those with their work as far as is practical. The management attitude shows respect for the workers and a willingness to let them exercise considerable control over at least the "listening environment" in which they work. And the workers inturn are more happy, motivated, and productive thanare most work forces performing routine, repetitive tasks. ■

MOTIVATION IDEA 1

Rewarding Each Individual's Performance

Maybe you routinely reward individual performance. If so, great. But in the majority of workplaces, teams and other groups are the basic unit when it comes to motivation and rewards. Which makes sense considering that much of the important work employees do is done in groups. Yet individuals really like their own performances to be recognized. According to a Society for Human Resource Management report on a study by Sibson and Company, U.S. workers want their rewards focused individually, and they feel a "deep, profound dissatisfaction with the way their performance is evaluated and rewarded." That's because many of them are not recognized for good performance. Many people feel they work in a partial vacuum, in which not even their direct supervisor understands or appreciates what they do.

So the obvious solution is to pay close attention to individual performances. To make it clear that you notice and care when someone puts in a good effort, takes on a new challenge, or overcomes a problem. Perhaps one team really deserves that big end-of-year reward. But most of the people on all of the teams deserve plenty of recognition for their individual contributions throughout the year. And according to the studies, that lower-key, more frequent, individual recognition is the real key to motivation. Treat each individual as if their performance is important, and they will feel their performances are important, too.

Our approach is not going to take us a lot farther because it runs counter to some of the basic principles of human nature. Our approach focuses on limiting the downside of human performance. It makes sure people show up. Makes sure they are focused on assigned tasks. Keeps an eye on them to prevent them from messing up or slipping away before they are done. Our approach focuses on the weaknesses of our people instead of their strengths.

As a result, motivation and rewards are used to push people up the hill, not to help them find hills they really want to climb. One of the important concepts this book explores is the distinction between motivation that wells up from within and motivation that is imposed from without. A reward can represent and amplify either kind of motivation. If your employees work for the reward, then it is the thing they are motivated by, and it is external, or *extrinsic* as psychologists say.

But if the reward recognizes and praises employees for doing what they want internally or *intrinsically* to do anyway, then it is a far more potent thing.

People want to do . . . what they want to do! It's that simple. If your people aren't working as hard and well as you know they can, the problem is they don't want to. You'll never break through to higher performance levels until you fix that problem. Until you get them doing what they want to do.

The good news, as you read this book, is that you don't have to change their jobs dramatically to create tasks that people are intrinsically motivated to perform. You need to change your own behavior to make sure they get plenty of the feedback they need to make those jobs challenging and rewarding for them. And you sometimes need to fiddle with the work environment or the way the job is structured or supervised, too. But such changes are modest and within every supervisor's reach. This is not a book about how to transform your company into some new sort of beast that the owners or customers would never support. It's simply about transforming the daily interactions with your people in small but powerful ways in order to help them achieve what they want anyway: engaging, engrossing work that they are intrinsically motivated to perform at peak levels.

This compelling vision of employees who want to work and are motivated by their own excitement about what they can accomplish is reminiscent of a recent finding from the field of sports psychology, as reported by the magazine *Psychology Today*:

> **Those who were "intrinsically motivated"–who played in order to understand the game, develop their skills, or accomplish a personal goal–could actually see better than those who played with a trophy or a championship in mind. Their vision was sharper and their reaction times quicker because the concentration crucial to acute vision is more available to those deeply immersed in an activity. Intrinsically motivated athletes are self-starters. They draw on the energy generated by their own goals and aspirations.**

A major study of 2,500 U.S. employees across the nation reveals that while workers believe they are contributing to their companies' record performance, they doubt that their hard work is being fully recognized or rewarded.
—JOSEPH CONWAY, TOWERS PERRIN

My goal is to make it clear that there is a better alternative

Too often, in sports, work, and life, we try to motivate with trophies and other external rewards. We ignore the consequences. We blind our own people to ambition. We control instead of inspiring. And that is why it feels like something is missing in the average workplace. It is. We are missing that spark of excitement and inspiration that is found wherever people are inspired to pursue excellence and do their best. And nobody does their best unless that is their purpose.

My goal in writing this book—and it was an inspiring one indeed—was to make it clear for supervisors and managers everywhere that there is another, better alternative to the one they've learned and used for many years. And I want to make that alternative readily available for those who wish to strive for it. If you become even half as excited as I am about the potential for your people, then you will have the motivation you need to join me on this exciting quest for high motivation in the workplace.

I can't promise you that it is a simple, overnight transition. But I can promise you that you can do it. It may take some study and effort, but heck, you are working every day anyway. Might as well work on something really rewarding and worthwhile!

And I can't think of anything more worthwhile than bringing out the true potential of your people. I think you will discover along the way that you have a great deal more potential than *you* have realized and utilized to date as well. So enjoy your quest. I'm glad to have you aboard.

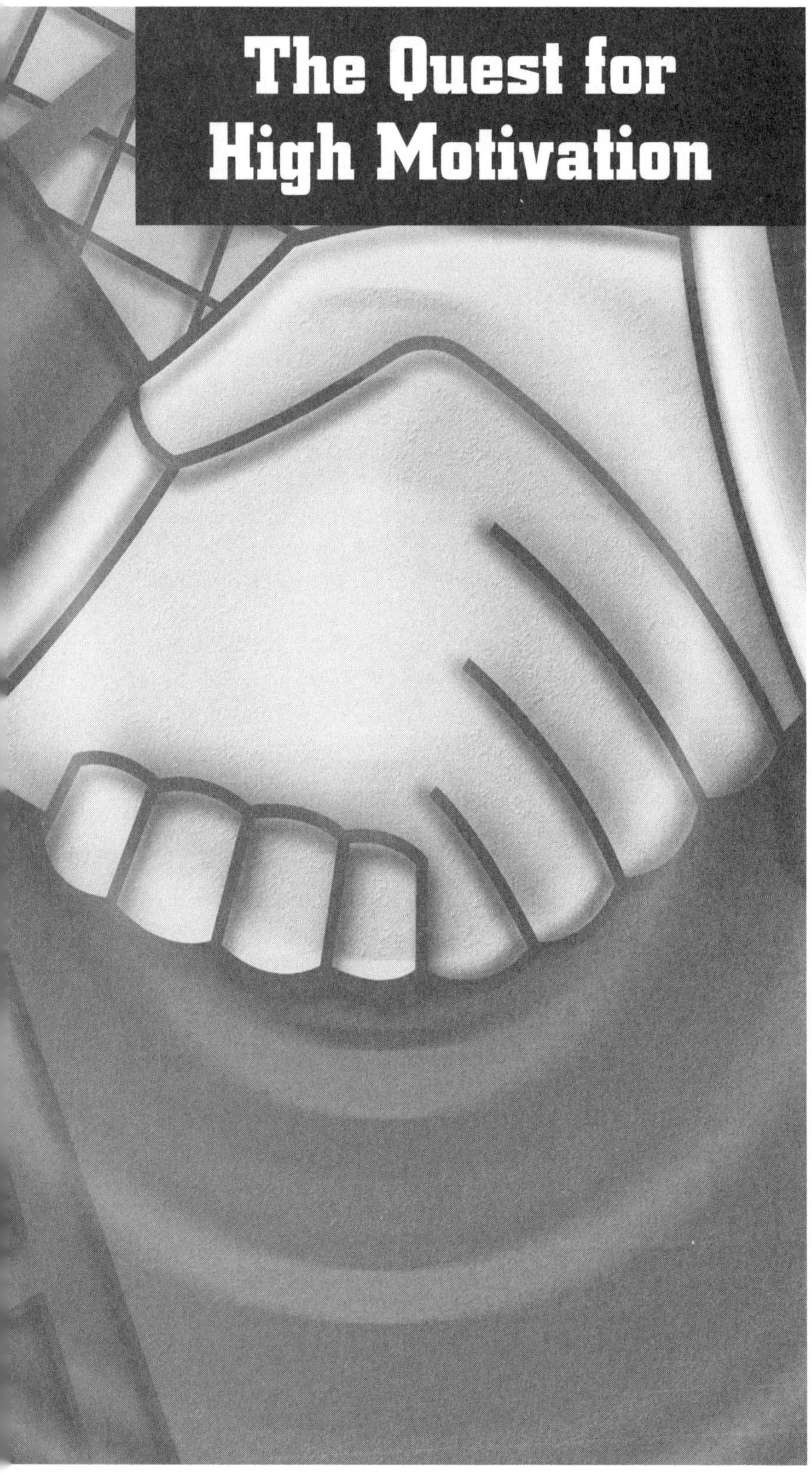

Chapter 1

> No matter how many ideas we try, it all comes back to people—their ideas, their motivation, their passion to win.
> —Jack Welch, General Electric

You want to motivate your employees. You want to say or do something that makes them perform better. And you are certain they *could* perform a whole lot better *if* they had more motivation.

You're right, of course. Most people perform far below their potential most of the time. And your quest for the right things to say or do is a sensible one. There are better strategies, many of which you'll find in the pages of this book.

You are not alone in seeing your challenge this way. Every manager senses the potential for higher motivation and better performances in his or her people. Every manager suffers from the same frustrations. And every manager wishes to motivate employees (or students, or children, or team members, or even pets). Why? Because:

> **Whenever we must accomplish our goals through others, their motivation is our greatest limiting factor.**

But if you are like most managers, you actually don't do a great deal about this employee motivation problem each and every day. You probably feel some frustrations about their motivation levels most days, but it is hard to find the time to research and try out new options in your busy schedule. It is all too easy to stick to the old routines and let your frustrations simmer on the back burner of your mind.

Even when you try something new, you may find the result disappointing, since the vast majority of incentive and reward schemes fail to create lasting improvements in motivation or performance. And that tends to discourage us from further experiments (although it ought instead to encourage us to admit our conventional approaches are flawed, as you will learn in the coming pages).

Let's start by reaffirming your instincts here. Your frustrations with your employees' level of motivation are right on target. Listen to that inner voice! Don't let lethargy, tradition, or frustration keep you from cracking the motivation nut.

Your gut says motivation is the key issue, and your gut is definitely right. Just because most managers do more grumbling than real fixing is no reason for you to push the motivation problem to the back corner of your desk.

In fact, if you'll follow your nose on this for one more minute, you'll soon discover that the motivation problem is a lot bigger than any of us likes to admit out loud. (That's the bad news. Fortunately, there is also good news because if you solve the motivation problem, a lot of other good things begin to happen almost as if by magic!)

"Average" Motivation Is Actually Quite Low

We are *used* to the average motivation level of employees in a typical workplace, so it seems reasonable to us. By long custom, supervisors create average expectations and employees more or less fill those expectations, and everything seems "normal," "okay," and "fine." ("How's it going in your department, Joe?" "It's okay. Everything's fine. How about you?")

But if you think more deeply about motivation, you'll agree with me that normal is not just fine. The reason is that:

> **People are capable of *far* higher motivation and performance levels than we see in the average workplace.**

I'll support that statement with evidence in a minute, although I think you probably agree with me once you see it written in black and white. And you no doubt "get" the implication of it, too: that the average workplace evidently does not motivate people to a large degree.

> It's amazing what people can do if they really try.
>
> —OLD-BUT-TRUE SAYING

And yet it took me a long time to come to these simple conclusions. In researching this book, I decided after talking with hundreds of people in conventional workplaces to "get out of the box" and search for peak motivation and performance levels wherever they could be found.

I wanted to recalibrate my sense of what true motivation looks and feels like. And I was sure I'd seen true motivation in many contexts, in fact, wherever people strive for things they believe in and wish to accomplish. So I went farther than the typical companies of the consultant/trainer beat. I looked for highly motivated people everywhere and anywhere, and I found them on sports fields, in medics' uniforms on the field of battle, in ministries, and in the lonely struggle of the eager entrepreneur. I found them in places like:

I'd hate to see all that youthful enthusiasm and commitment give way to the average employee's punch-the-clock mentality.

- The collectively owned copy shop on the ground floor of my office building, where the employee-owners cheerfully work long days and nights, and always go the extra mile to satisfy their customers, while managing to make enough extra money to set 10 percent of all their profits aside for local charities.
- The members of the youth soccer teams I've coached who voluntarily work themselves to exhaustion for zero compensation. They taught me the true value of motivation by showing me that when I built commitment to the sport and the team and gave them lots of positive feedback and learning opportunities, they would transform themselves from bumbling beginners to league winners in the course of a single season. I hope they'll still be able to teach that lesson when they grow up and go to work for some manager who hasn't learned it yet because I'd hate to see all that youthful enthusiasm and commitment give way to the average employee's punch-the-clock mentality.
- A photographer whose work I admire (one of his photos is in this chapter) who, like most artists, works entirely on his own, often photographing from early in the morning to sunset, and then logs long, difficult hours in the darkroom, in order to prepare for an exhibition or deliver new prints to one of his galleries. Not only do artists do tougher work for longer hours than any employee could legally be required to do, but they continually struggle to perfect their art. And all this with no one to supervise, motivate, or reward them but their own desire to create great art.
- The amateur mountain climbers and triathletes who spend many hours before or after work each day training for their sport. As I write this book, I'm sitting in a turret office in an old summer house in Woods Hole, Massachusetts, and there is a steady stream of runners passing by my window at all hours of the day. They are training for the Falmouth Road

Race, which starts a couple of miles from here and is a high point of the summer in these parts. So all I have to do is look up from my pile of papers to see what true motivation looks like. Tens of thousands of ordinary employees and managers train all spring, then plan their vacation time to compete in this race. How many of them display the same level of dedication and commitment to their work? Some, I'm sure, but certainly not the majority. I'll bet many of them sneak time away from the office if they can to spend more time on training. Some are no doubt "out sick" today so they can get here early to practice on the course.

- The foster parents who adopt a dozen homeless children just because it feels like the right thing to do. Well, I know what's right, too, but I sometimes have a hard time doing it. (For example, I struggle to find the money in my large household's budget to make substantial donations to charities. I can't imagine how we could take on many more children, but somehow people do.)
- The volunteers who rush to a disaster area to give aid to the victims. I remember when Hurricane Bob smashed into Cape Cod a few years ago and devastated the towns of Woods Hole and Falmouth. We were without water or power for quite a while, and I was amazed to learn that utility workers from other states had volunteered to come to our communities and get our power lines up and running again. They were staying in makeshift shelters and working round the clock to do a job that they probably took far less seriously under more normal circumstances, when there wasn't a disaster to motivate them. What makes it a job on some days and a calling on others?

> There are times when you can inspire people, but motivation, the reason to act, comes from within.
> —BARRETT JOYNER, SALES V.P., SAS

All these people exhibit remarkably high motivation levels. They sustain a high level of motivation and achieve performance peak after performance peak in spite of (or perhaps because of) the lack of traditional supervision and rewards.

Nobody tells them to do it. Often nobody even pays them for doing it. Most remarkably, nobody offers them special rewards or incentives in order to induce them to do it. Sure, a "thanks," a "good job," or an occasional trophy help. But the motivation is independent of these external factors. It bubbles up from within.

Far from having to make these people perform, you simply need to let them perform. You probably couldn't stop them from performing if you tried! The opportunity they pursue is so personally compelling that they are highly self-motivated. If only people could be so motivated in the work they do for you. (And they can! In this book, we'll explore the secret of achieving true motivation. Stay tuned.)

I've never worked so hard in all my life for so little pay. And I loved every minute of it!
—PEACE CORPS VOLUNTEER

The Dark Side of Motivation

My research also led me to another, more sobering example of high motivation. Inexpensive freight transportation has made it easy to subcontract manufacturing abroad, and as an unfortunate result, abusive labor conditions involving lock-downs, captive workers, child labor, and unsafe working conditions are increasingly common in many countries. According to the experts at Verité, a nonprofit that inspects overseas factories for U.S. companies, the odds are good that one or more of the articles of clothing you now wear was made under inhuman working conditions for just pennies an hour.

In these sweatshops, employees work twice as long hours as your employees do, typically in work spaces that are dirty, excessively loud, and poorly lit. And they endure much higher injury and death rates, in exchange for roughly a hundredth of your workers' pay. Sometimes they aren't paid at all. In such circumstances, doing even an adequate job is a remarkable thing.

How can they sustain motivation under such extremely unrewarding conditions? Because they face severe threats. Living in poverty, they may have no other options for supporting themselves and their families. And once caught up in an abusive job situation, they are fearful of the consequences of resistance. Many of these factories are patrolled by heavily armed guards; beatings by supervisors are common; and even access to water, food, and bathrooms may be withheld.

Under such threatening conditions, survival is a highly motivating proposition. People will do amazing things when their backs are against the wall. If you doubt this, talk to a mugger about motivation. Muggers can get you to do something you don't want to do, and you pay them instead of the other way around! To a mugger, motivation is as simple as a shiny gun displayed near someone's torso, along with some variant of that magically motivating phrase, "your money or your life."

If you wish to truly understand motivation, you must consider the full range of situations in which people are highly motivated. And some of those situations are ones in which extreme coercion is applied, and people are motivated by the desire to survive, rather than the desire to succeed. Although you obviously don't intend to apply this lesson directly to your people, there is still much to be learned from it. For starters, I'm sure you noticed, as I did, that the strongest levels of motivation come from within, whether they are based on the desire to succeed or to simply survive.

Rethinking Motivation

And so my search for the extremes of motivation led me to redefine the motivation spectrum. It led me to see that high motivation is commonplace where there is either great opportunity or great threat. People rise to either occasion, but are typically less motivated between these extremes, as Figure 1-1 illustrates.

> With my 30 years of personal management experience it has become clear that people have to motivate themselves.
> —DAN ECKERT

Yet the average workplace is about midway between the extremes of high threat and high opportunity, as shown in the figure. The personal stakes are relatively low. The threats are nothing like those imposed by a mugger or a sweatshop boss. Unless your company is faced with a major disaster, there is no way you can create survival threats sufficient to sustain a very high level of motivation, even if you wanted to. And you don't. We all know motivation by threat is a dead-end strategy, and we are naturally more attracted to the opportunity side of the motivation curve than the threat side.

Yet it is also an unfortunate truth that most supervisors make casual use of threats, forgetting that they do not have, or want, the coercive power to motivate by fear alone. Threats, of course, move people toward the survival side of the motivation curve, which moves

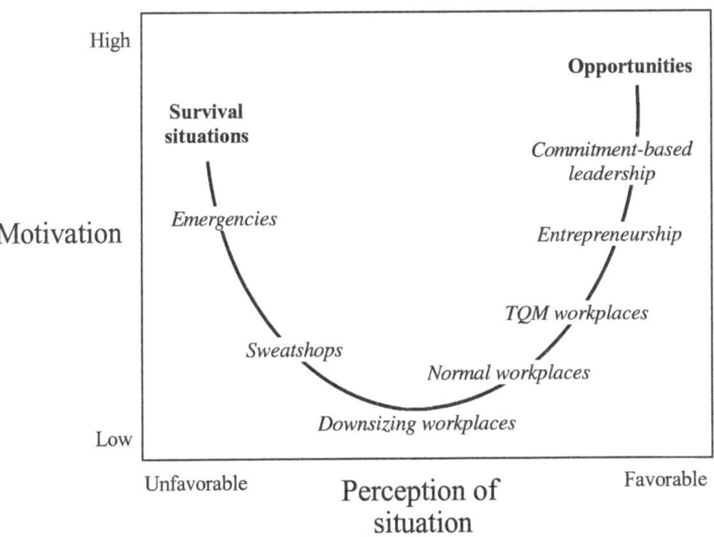

Figure 1-1

them away from the opportunity side. So threats tend to move people away from the high motivation of genuine opportunities. Yet they generally fail to move them up the survival side of the motivation curve sufficiently to create high fear-based motivation. So threats are generally counterproductive. In fact, we can state as a general rule that, in any civilized workplace:

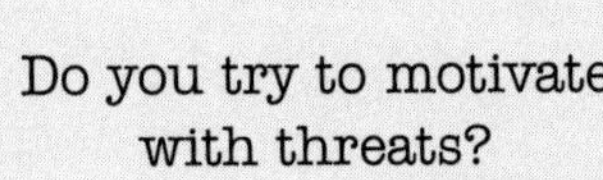

Threats are always demotivating.

Do you use threats in a misguided effort to motivate your employees? Of course not! Threats are not nice, and you see yourself as a fundamentally nice person (and I bet you are right). Most managers say they never or rarely use threats.

But *most employees say their supervisors do hold threats over them on a routine basis.* Most employees feel that their bosses use their power to withhold opportunities and rewards and on occasion to actively punish and do harm. In my work, I've interviewed and surveyed thousands of employees in all sorts of organizations, big and small, and I'm willing to bet that your employees are convinced that you use threats to try to coerce them into doing what you want.

And if your employees think you use threats, then you do. What matters in motivating (or trying to motivate) people is what they perceive. Their understanding of the situation drives their behavior, so your understanding of the situation is really quite irrelevant.

You need to "get into their heads" and understand how they see you so you can manage the impression you make, not just your intentions! Ken Blanchard, a wonderful trainer who says his goal is "to take the B.S. out of behavioral science," often tells audiences that "motivation is a six inch job. It all comes down to the space between your ears." Then he holds his hands up to his ears to demonstrate that it's what people hear and what they think of it that matters. Anything outside the space between the ears is superfluous!

And the truth is that most people hear the following comments and actions as *threats*:

Employees feel their bosses use threats to coerce them, even when the boss denies it.

- Annual performance reviews in which the supervisor tells them what they did wrong, and also how much of a raise they will or won't get. The link between the manager's judgment of long-past events and the manager's control over compensation is powerful in employees' minds, so formal performance reviews are actually the worst place to review performance. Many managers sense this and tend to overreport performance so as to minimize the "damage" their people feel from the reviews. Then companies say they have a problem because managers won't report employee performance accurately enough. Well, believe me, it's a much bigger problem than that. And it's called threat-based management.
- Cash rewards and incentives in which managers have control over the allocation of the rewards, whether based on individual supervisor judgment or committee. Often employees focus on who *didn't* get the rewards (the majority don't after all). And they may feel there is a veiled threat of withholding rewards from those who don't "kiss ass" and "suck up to" their supervisors. It is sad but true that employees will often

view a well-intentioned reward program in this contrary and negative light.

- Bonus programs often degenerate into threat-based motivation, too. When employees see it as a case of "If you don't do X, you won't get a bonus," then it's a threat, not a reward. And that is what happens all too often because employees come to see bonuses as their due, not as something out of the ordinary. And when management withholds something you feel you are due, that pushes you down and away from the positive side of the motivation curve.
- Supervisors sometimes say things like, "If you don't get this project on track by the end of the month, I don't know what I'm going to say to the V.P. You know they're looking for ways to cut the payroll." But is this a genuine sharing of vital information, or just a veiled threat of downsizing? Most employees will take it as a threat and feel angry or resentful rather than motivated.

Most employees will take it as a threat and feel angry or resentful rather than motivated.

- Whenever decisions are "handed down" from on high, those affected by them tend to see them as attacks. Lacking access to the dialog behind the decisions, they immediately worry about the personal impact of those decisions. Arbitrary, apparently random, and heartless changes reduce one's sense of control and create resistance and fear. The result is the exact opposite of the optimism and hopefulness that characterizes the truly motivated individual. Every time somebody makes a decree, everybody else feels threatened by their raw use of power. And the result is demotivating instead of motivating, as are threats in general.
- When a supervisor loses his or her temper at a "difficult" employee, he or she usually resorts to direct personal threats. "This will go in your file." "I'm keeping track of the number of days you've been late this month." "That's grounds for dismissal." These are direct personal threats, of course, and even the supervisor giving them perceives them as threatening and negative. So if we see them that way, and we know the employee does, it shouldn't be hard to kick the habit. But does that mean you have to be a pushover? Not a

> bit of it. The ultimate sign of strength is to make no threats and to take firm, appropriate action only when necessary. If someone really messes up, just make the proper note of it for his or her file. But never threaten to do so! Then, if your positive approach to motivation (the one I *know* you'll have by the end of this book) brings your employee around, you can make a note of that improvement for his or her file, too.

So please rethink your own behavior as a supervisor in order to ferret out any unintentional or intentional uses of threats. Threats don't motivate. Opportunities do. Move them toward the positive side of the motivation curve, not the negative side please! All threats do is create distrust and fear.

Threats don't motivate. Opportunities do.

Are They Afraid of You?

I've often slipped a few questions into employee surveys to find out if they fear their managers. And guess what? They usually do. Distrust and fear are in fact the norm in traditional workplaces. The same workplaces where managers keep trying motivation programs, and keep complaining that the programs are no darn good.

Oh, I know what you are thinking. You are thinking that a good spanking used to be considered healthy for a child. Or that the "real world" is tough and you have to be, too. Maybe you've read an interview with one of those tough-ass execs like "Chainsaw" Al Dunlap, whose plan for Coleman when Sunbeam acquired it (according to a *Wall Street Journal* article of August 19, 1998) was to "start whacking people." Well, just remember that you can't find examples of highly motivated people in negative, threat-driven environments. Not unless you are willing to go all the way to survival issues, like a sweatshop or a mugging. And even then, compliance is the best result you can hope for, not personal development and excellent performances. Threats are no substitute for true positive motivation.

By the way, Al Dunlap was fired by his own board shortly after he made that comment about whacking people. His threats cost a lot of people their jobs, including many of the best who quit because they couldn't stand working for him. But threats failed to produce

Weed out trouble makers right away, because they're like a cancer and if you don't, they'll grow back.

—AL DUNLAP, EX-PRESIDENT OF SUNBEAM

the performances Sunbeam and Coleman needed to succeed in the marketplace. So I guess Chainsaw Al taught us a valuable lesson about management after all.

Unlike self-proclaimed tough guys like Dunlap, you probably make only casual, even accidental, use of threats. You probably follow your more sensible instincts and focus on the positive side of the motivation curve much of the time. But what happens when you send mixed signals, some positive, some negative? You get an average at best–in general, negatives outweigh positives about four to one in terms of their emotional impact. So the occasional threat can undo a lot of positive efforts. And when you cancel out, you end up in the middle, which is the *lowest* part of the motivation curve. Oops.

Moving Up the Motivation Curve

If you focus on the opportunity side of the motivation curve in Figure 1-1, you can think of your challenge as moving your people up the curve, toward higher levels of opportunity.

You know that people who are pursuing compelling personal opportunities are highly motivated. So "all" you must do to break through to higher levels of motivation is to *increase the opportunities for your people.* (That is in fact easier said than done until you learn new approaches to management, which is why there is more than one chapter in this book. But it isn't nearly as hard as motivating them any other way since it actually works and other methods don't.)

We do not walk on our legs, but on our will.

—SUFI PROVERB

If you stop thinking about it as a motivation problem, and start thinking of it as *an opportunity problem*, you will theoretically be able to bring employee motivation and performance levels to the extremes you see in special circumstances, but so rarely see in your own work force. As you develop creative ways to put this theory into practice, you will be surprised at the amount of natural, internal motivation you release in your employees. To help you implement this theory, I've sprinkled motivation idea boxes like the following one throughout the book. And you will also find that later chapters explore different aspects of implementation in detail.

The concept that we can motivate people to their highest levels of potential by presenting them with opportunities to succeed instead of telling them what to do is a theory I arrived at after researching and working on motivation for many years, and I have subsequently been able to find compelling examples of its validity, and to collect and develop lots of practical ways to put it to use. When I realized that none of the so-called employee motivation programs could motivate people as well as an opportunity to succeed at something they cared about, I stopped looking for external "motivators" and began to seek ways of "turning on" people's natural internal motivation to succeed. (It's interesting that the word *motivator* isn't even in many dictionaries.)

In truth, there is no such thing as a motivator. You can't just apply the right treatment and "get" employee motivation, as if you were doing some chemistry experiment. People who are highly motivated are self-motivated. Period. They have a strong will to achieve, to succeed, to learn, to perform. External factors are insignificant in comparison with internal motivation to succeed. Impose external threats *or* incentives in too heavy-handed a manner, and these self-motivated people will lose their strong commitment and become as careless as the rest.

Why People Think They Need New Careers

As Edward Deming, the father of modern quality management methods, was fond of saying, nobody goes to work to do a bad job. And, I might add, people don't go to work to do a mediocre job either. Doing a bad job makes people feel bad. It's demotivating. It leaves you feeling that your work was a meaningless exercise in pushing paper or punching the time clock. It makes you feel that life is passing you by.

But the truth is that, in the typical workplace, people are doing something far short of a great job. They are not performing anywhere near their potential. They are not reaping that most compelling of all rewards, the satisfaction in a job well done.

MOTIVATION IDEA 2

The Measure of Their Success

Teach employees to measure and track their own performances using charts or graphs. (Basic techniques from statistical process control or total quality management can be applied if you wish.) For instance, if a hotel wishes to encourage employees to thank customers by name, then create a chart with number of thank-yous-by-name plotted by day for the month. Then give employees a pocket version of it and a pen to add ticks as they work. Or a counter to stick in their pocket and click each time they do it right. You can even have prizes or awards they earn when they reach certain milestones. And you can allow them to present their graphs to collect the prizes.

Benefits. Shows a high level of trust in their honesty and responsibility. (Whether you really trust them or not, they will become more trustworthy because you communicated trust to them.) Teaches them to monitor their own behavior. Increases sense of self-control, which leads to internal (intrinsic) motivation, the most powerful kind. Raises self-awareness of performance. And highlights a performance goal at least as effectively as conventional management-controlled rewards or measures.

It is not our nature to un-excel. We don't even have words in our language for the opposites of words like *motivation, potential, excel,* and *excellence*. That's not a place we want to go. Who'd bother getting up in the morning if his or her goal was to "mess up" or "blow it" or "perform well below my potential"? Yet we've just agreed that that is what many employees are doing. We've just agreed that the typical workplace keeps people in the unrewarding middle of the motivation curve. We've just agreed we have a motivation problem.

> One of the greatest diseases is to be nobody to anybody.
> —MOTHER TERESA

And if it's a problem for managers, believe me, it's a far greater problem for employees.

I have an interesting perspective on employee motivation because I wrote a little book called *Adventure Careers* many years ago with an adventurous friend. We interviewed people who were doing really amazing and different things with their lives. Then we told their stories to "the rest of us" in the book.

I've written a lot of books over the years, but I've never gotten as strong, as many, or as emotional reactions as I did from that little book. At book signings, people followed me around as though I were their guru, begging me to help them figure out what to do. And people continue to send letters requesting help or effusively thanking me for inspiring them to transform their lives. Why? What nerve did we touch, and why is it so amazingly sensitive?

The common theme in every one of the many and varied personal stories I heard was a quiet sense of desperation. People feel trapped in dead-end lives, even if their careers appear to be on track. Their work simply is not fulfilling. It's a job, not a calling. It pays the bills, but who wants to live for bills? It gives them some small successes, but it never allows them to truly spread their wings and find out what they are fully capable of doing. And it keeps them busy, but they often feel that it does little or nothing to improve the world or benefit anyone else. In short, their work is meaningless.

And you would be amazed at the people who echo this refrain. Many of them hold jobs others would die for. I remember being interviewed by a successful, grossly overpaid host of a television show who confided to me during a commercial break that he wished he could have an adventure career but was too afraid to quit and start all over again in some new field.

I told him that hosting a TV show is one of the most popular "fantasy" careers for Americans. But he just shook his head and said, "not after you've done it a thousand times."

In a sense, jobs are like relationships. Once the blush is off the rose, once the honeymoon is over, it is easy to fall into boredom and dissatisfaction unless you make a real effort to grow the relationship and develop it into something that is constantly new and rewarding.

But most people's jobs don't offer them that kind of development path. Most jobs are emotional dead ends. Most workplaces keep people in the dull middle of their motivation curve. Where you soon long for adventure and worry that your life is becoming a meaningless routine.

Most jobs are emotional dead ends.

Since their employers don't give them the opportunity to move up the curve, employees seek their own opportunities. They naturally need to find meaning in their work and lives, to seek a calling, to increase their value to society. But the workplace stifles these healthy urges. So they desperately seek other avenues of growth.

That's why so many people came to my book signings when I wrote *Adventure Careers*. But for many of them, a radical new direction in life was economically risky and difficult to undertake. A far more practical and simple approach is to make their current job more meaningful and challenging. Why should people feel trapped in their jobs? Why should they have to "give it all up" and start all over again in order to find the challenge and meaning their work fails to provide? A far better solution to their problems is to help them move up the motivation curve in their current work.

And you know what? Giving people meaningful adventures in their current jobs is not some soft-hearted exercise in spoiling your employees. Nor is it an expensive perk or special benefit. It is the simplest and least expensive way to get them moving up that motivation curve. The solution to their problem is the solution to your problem, too.

> The most powerful reward of all is satisfaction in a job well done. And it's absolutely free!
> —ANONYMOUS

The Psychology of Optimal Experiences

It is sometimes hard to understand why one task or activity is highly motivating and rewarding for a person and another isn't. Why does your employee find it boring to do that project you really need her to do? Why doesn't it turn her on, no matter how hard you try to get her excited and motivated? Until we get good at understanding why certain activities are intrinsically appealing, it is hard to match people with the right opportunities to keep them motivated.

And one very good answer to this question comes from the work of psychologists who study what is termed *optimal experiences,* or experiences where people are totally caught up in what they are doing, wholly focused on it, and able to perform at a very high level with ease. The condition is also termed *flow,* and you want your people to experience flow because it is an excellent indicator that they are properly prepared for and aligned with the right activities to make them highly motivated.

The easiest way for me to explain flow is to describe my own experience of it. When I write, it's a flow experience. When you do, it probably isn't, since writing for most people is a difficult chore. But when I sit down to write, my mind clears itself of extraneous thoughts and worries. (I'm writing right now with a huge pile of unopened bills next to me, and it doesn't bother me in the least!) My thoughts bubble up eagerly, and my hands fly over the paper or the keyboard. I feel a sense of exhilaration and pleasure when the writing goes well. It's hard work, sure, but I can sustain it for many hours without a break because it just flows and carries me along with it. As a result, I am a very productive writer–people are often surprised by the amount of work I do. But I don't feel worn out by my writing. In fact, it gives me energy. And I sometimes experience flow in other situations, too. When I'm giving a presentation or when I'm doing my favorite sports, for example.

Your optimal experiences are probably different ones from mine, but they nonetheless *feel* the same. Golf is torture for me and I'm terrible at it. But when I watch Tiger Woods play I can tell it just flows for him, as writing does for me. I know how he must feel when he plays, and I know that he couldn't have achieved such mastery without first learning how to make golf into a flow experience.

Interestingly, psychologists have discovered that the pleasures of these optimal experiences are sufficiently great that most people describe themselves as more happy when in the flow state than when relaxing or hanging out. When we look back on our lives, the times we remember most fondly are by and large these optimal performances in which we were experiencing flow. In other words, life's peaks coincide with periods of peak motivation as well. Please read the quote in the margin to see how a leading researcher explains it.

Children instinctively understand this point, without the need for a psychologist to tell them. They constantly badger their parents with the complaint, "I'm bored. I don't have anything to do." Of course, they do have many things they could do, but they need a little help getting involved in the right activity so that they can "get in the groove" of another flow experience. Csikzentmihalyi points out that optimal experience is "something that we make happen," and observes that, "For a child, it could be placing with trembling fingers the last block on a tower she has built."

Parents rarely appreciate the need to help children make these optimal experiences happen. They take the "I'm bored" comment too literally, and simply offer any old alternative instead of creating the next optimal experience. The truly great teachers, on the other hand, are keenly aware of the distinction between a generic activity and a truly engaging, optimal one, and they are able to transform a rowdy classroom into a productive one just by offering the right activities.

The motivational manager would do well to make a study of optimal experiences. What things catch people up and keep them engaged and alert? What things don't? Do you need to increase or reduce the level of challenge to make something more optimal? Or is it that the activity doesn't seem important? Or is it that the feedback about personal performances is too unclear to make it engaging?

These helpful questions are actually formalized in a method for leading people to high motivation called commitment-based leadership. I'll show you a detailed method for designing tasks and managing performances that increases the amount of flow in your

> Contrary to what we usually believe, the best moments in our lives are not the passive, receptive, relaxing times—although such experiences can also be enjoyable, if we have worked hard to attain them. The best moments usually occur when a person's body or mind is stretched to its limits in a voluntary effort to accomplish something difficult and worthwhile.
>
> —MIHALY CSIKZENTMIHALYI (IN *FLOW: THE PSYCHOLOGY OF OPTIMAL EXPERIENCE*)

workplace in later chapters, when I introduce you to the commitment-based leadership model. But a general sensitivity to the flow issue will stand you in good stead whether you adopt that specific methodology or not.

And it is vital to remember that, when people move up the motivation curve, it is generally by becoming highly engaged in their work. High motivation produces, and is produced by, flow experiences.

Parting Shots

In this chapter, I've shared an exciting new perspective on motivation and encouraged you to go with your instincts and treat your current level of employee motivation as the beginning of a journey, not the middle or end. I've shared my own quest for a deeper understanding of what motivation is really about. This quest for motivation reveals a number of essential insights for all who wish to achieve higher employee motivation and performance levels.

Work is far less meaningful and rewarding than it ought to be.

First, it reveals that we as a species are capable of amazing feats of endurance, commitment, and determination, and that these often take place outside the traditional structures of the workplace. Though we can truly "walk on our will" instead of our feet as the saying goes, we rarely do so at work. And as a result, work is far less meaningful and rewarding than it ought to be. It is no wonder most supervisors and managers are frustrated with the levels of motivation their people display. And it is no wonder that so many people report they are dissatisfied with their work and seek new adventures and alternatives. As Deming said, we don't go to work to do a bad job. So when work leads us to do anything but our best, we feel bad somewhere deep inside.

Second, our quest for motivation reveals that the truly motivated people are moved far more from within than from without. Yet most workplace approaches to motivation seem to use external influences, from compensation and benefits to incentive and reward programs, to try to motivate people.

Third, it reveals that when people are pursuing compelling opportunities, they behave very differently from when they are just "doing their work." It is no longer a job when you are excited about the potential opportunities it represents, whether they are opportunities to accomplish personal goals or to do something for the good of others (and in the highest levels of motivation, these two coincide).

Fourth, it reveals that the work is its own greatest reward when you are pursuing a compelling goal and are able to perform "in the flow" by becoming totally absorbed in your task. People who regularly work in this optimal state are far more motivated, enthusiastic, and healthy than those who don't. Yet we are not particularly good at creating these flow experiences that make work intrinsically motivating and enjoyable to do.

Work is its own greatest reward when you are pursuing a compelling goal and are able to perform "in the flow" by becoming totally absorbed in your task.

And fifth, it reveals that we are all naturally inclined to pursue higher levels of motivation. *The motivation curve calls to all of us.* And when work fails to satisfy this natural urge, we feel trapped and defeated and fantasize about finding something new and better to do with our days. But this is simply the employee's side of the motivation problem. Employee and manager alike benefit from any efforts to move employees up their motivation curves. It's a "win-win" solution and a natural one that all of us are eager and able to pursue once we recognize the wisdom of this positive approach to motivation.

What Does True Motivation *Look* Like?

I want to end this first chapter with something special. It's a photograph, a photograph by a noted photographer who has generously permitted me to reproduce it for your use (see Figure 1-2).

Now, the interesting thing about this photograph is that it is, to my eye, the perfect illustration of internal motivation in its strongest, most natural form. I bet it reminds you of moments in your life, perhaps in childhood, when you were so completely caught up in the joy and excitement of what you were doing that it was perfectly natural to throw yourself into it 200 percent.

Perhaps you remember from your own or your children's youth that children don't really "do" walks. Younger children can't really walk a long distance. They quickly tire and want someone to carry them.

Photo courtesy of ©1998 Ken Kipen Photography.

Figure 1-2

On the other hand, these same children can play far harder than adults for far longer. They are absolutely tireless when they are excited (and they are usually excited at bedtime, alas).

Here at the summer cottage where I'm writing this chapter, there is a long grassy hillside leading down to a set of long wooden steps leading down to a beach. My daughter Noelle could not walk the entire way for many years. But one day one of her older brothers showed me how to avoid the arduous task of carrying her up the hill. He simply said three magically motivating words: "I'll race you!" Now it was no longer a boring walk. It was an all-or-nothing challenge, a thrilling game. (My sons were wise enough to set their pace so she could stay in the game, since it's no longer fun if the challenge is unrealistic. And when the racing finally grew dull, my daughter became a bird and "flew" up and down that hill with a beach towel fluttering behind her. Our ability to motivate her was limited only by our imagination.)

We are older and wiser than kids on the way home from the beach, I suppose, but we are still the same people deep inside where our motivations take root and grow. The average dull job is like that

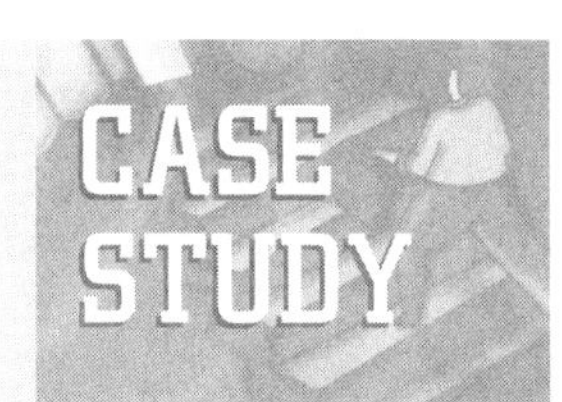

Rewarding Each Other at Chevron Chemical

Chevron Chemical, a part of Chevron Corp., permits its employees to recognize each other for behaviors such as doing something special to help out or acting in the best interests of the entire company. The rewards are given to people whose behavior forwards the company's quality objectives and corporate vision. There is no review committee or other management control (as in most such programs), so employees really are trusted to make the right decisions about who should get the rewards. The rewards are certificates redeemable for $25 worth of prizes. (Chevron contracts with BI Performance Services of Minneapolis, Minn., to offer *AwardPerqs* certificates.)

At the beginning of each year, Chevron Chemical employees receive three certificates worth $25 each that they may give to other employees as they see fit. The only control is that each certificate is a three-part form that is filled in to explain the employee's decision. One copy goes to the winner of the reward, another copy goes to the winner's supervisor so that the winner can be recognized at a meeting or function, and the third copy goes to the person who administers the program in order to create a central record for tracking and studying the program.

About 70 percent of Chevron Chemical employees hand out peer rewards, and 92 percent say they are satisfied or extremely satisfied with the program according to an annual survey used to track it. Satisfaction scores are higher for this program than for any other Chevron Chemical has tried.

Thanks to BI Performance Services and Chevron Chemical for providing this case.

Analysis. Wow! A reward program run not only for but *by* the employees. It certainly simplifies the decision making to let employees hand out rewards to their peers. And it gives each and every employee one of the biggest incentives of all: power. Incentive programs in which supervisors hand out rewards can easily fall from rewarding to controlling, but this one end-runs the problem.

What this program delivers is positive peer feedback about behaviors that advance the company's vision and mission. And that sort of feedback is likely to be informative and thus good for self-motivation, rather than controlling. It shows employees how their behavior is seen by their peers—a good reality check on their own self-perceptions. And the fact that a majority of employees participate in Chevron Chemical's program means that employees find the rewards helpful.

To make sure you keep this kind of program informative and empowering, don't make the guidelines for giving awards too specific. That would push it toward the control end of the spectrum, which gets you off the opportunity side of the motivation curve. Instead, create a form in which employees are encouraged to describe the behavior they liked and why they liked it. This informs the recipient and those who learn about the reward about desirable behaviors. It also encourages those who give rewards to think about and define exemplary behaviors. Which means *they* are more likely to engage in those behaviors, too!

Idea. One of the best features of this program is that it stimulates positive peer-to-peer feedback. Employees, like managers, tend to provide too little and too negative feedback to others unless trained in effective uses of feedback. So consider kicking off a peer-to-peer reward program with employee training in peer-to-peer feedback. Then you'll get informal, daily peer-to-peer feedback along with the less frequent, more formal peer-to-peer rewards. And this takes pressure off supervisors so they can concentrate on finding challenging development paths for each employee instead of having to worry about providing daily reinforcement or policing of employee behavior.

long, hot walk home from the beach. The average manager is like that well-meaning father or mother who keeps carrying, encouraging, and threatening in turns to get us to walk up the hill. And the truly inspired manager is like the older brothers who turn the trip into a race and leave the parent huffing and puffing far behind.

The average manager is like that well-meaning father or mother who keeps carrying, encouraging, and threatening in turns to get us to walk up the hill.

But I've forgotten to tell you about this photograph. Let's take a close look at it.

It shows a young boy running for all he is worth down a very long dock. The dock dead-ends in a boathouse, so we know the boy will simply have to turn around and walk back when he reaches the end. But we know that doesn't dampen his enthusiasm in the least.

We also suspect (and the photographer confirms) that the boy is simply running down that dock for the pure joy of running and the excitement of being a part of the photographer's project. Why not? What fun! Here I go!!!

You don't have to pay a boy to do something like that. You don't have to convince him to do it. Or threaten him with consequences if he doesn't. It is simply the right task at the right time in his life, and he really wants to do it. In fact, the photographer nearly lost the opportunity to take the picture because the boy took off so quickly in his excitement to do the job.

I love this image, not only because it is such a fine picture in its own right, but because it is a powerful image of what true motivation looks like. I want you to hold this image in your mind as you read the rest of the book and as you take ideas and methods from this book to your employees, children, or any others you wish to motivate. You'll know you've done your job when they take off like this boy, racing down some pathway just because it's there and it appeals to them. Motivation can be this powerful, and often is—outside the workplace. Let's bring that same excitement to your job and the jobs of your employees. There is an eager child within each of us waiting to jump up and sprint forward. What are we waiting for? Let's go!

Measuring and Managing Motivation

Chapter 2

Most people think about motivation as a matter of applying the right motivators to "make their people" do what they should. As we learned in Chapter 1, this is a mistaken view of motivation. People don't achieve high levels of performance and motivation until they are aligned with the right opportunities, opportunities that permit them to get engaged in challenging, inherently interesting work. And because we aren't traditionally very good at creating those motivating opportunities for employees, there is a far greater motivation problem in the workplace than anyone likes to admit.

> Only mediocrities rise to the top in a system that won't tolerate wave-making.
>
> —Lawrence J. Peter (discoverer of the Peter Principle)

One reason—the biggest reason—why most managers have a motivation problem is that our conventional thinking about motivation is all wrong. We ignore much of our employees' potential and allow them to operate near the bottom of the motivation curve. And we fail to appreciate that people are ready and willing to self-motivate—but only when faced with real personal threats or opportunities. Instead of working toward the top of the motivation curve, most of us fool around with messy low-powered external motivators that don't move employees far from the bottom of the curve.

But Does All This Apply to *You?*

So far, I've generalized about employees in the workplace. I've argued that most workplaces underutilize their people, leaving both managers and employees frustrated and unable to achieve their objectives. But each workplace is unique, so let's look at yours more closely. Do the generalizations about motivation apply to *your* people?

You know you have a motivation problem if:

- You have to keep an eye on your people to make sure they actually do their work.
- Your people just don't seem to care enough to perfect their skills and learn from their mistakes.
- You are the only one who takes serious problems seriously.

- You have the unpleasant feeling that most of your people think they deserve good pay and promotions just for showing up and doing the minimum.
- Your people are cynical about most of the incentives your organization offers and seem to "go along" with the latest initiatives and programs just to "keep management happy."

Let's stop for a minute and think about that last point. Are most employees cynical about management efforts to motivate them? We hate to admit it, but survey after survey shows it is true, so it's probably true of your people, too. The employee whose boss reads the latest bestseller and starts dishing out regular dollops of praise and pats on the back is eyed with serious suspicion by most employees. An employee may act out his or her side of this drama, but inside, is usually thinking, "Okay, what's the hidden agenda here? When's the other shoe going to fall?"

As a management consultant, I've often had opportunities to interview employees "off the record" when I'm working with companies that are implementing some new program. And you know what employees usually say when they feel safe that the boss isn't listening? They say something like this: "Oh sure, we'll play along with the new program for a while. But we know it'll blow over and we'll go back to business as usual. At least that's what will happen if I don't lose my job in the interim."

I also hear another comment all the time, especially when these new programs are accompanied by heavy-handed incentives and rewards for compliance.

What employees say is:

"Actually, I'm insulted by these incentives. They're treating us like children."

Now, those are pretty negative comments, and there are plenty more where these came from. There is zero "buy in" for most motivational programs, to use a favorite management term. There is a

My new boss does all that empowerment stuff. He tells us our opinions really matter. But he never really listens to us. He never does anything with our suggestions. How stupid does he think we are?

—FROM ANONYMOUS EMPLOYEE INTERVIEW

deep-rooted cynicism about management and "what they're up to now" that is, unfortunately, a natural and rational response to a workplace in which:

- Major reorganizations and layoffs are arbitrary from the employees' perspective since their performance doesn't "predict" what will happen to them.
- There is no real loyalty since companies are happy to replace experienced employees with new ones, temp workers are increasingly popular, and job tenure rates have been declining for many years.
- It seems clear to most employees that companies are far more interested in getting the most out of people for the least amount of money than in helping people develop and succeed.
- Unfortunately, it just takes one traumatic experience at work to "spoil it" for an employee. And when I interview employees, most have experienced a trauma within the last year, such as what they see as unfair treatment by a supervisor; the unexpected loss of status, an opportunity, or a job; or the unexpected addition of extra workloads when someone else is laid off or leaves and is not replaced. Employees may "nurse" such injuries for a long time but never feel free to talk to their managers about them!

Experienced employees keep their guard up when it comes to motivation and reward programs.

As a result of such events and observations, experienced employees are aware that their employer's goals are often at odds with their goals as individual employees. And they keep their guard up when it comes to motivation and reward programs.

Only when you find opportunities to move people up their motivation curves can you align personal and organizational interests and overcome this negative climate. And only when you align interests, even temporarily, can you achieve truly high motivation and performance levels. Someone who is riding in a canoe but doesn't approve of the direction it is going cannot be counted on to paddle with all his heart!

Let's Measure Motivation in Your Workplace

There is a clear us-and-them framework underlying employer–employee relations at most companies. Is there a similar attitude at your company as well? Do your employees feel that your organization's opportunities are their own, or is there some suspicion that the organization's interests conflict directly with theirs?

These are tough questions. The surest way to answer them is to simply measure employee motivation levels. Here is a simple assessment tool I developed for my consulting and training work, but you can use it yourself. Fill it in to find out where your people fall on the motivation curve. If you take just a few minutes to fill it in and tally the score, you can rate your employees' current level of motivation. And that way, you can have a benchmark to tell you exactly where your quest for motivation begins, and to give you a reference point as you track progress in the future.

So please grab a pencil and fill in the following inventory.

> A person is not the sum of what he has but the totality of what he does not yet have, of what he might have.
>
> —Jean-Paul Sartre

JML Inventory

Instructions. How well do the statements below describe your current work force? Please rate your level of *disagreement* or *agreement* with each of the statements.

Here is the scale:

1 = very strongly disagree
2 = strongly disagree
3 = disagree
4 = neither disagree nor agree
5 = agree
6 = strongly agree
7 = very strongly agree

(For example, if you were asked to disagree or agree with the statement, "I am alive," you would probably circle 6 for strongly agree or 7 for very strongly agree.)

Statements

Set A

1 2 3 4 5 6 7 They put lots of extra time into their work.
1 2 3 4 5 6 7 They don't stop working until they're satisfied they've done everything they can in a day.
1 2 3 4 5 6 7 They don't take as much time off as they could.
1 2 3 4 5 6 7 They rarely miss a day of work.
(Sum of Set A answers = _______)

Set B

1 2 3 4 5 6 7 They work harder in this job than they did in past jobs.
1 2 3 4 5 6 7 They work a lot harder than most people do.
1 2 3 4 5 6 7 They put a great deal of energy into their work.
1 2 3 4 5 6 7 They put a great deal of enthusiasm into their work.
1 2 3 4 5 6 7 They choose to work a lot harder than the average person does.
(Sum of Set B answers = _______)

Set C

1 2 3 4 5 6 7 When they're working, they don't like to be interrupted.
1 2 3 4 5 6 7 They rarely take breaks.
1 2 3 4 5 6 7 They concentrate very hard on their work.
1 2 3 4 5 6 7 When they're working, they often lose track of time.
1 2 3 4 5 6 7 When they're working, they tend to forget about everything else.
(Sum of Set C answers = _______)

Set D

1 2 3 4 5 6 7 For them, work is its own reward.
1 2 3 4 5 6 7 They really enjoy the work they're doing right now.
(Sum of Set D answers = _______)

Set E

1 2 3 4 5 6 7 They're happy with their current jobs.
1 2 3 4 5 6 7 They can't imagine doing anything else right now.
1 2 3 4 5 6 7 They are not looking for other jobs.
(Sum of Set E answers = _______)

Set F

1 2 3 4 5 6 7 They are performing at a very high level right now.
1 2 3 4 5 6 7 They are doing better work right now than they've ever done before.
1 2 3 4 5 6 7 They are performing better than they thought they were capable of.
1 2 3 4 5 6 7 They do exceptionally good work.
(Sum of Set F answers = _______)

Set G

1 2 3 4 5 6 7 They often do something extra to help out at work.

1 2 3 4 5 6 7 They often volunteer to take care of something that they see needs doing.

1 2 3 4 5 6 7 They like to put in that extra effort that makes the difference between mediocrity and excellence.

1 2 3 4 5 6 7 They do whatever they have to in order to complete their work properly.

1 2 3 4 5 6 7 They are not satisfied until the job is done to their own personal standards of excellence.

(Sum of Set G answers = _______)

Good work. Okay, now go back and analyze your answers according to the following instructions.

Calculating Component and Overall Scores

Set A scores total _______ ÷ 4 = _______ = Amount score
Set B scores total _______ ÷ 5 = _______ = Effort score
Set C scores total _______ ÷ 5 = _______ = Focus score
Set D scores total _______ ÷ 2 = _______ = Enjoyment score
Set E scores total _______ ÷ 3 = _______ = Intention score
Set F scores total _______ ÷ 4 = _______ = Overachievement score
Set G scores total _______ ÷ 5 = _______ = Volunteering score

Sum of component scores : _________
Divided by 7 = ________ = Job Motivation Level

Interpreting Job Motivation Level Scores

If your employees score high on the job motivation level (JML) inventory, you don't have a motivation problem right now. Congratulations!

But *most* scores are in the middle to low end of the range, so yours probably are, too. Don't worry if your people don't rate a high JML score, because 95 percent of work forces fail to score at the top of the motivation range. You're not alone! And besides, it's actually good news, not bad. Untapped motivation potential means that your employees could perform far higher than they currently do. Awfully good news when you think about it. All you need is some streetwise ideas for how to tap into their natural motivation, and you can achieve significantly higher performance.

Think how boring it would be if they were already at the top of the scale. Then you wouldn't have an exciting challenge to keep *you* motivated! Heck, you'd have to find a new, more challenging scale to measure motivation on.

MOTIVATION IDEA 3

Rewarding with Knowledge

Offer employees a subscription to the publication of their choice from your list of approved titles. And develop a list of educational trade publications and general business magazines and newspapers that are relevant to the work of your company and the specializations within the company. That way you know that, whatever they choose, it is valuable to their development as employees. (Also give them the choice of where they want the subscription sent to them, at home or the office. Choices are motivational!)

The Importance of Measuring Motivation

One reason that employees are generally operating at the unproductive bottom of the motivation curve is that we don't bother to measure motivation. How many businesses track revenues? How many track motivation? And yet we know that motivation drives revenues and profits, so it seems as if we are failing to track an absolutely vital measurement. (Please see Appendix B, Is It True?, to explore the proof of these relationships.)

But there I go generalizing again. Let's talk about *your* employees. How often do *you* look at objective statistics on their motivation levels?

Hmm. Did I hear you say "Never"?

We both know full well that *nothing happens in business until you measure it.* How many businesses would turn a profit if nobody bothered to calculate the P&L? You wouldn't think of leaving any important bottom-line variable to chance. To manage, you

> To be what we are, and to become what we are capable of becoming, is the only end in life.
>
> —ROBERT LOUIS STEVENSON

must measure. (I think the one saying I've said more often than any other in my consulting career is, "You are what you measure!")

Don't ask me why we traditionally fail to follow this obvious rule that you don't get results until you measure them when it comes to employee motivation. The closest most organizations come is to do the occasional survey of employee satisfaction. Which is all well and good. And, in fact, satisfaction often reflects motivation levels along with a lot of other things. But satisfaction is not motivation. I know lots of satisfied people who aren't motivated to do anything. You can be satisfied with doing nothing, after all. So satisfaction measures don't tell us everything we need to know about motivation levels.

You just completed a version of the JML inventory. JML is a specific measure of job motivation level. It measures motivation level by looking at seven key components or indicators of job motivation level:

JML FACTOR	EXPLANATION
A. Amount	How much they work
B. Effort	How hard they work
C. Focus	How involved they are in work (difficult to distract; experiencing flow)
D. Enjoyment	How much they enjoy doing their work
E. Intention	Whether they plan to stay in their current job
F. Overachievement	Whether they are performing at or above apparent level of ability
G. Volunteering	Whether they take on extra responsibilities

Each of these seven dimensions is a valuable measure of job motivation level, and taken together, they give you a good overall indication of how motivated employees are–or aren't.

In the first chapter, I gave you a striking visual image of a boy sprinting down a long dock and asked you to keep this image in mind so you would remember what true motivation looks like. Well, when you get to measuring true motivation, the seven JML factors give you another view of what it looks like. The point of any measurement is to allow you to "see" the thing you want to manage. We can see motivation level by tracking amount, effort, focus, enjoyment, intention, overachievement, and volunteering.

You can also perform an informal, "eye-ball" measure of motivation if you remember these components, now that you know what they "look" like. Does someone seem to be reasonably high on all seven of them? If so, you can make a well-informed judgment that they are highly motivated, and therefore ready to rise to any appropriate new challenge you present them with. But if not, then your ability to "see" their motivation problem gives you the power to start working on it right away. In which case, you will know to focus on the "people" side of management before you work on the task side. And once you "get the people right," the task will generally take care of itself!

I strongly advise you to make occasional formal measurements of job motivation levels. I know you just filled in the JML inventory I included earlier in this chapter, so I am including a second, blank copy of it as an appendix to this chapter. Don't write in that one! Use it as a master. You have my permission and encouragement to photocopy it as much as you want in order to be able to track employee motivation with a consistent measurement tool over time. You will find it much easier to boost motivation if you do periodic, say monthly or quarterly, measures of the average job motivation level in your organization.

And I recommend that you give copies of it to other managers, too, for them to use in tracking their employees' motivation levels. Just don't expect to be able to compare your results directly with theirs since individual managers tend to have their own biases in how they fill in such forms. The best use of this assessment is to compare your historical results with current ones so you can track your own progress with your people over time.

Compare your historical results with current ones so you can track your own progress with your people over time.

If you really want to compare motivation levels in different units of an organization, you'll have to have employees fill in their own version of this assessment instead of relying on management judgments.

I'll include an employee-oriented version of the JML assessment in the appendix, too.

Should Your Employees Measure Their Own Motivation?

> A man can succeed at almost anything for which he has unlimited enthusiasm.
>
> —Charles Schwab

There is another way to go about measuring JML that I also want you to know about. Instead of your filling in the form, you can have individual employees do so. It takes a form with somewhat different wording, but the principle is just the same. I'll include a copy of that self-assessment version in the back of this chapter, too, in case you want to try.

As an outside consultant and trainer, I generally prefer to let people measure their own level of motivation. They are likely to give me more accurate impressions of their own state of mind than their bosses can. (And many bosses overstate employee motivation levels because they feel low motivation reflects poorly on them, not realizing that it is endemic in business organizations.)

To get accurate, honest answers from employees, you have to give them an assessment such as the JML in a "safe" manner. I can do that as an outsider, as long as I collect multiple copies anonymously, and promise to report only the overall average to management. If you just tell an individual employee to fill it out and hand it in to you, anyone with half a brain will figure out that it looks best to give high answers. Then you are measuring their fear of your wrath instead of their motivation. Which means a high score is probably an indicator of low motivation, not high motivation. Oops!

So if you decide to go for accuracy and have employees report their own job motivation levels, make sure you do it in a way that reassures them there are no individual repercussions. Make sure they feel safe from the possible anger of the managers who see the scores. Protect their privacy with a process that looks and feels extremely safe.

Dialing for Awards at Mazda

Mazda tested a traditional cash incentive program for motivating car salespeople against a program in which salespeople called a toll-free line after selling a vehicle in order to receive computerized award points ranging from $25 to $250 (average payout $75 in each program). The award points could be traded in for a wide variety of merchandise and travel options offered by the incentive firm that worked with Mazda to develop the program, BI Performance Services (of Minneapolis, Minn.).

According to Clark Colby, Incentives Manager at Mazda Motor of America, Inc., "The possibility of 'hitting it big' adds to the excitement of the program," and as a result, the program produced sales 15 percent above objectives. In contrast, comparable cash awards were less exciting and raised sales only 2 percent above objectives in the districts where the cash incentive was used. Mazda was pleased with the result, but surprised that cash awards were not as powerful as the company and industry traditionally consider them. In explanation, Colby theorizes that "the emotional impact of an offer of tangible rewards, i.e., merchandise and travel, is more powerful, from a behavioral change point of view, than is an offer of an equivalent sum of money."

Thanks to BI Performance Services for contributing this case. Additional source: Clark B. Colby and John M. Jack, *Testing the Popular Wisdom: A Comparative Study of the Effectiveness of Incentives*, BI Performance Services, 1996.

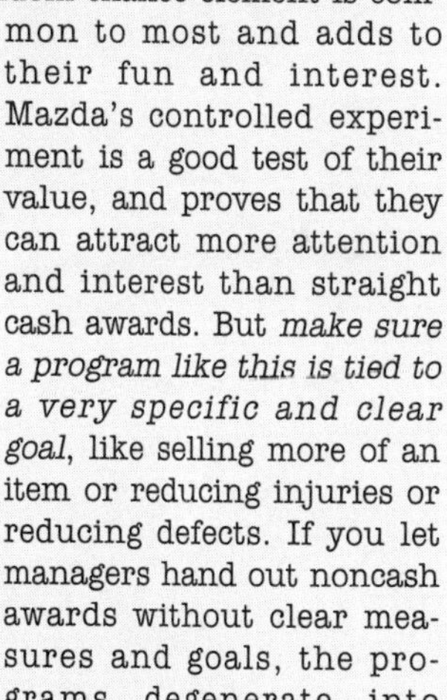

Analysis. A number of companies offer off-the-shelf incentive systems like the one Mazda used, in which some kind of coupons or points are awarded to employees who achieve performance goals. The random chance element is common to most and adds to their fun and interest. Mazda's controlled experiment is a good test of their value, and proves that they can attract more attention and interest than straight cash awards. But *make sure a program like this is tied to a very specific and clear goal*, like selling more of an item or reducing injuries or reducing defects. If you let managers hand out noncash awards without clear measures and goals, the programs degenerate into arbitrary, controlling rewards. And those are demotivating, no matter how appealing the prizes! Also, expect these programs to have strong impact when first introduced, but (unless you modify them) to gradually become old hat. So pick an *attainable* goal, and run the program only for the time needed to attain it, as Mazda did.

Once You Measure Motivation, *You* Have to Fix It

It is a radical thing to say the average employee might be as motivated as a star athlete or enthusiastic entrepreneur. Yet that is what the quest for high employee motivation is all about.

If you are like me, you want to hear more specifics about how to put that theory into action. Sure, your employees may be far more motivated by off-the-job activities than by their work. But since that's the norm around the world, what can *you* do to fix it? For that matter, once you begin to track and measure motivation like other key business variables, you will soon find yourself (or worse, your boss) thinking that *you* have an obligation to *raise* motivation levels.

> Every calling is great when greatly pursued.
> —Oliver Wendell Holmes, Jr.

Sorry, but what else could be more important for a manager to take on than the responsibility to motivate his or her employees? I wouldn't duck this one if I were you.

Sure, it's a big project, but then again, you are only at the beginning of a very rewarding journey. And you've already taken the most important step: you've recognized and measured the problem. That puts you way ahead of 99 percent of managers.

And I promise that you will find that upcoming chapters give you lots of solid, commonsense answers you can use to fix your motivation problem and get your people performing way above average. That's *your* opportunity, and with the right support from me, you should find it an inspiring opportunity to pursue!

Parting Shots

In sum, we've agreed (I trust) that motivation is a problem, even in your own above-average group of employees. In fact, it's the key issue in getting others to accomplish your goals. And it's a bigger problem than we like to admit, so until we begin to measure motivation it's very hard to keep focused on managing and improving it.

Motivation is a big problem because our conventional approaches to it don't work very well. Regrettably, typical motivation methods and programs have a minor impact on motivation, not a major one. Managers have insufficient influence over employee motivation because they have inherited some serious misconceptions

Self-Directed Development at DELTA Dallas Staffing

This recruiting and temporary staffing firm is a fast-growing regional success story. CEO and President Linda Crawford runs a corporate staff of thirty employees, who in turn field more than three hundred temporary employees for client companies. DELTA Dallas uses goal-setting sessions with each employee to define development goals and measures. According to Crawford, employees set goals for themselves. And each employee is "invited to annually write their own Strategy for Excellence by answering questions such as, 'What motivates your top productivity?' and 'Do you see yourself taking on more of a leadership role in the coming year and in what capacity?'"

In addition to writing their own plans, employees meet one on one with team leaders each year to discuss and develop the company's objectives and goals. This input gives employees a chance to shape the company's plans, and it helps align personal and organizational objectives.

DELTA Dallas's uses of employee goal setting reflect Crawford's belief that "My goal as a leader is to help others make their goals."

Thanks to *Workforce* for researching this case. (For more information, see *Workforce*, January 1998, pp. 16–17.)

Analysis. This company puts one of the best but least used motivation methods to work. It uses employee–employer goal-setting sessions to develop employee-defined performance and development objectives. When employees feel that they have a significant voice in setting the level and direction of their development goals, their work is transformed into opportunities for personal development and growth. They can pick compelling goals, and they can set achievement levels that are challenging but attainable. At its best, this kind of program is highly motivational because it taps into the intrinsic motivation of *opportunity*.

But be careful not to overpromise. If you tell employees they can set their own goals, but then find you have to veto many and make others more challenging in order to make employee goals relevant to company goals, the program will fall flat. Organizational needs and plans have to provide the stage for employee plans but shouldn't overshadow them. One way to do this is to follow DELTA Dallas's lead and have employees participate in organizational planning first so that they understand the context in which their own personal plans must function. ■

People are motivated by compelling opportunities, not by jelly beans.

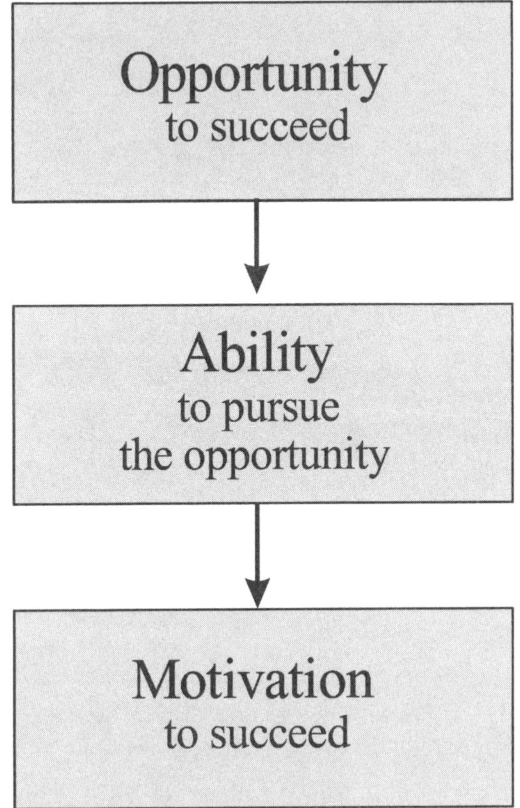

Figure 2-1

about motivation. Our beliefs and traditions are misguided at best. Much of what we think we know about human motivation is wrong.

For starters, there are not really any magic motivators that can create sustained high-level motivation. People are motivated by compelling opportunities, not by jelly beans. But when you align your supervisory goals with employee opportunities to succeed, you can achieve exceptional levels of motivation, as Figure 2-1 illustrates.

This relationship between opportunity and motivation is key and will be our primary focus as we explore ways of achieving high motivation in your work force. The streetwise manager knows that you must "tap into" employees' self-motivation by giving them motivating opportunities to succeed. In the upcoming chapters, I'll show you how–and how not–to accomplish this exciting goal.

> An empty bag cannot stand upright.
>
> —BENJAMIN FRANKLIN

Job Motivation Level Inventories

Here are two versions of the JML inventory, one for distribution to employees and one for use by managers. (If you hand out copies of the employee version, be sure to collect them anonymously and average the scores.)

Use these as masters to photocopy as many copies as you need for use within your own organization, or call HRD Press in Amherst, Mass., at (800) 707-7769 or (413) 253-3488 to obtain the latest professional versions of the JML inventory and supporting materials for use in employee assessment and training.

JML Inventory

Employee Version

Instructions. Please rate your level of *disagreement* or *agreement* with each of the statements.

Here is the scale:

1 = very strongly disagree
2 = strongly disagree
3 = disagree
4 = neither disagree nor agree
5 = agree
6 = strongly agree
7 = very strongly agree

(For example, if you were asked to disagree or agree with the statement, "I am alive," you would probably circle 6 for strongly agree or 7 for very strongly agree.)

Statements

Set A

1 2 3 4 5 6 7	I put lots of extra time into my work.
1 2 3 4 5 6 7	I don't stop working until I'm satisfied I've done everything I can in a day.
1 2 3 4 5 6 7	I don't take as much time off as I could.
1 2 3 4 5 6 7	I rarely miss a day of work.
	(Sum of Set A answers = _______)

Set B

1 2 3 4 5 6 7 I work harder in this job than I have in past jobs.
1 2 3 4 5 6 7 I work a lot harder than most people do.
1 2 3 4 5 6 7 I put a great deal of energy into my work.
1 2 3 4 5 6 7 I put a great deal of enthusiasm into my work.
1 2 3 4 5 6 7 I choose to work a lot harder than the average person does.
(Sum of Set B answers = _______)

Set C

1 2 3 4 5 6 7 When I'm working, I don't like to be interrupted.
1 2 3 4 5 6 7 I rarely take breaks.
1 2 3 4 5 6 7 I concentrate very hard on my work.
1 2 3 4 5 6 7 When I'm working, I often lose track of time.
1 2 3 4 5 6 7 When I'm working, I tend to forget about everything else.
(Sum of Set C answers = _______)

Set D

1 2 3 4 5 6 7 For me, work is its own reward.
1 2 3 4 5 6 7 I really enjoy the work I'm doing right now.
(Sum of Set D answers = _______)

Set E

1 2 3 4 5 6 7 I'm happy with my current job.
1 2 3 4 5 6 7 I can't imagine doing anything else right now.
1 2 3 4 5 6 7 I'm not looking for other jobs.
(Sum of Set E answers = _______)

Set F

1 2 3 4 5 6 7 I am performing at a very high level right now.
1 2 3 4 5 6 7 I am doing better work right now than I've ever done before.
1 2 3 4 5 6 7 I am performing better than I thought I was capable of.
1 2 3 4 5 6 7 I do exceptionally good work.
(Sum of Set F answers = _______)

Set G

1 2 3 4 5 6 7 I often do something extra to help out at work.

1 2 3 4 5 6 7 I often volunteer to take care of something that I see needs doing.

1 2 3 4 5 6 7 I like to put in that extra effort that makes the difference between mediocrity and excellence.

1 2 3 4 5 6 7 I do whatever I have to in order to complete my work properly.

1 2 3 4 5 6 7 I'm not satisfied until the job is done to my own personal standards of excellence.

(Sum of Set G answers = ________)

Thank you for your assistance.

JML Inventory

Manager's Version

A Human Interactions Assessment & Management Product
Distributed by HRD Press, Amherst MA (800) 822-2801

Instructions. How well do the statements below describe your current work force? Please rate your level of *disagreement* or *agreement* with each of the statements.

Here is the scale:

1 = very strongly disagree
2 = strongly disagree
3 = disagree
4 = neither disagree nor agree
5 = agree
6 = strongly agree
7 = very strongly agree

(For example, if you were asked to disagree or agree with the statement, "I am alive," you would probably circle 6 for strongly agree or 7 for very strongly agree.)

Statements

Set A

1 2 3 4 5 6 7 They put lots of extra time into their work.
1 2 3 4 5 6 7 They don't stop working until they're satisfied they've done everything they can in a day.
1 2 3 4 5 6 7 They don't take as much time off as they could.
1 2 3 4 5 6 7 They rarely miss a day of work.
(Sum of Set A answers = _______)

Set B

1 2 3 4 5 6 7 They work harder in this job than they did in past jobs.
1 2 3 4 5 6 7 They work a lot harder than most people do.
1 2 3 4 5 6 7 They put a great deal of energy into their work.
1 2 3 4 5 6 7 They put a great deal of enthusiasm into their work.
1 2 3 4 5 6 7 They choose to work a lot harder than the average person does.
(Sum of Set B answers = _______)

Set C

1 2 3 4 5 6 7 When they're working, they don't like to be interrupted.
1 2 3 4 5 6 7 They rarely take breaks.
1 2 3 4 5 6 7 They concentrate very hard on their work.
1 2 3 4 5 6 7 When they're working, they often lose track of time.
1 2 3 4 5 6 7 When they're working, they tend to forget about everything else.
(Sum of Set C answers = _______)

Set D

1 2 3 4 5 6 7 For them, work is its own reward.
1 2 3 4 5 6 7 They really enjoy the work they're doing right now.
(Sum of Set D answers = _______)

Set E

1 2 3 4 5 6 7 They're happy with their current jobs.
1 2 3 4 5 6 7 They can't imagine doing anything else right now.
1 2 3 4 5 6 7 They are not looking for other jobs.
(Sum of Set E answers = _______)

Set F

1 2 3 4 5 6 7 They are performing at a very high level right now.
1 2 3 4 5 6 7 They are doing better work right now than they've ever done before.
1 2 3 4 5 6 7 They are performing better than they thought they were capable of.

1 2 3 4 5 6 7 They do exceptionally good work.
(Sum of Set F answers = _______)

Set G

1 2 3 4 5 6 7 They often do something extra to help out at work.

1 2 3 4 5 6 7 They often volunteer to take care of something that they see needs doing.

1 2 3 4 5 6 7 They like to put in that extra effort that makes the difference between mediocrity and excellence.

1 2 3 4 5 6 7 They do whatever they have to in order to complete their work properly.

1 2 3 4 5 6 7 They are not satisfied until the job is done to their own personal standards of excellence.
(Sum of Set G answers = _______)

Thank you for your assistance.

Analysis and Interpretation

Calculating component and overall job motivation level scores

Set A scores total _______ ÷ 4 = _______ = Amount score
Set B scores total _______ ÷ 5 = _______ = Effort score
Set C scores total _______ ÷ 5 = _______ = Focus score
Set D scores total _______ ÷ 2 = _______ = Enjoyment score
Set E scores total _______ ÷ 3 = _______ = Intention score
Set F scores total _______ ÷ 4 = _______ = Overachievement score
Set G scores total _______ ÷ 5 = _______ = Volunteering score

Sum of component scores : _________
Divided by 7 = ________ = Job Motivation Level

Range

JML scores and individual component scores range from 1 (very low) to 7 (very high). Scores above 4 indicate some positive motivation on the part of employee(s). Scores of 4 or less indicate demotivated employees.

Definitions

Job motivation level. How enthusiastic and eager workers are to do their work, based on observations or self-reporting of their job performance.

Amount. How much they work.

Effort. How hard they work.

Focus. How involved they are in work (difficult to distract; experiencing flow).

Enjoyment. How much they enjoy doing their work.

Intention. Whether they plan to stay in current job.

Overachievement. Whether they are performing at or above apparent level of ability.

Volunteering. Whether they take on extra responsibilities.

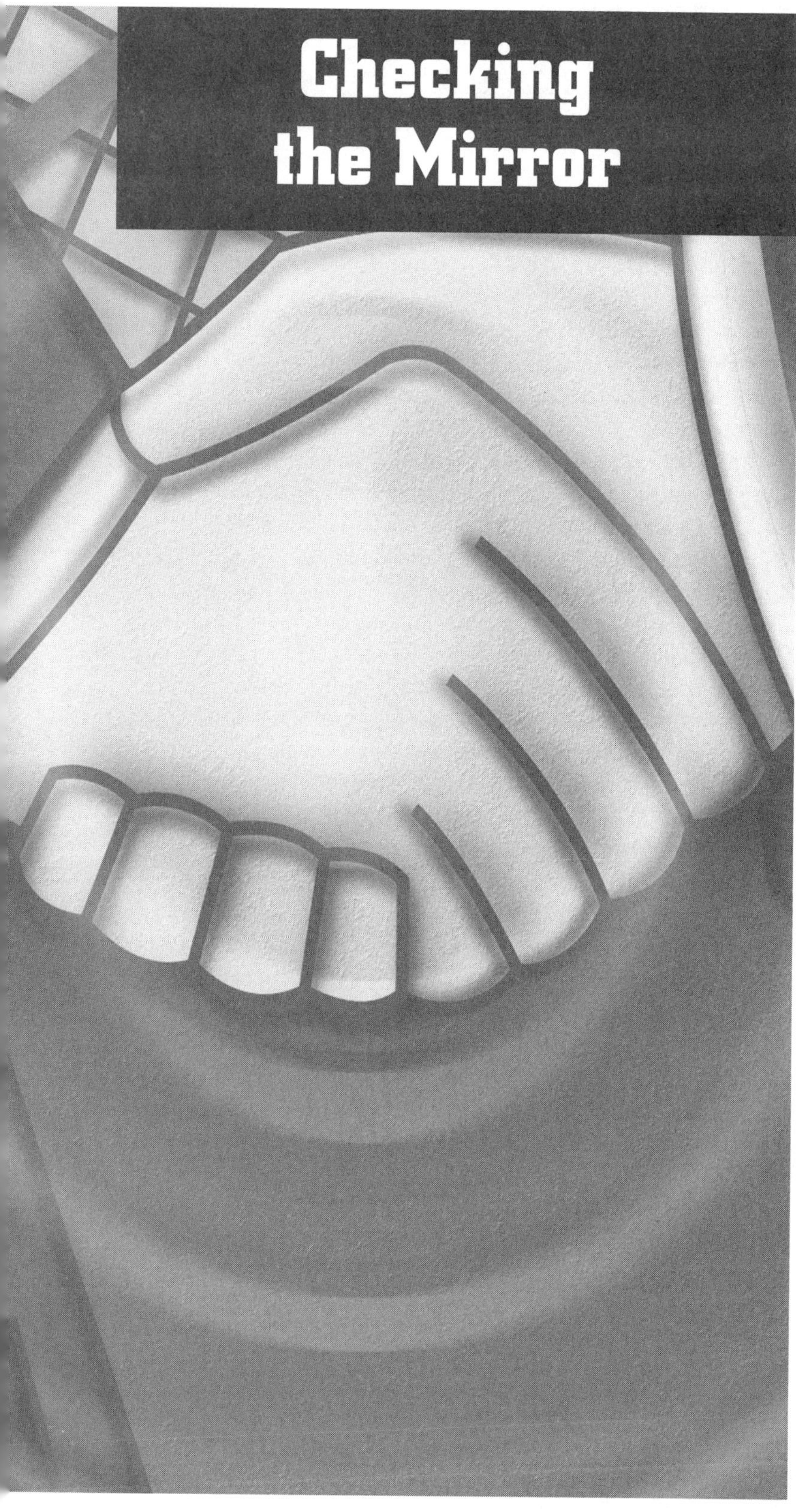

Checking the Mirror

Chapter 3

In the first chapter of this book, I argued that your management instincts are 100 percent right. You do have a motivation problem. (Or is it an opportunity problem? Anyway, it's certainly a problem!) Most employees routinely perform far below peak motivation levels. If you measured employee motivation with the job motivation level (JML) inventory in Chapter 2, you now have a hard number to tell you just how far below their peak your people are.

This is both the bad news and the good news, of course, because it's a wonderful opportunity for you when you recognize that there is a large amount of untapped potential in your work force. It's exciting to realize that employees are currently operating on the low to middle portion of the motivation curve. It gets you thinking what will happen when they move up that curve.

The first step toward moving employees up the motivation curve is realizing that there *is* a serious motivation problem. Until you listen to that voice, and begin to acknowledge and measure motivation levels, you won't give that motivation problem enough attention to do anything about it. You'll be stuck in the status quo like the rest of them.

But we worked on that issue in the first two chapters. This is Chapter 3. So let's deal now with the next major barrier to high employee motivation. (Oh, you didn't expect multiple barriers? Sorry, but this is the real world and worthwhile endeavors are always challenging to achieve!)

Is it *their* motivation problem—or is it yours?

What is the next issue? Now that we agree we have a problem and are confident we can measure and track it, we have to decide *whose* problem it is. And this is another place where lots of managers go wrong. They never stop to ask whether it's the employees' problem or whether *it might actually be management's problem instead.*

Yet in 99.999 percent of the cases where employees are lacking in motivation, the problem can be traced to management, not the employees. So you always must ask . . .

Is It *Us* or Is It *Them*?

"I'm dissatisfied with my employees."

"Why?"

"They just don't seem to be motivated. I guess they don't care how we do."

"Why don't you try some new incentives? I've got a new catalog of employee rewards."

Stop!

I hear discussions like this all the time. And they make me crazy! The problem is that people usually answer that "why?" question thoughtlessly. And thoughtless answers always seem to be about your employees: *their* attitude, *their* motivation, *their* values. Which leads to programs designed to change your people's attitudes, motivation, and values. But these are hard things to change, and they are seldom at the root of the problem anyway. The first place a manager should look whenever employees underperform is in the mirror.

It's hard to take that honest closeup look at yourself, I admit. But the good news is that, once you do, the "fixes" are usually far easier and more effective. Because:

It's considerably easier to change yourself than to change everyone else!

Whenever you find yourself asking why employees don't seem to be motivated, take the time to explore the reasons fully. There are always at least two types of answers to that question, so check that you have covered the following two groups of answers, not just one.

> The manager/supervisor's responsibility is to make sure he understands and manages the environment for employees to be motivated in.
>
> —Dan Eckert

Them Answers vs. Us Answers

The first group, the one we typically give, is answers that have to do with Them. The second group, the one we usually overlook, is answers that have to do with Us.

But the Us group generally is at the root of Them problems. For instance (to make it very simple), if one of the things about us is that we are not nice to them, then they will have a negative attitude toward us. But programs designed to work on their negative attitude will fail because that is not the real problem; it's just a symptom of our behavior.

I'll tell you a personal story to illustrate this point, even though it is a bit embarrassing. I was worried at one stage that my two older boys were developing bad tempers because they often cursed when they encountered a minor frustration. I took a tough line on cursing, telling them in no uncertain terms I never wanted to hear it again. And I also explained to them that instead of getting frustrated by minor setbacks, they ought to apply their problem-solving skills instead. But for some months, my admonitions went unheeded. Finally, one night when I was washing up after dinner, my wife said to me:

> *"There you go again. You'll never get the boys to clean up their act when you keep doing that."*
>
> *"Doing what?" I answered in surprise.*
>
> *"Aren't you listening to yourself?" she replied. "You just swore when you dropped that pan. In fact, every time you do the dishes, you curse a blue streak."*
>
> *"Oh."*

It's a lot easier to change yourself than to change your employees.

It's amazing the things we don't know about ourselves! I hadn't ever really thought about it, but in fact my boys were simply mimicking me. And once I broke my own habit, their bad habit disappeared without a trace. (Fortunately, that's the only bad habit I've ever had. Right?)

So when managers say their people have a motivation problem, they are probably "blaming the victim" as the old (and true) saying goes. Their natural use of Them answers may be blinding them to some simple Us answers.

Before you say, "My employees have a motivation problem," stop and think whether it is really them. Could it be you who has a problem? And if it is, then you have the less comfortable but far easier task of changing your own behavior, instead of theirs. Remember, when it comes to motivating and managing people, it is generally far easier and more effective to *Change your own behavior instead of theirs!*

Doing Formal Analysis of the "Motivation" Problem

One way to check on who should "own" any problem is to fill in an Us/Them table. This exercise not only clarifies whose problem it is, but also helps you figure out what is causing the problem–and of course, identifying the cause is always the best way to solve a problem.

Here is a sample Us/Them table that has already been used to analyze a motivation problem.

US/THEM TABLE

Problem: Employees aren't participating in our new suggestion system.

Why?

THEM REASONS	US REASONS
Bad attitude	We didn't get their input on program design.
Not motivated	We have a history of "not listening" according to them.
Don't care	They think we don't care about them.
Don't understand the importance	We aren't offering "important" rewards for their ideas.
Don't think we'll implement their ideas	It's been three months, and we haven't implemented any major ideas yet.

The group first aired lots of Them answers.

This table was developed in a management problem-solving session in which the group first aired lots of Them answers. Then we put up an Us/Them table, wrote down the main Them answers, and stared at the blank Us column for a while. Gradually, people began to think of things to put in the Us column, too.

To help, we asked questions like, "So *why* do you think they have a bad attitude?" Often the why *behind* the why is the one you want.

As a result of this exercise, the managers redefined their problem as a listening problem, not a motivation problem. And they realized the problem was that management didn't seem to listen to employees, not that employees weren't motivated. As a result of this insight, managers made a study of all the ways they failed to listen to their people. And they gradually changed their own behavior to become more open-minded listeners. For instance, they:

- Added "Your Turn" time blocks on all meeting agendas in which they invite employees to raise topics they want to discuss.
- Began to carry Employee Idea Notebooks in which they discipline themselves to write down suggestions or complaints from employees, as they hear them. This practice captures the input for later study, signals a new respect for employee input, and perhaps most important, keeps managers busy taking notes so they can't interrupt employees as early and often as they used to.
- Required all managers to prepare monthly reports describing the ideas and concerns they have collected from employees and to say why they did or didn't take action on each one.

Amazingly, these changes in management behavior eliminated the concerns about the suggestion system.

Amazingly, these changes in management behavior eliminated the concerns about the suggestion system. In fact, the managers collected so many ideas that it became easy to implement employee suggestions, and a new atmosphere of openness and creativity spread through the organization.

What this example illustrates is the powerful point that *you can often fix employee motivation problems or boost employee perfor-*

mance by examining yourself and making small changes in your own behavior.

If you were at a party at someone's house and everyone you talked to seemed to have a strange habit of staring at your hair instead of looking you in the eyes, what would you think was wrong?

Well, if you are thinking like a manager, you would conclude that the other guests all needed to see an optometrist.

But if you are thinking straight, you'd go check your hair in the mirror.

Same thing with motivation. If every time you ask employees to work harder and do better they seem to ignore you and resist your efforts, does that mean you've been stuck with a group of employees who are hard of hearing? I doubt it. Better check yourself in the mirror before you conclude you need to call an ear doctor.

What's the View from the Employee's Side?

It's actually quite difficult to check yourself in the mirror of employee perceptions, which makes that Us column of the Us/Them table difficult to fill in. (But please fill it in anyway, even if it takes all day!)

Employees don't see a simple visual image of you that an actual mirror can replicate. What they see is the net result of a variety of experiences that are quite different for them than for you. So it is remarkably hard for most managers to truly "see" themselves in the employee mirror. As a result, they find it difficult to sleuth out the factors in their own behavior that they can change to produce improvements in employee motivation.

So it is remarkably hard for most managers to truly "see" themselves in the employee mirror.

Even when we are willing to take ownership of the motivation problem, and decide we will seek ways to change our own behavior, it can be maddeningly hard to figure out what to do. So I realize I really need to give you more support and structure for this difficult task.

And one very good way to do that is to summarize the employee's view of supervisor and workplace by identifying the prominent features of this workplace landscape. What are the standout concerns shaping employee attitudes and experiences? Once you gain an appreciation of these important factors, you will be able to use them like a mental checklist to "see" how any specific action you might take looks from their perspective. You will also be able to take the temperature of the overall climate to see if it is motivational or not.

Key Motivation-Related Issues from the Employee's Perspective

When you look at your employees, you think in terms of how motivated and productive they are, how many mistakes they make, whether certain ones are difficult to deal with, which have special expertise you can call on when needed, and so forth. These are the supervisor's natural concerns and interests. For someone to see the workplace through your eyes, he or she would have to learn about and explore your interests.

But when you "check the mirror" to see how employees view the situation, you must set these concerns aside and ask yourself what *employees* see. What are they looking for in the workplace? What concerns and interests shape their perception of it?

Do you remember what it was like to be in a position like theirs?

Only when you appreciate their concerns and can see yourself and the rest of the components of their workplace through their eyes can you truly appreciate their *motivation landscape*, the context in which they interpret your aspirations for them.

One great way to get inside employees' heads and look at things through their eyes is to empathize with them. Do you remember what it was like to be in a position like theirs? For that matter, are you in a position like theirs now? You may also have a boss you report to and so another part of your head thinks like an employee, not a supervisor. It shouldn't be as hard as it seems to be for most of us to fully appreciate the employee perspective. The trick is to treat your employees the way you *wish* your boss would treat you, not the way he or she *does* treat you!

"What We Have Here Is a Failure to Communicate"

Yet employees and supervisors rarely see eye to eye because workplace communication patterns prohibit full disclosure of attitudes and opinions in *either* direction. The hierarchical structures of most businesses lead to a considerable amount of wall-building and concealment. Nobody is fully honest (or even 50 percent honest) with their boss!

In addition, many people are not exactly clear how they feel in their roles as employees or supervisors. They aren't used to articulating their inner attitudes. Just as we cannot explain exactly how our eyes see what they do, it is difficult to explain exactly how we feel about the workplace landscape.

So there is another powerful way to get inside the heads of your employees. That is to consult a checklist of the prominent factors that emerge from a wide variety of detailed surveys and studies of how employees think. I've compiled what I believe are the most significant of these factors in the following pages of this chapter, and because the list is lengthy, I've devoted the next chapter to it as well. They include things like fairness, responsibility, and trust.

For instance, it is clear from numerous studies that employees apply a *fairness criterion* to much of what they see in their workplace. Is it fair? Am I being treated fairly? If the answer is no in their eyes (regardless of the "truth" of the matter from your perspective), then they will carry a negative evaluation of the workplace around in their heads. They will see a major flaw in their workplace, and it will stand in the way of their giving full commitment.

> He's fair. He treats us all the same—like dogs.
>
> —FOOTBALL PLAYER HENRY JORDAN REFERRING TO COACH VINCE LOMBARDI

When they look at you, they will see this trust problem and it will distract them. You might as well have a big spider on your shoulder. Employees will not seem to be able to focus 100 percent on you when you try to motivate them. Their attention will be drawn to that spider, and you won't be able to figure out what's wrong until you "check in the mirror" and see the trust problem, too.

On the other hand, if they see their supervisor as fair, or as increasing the fairness by reducing some of the unjust things, then this will tend to boost their motivation by increasing the appeal of the workplace.

Motivation Idea 4

Free Lunches

Why should there be no such thing as a free lunch? Once a week, take a randomly selected group of three employees out for a nice lunch. You can bill it to the company if you use the time to interview them for their views on how things are going and to ask them for ideas on how to fix problems and improve performance. Take your Idea Notebook to record their input.

Suggestions. Do the drawing on Monday and then ask the three which day that week works for all of them. Let them select the restaurant, too. And don't interrupt or argue with them when they try to answer your questions. Just write down what they say and try to listen without becoming defensive! Employees want choice. They want control. They want respect and open communication. So give it to them!

Evaluative Criteria: How Employees See Their Jobs

Factors like fairness and trust are, technically speaking, the employee's *evaluative criteria.* This is a term that's often used in marketing to explain the factors we use to evaluate something before deciding whether to buy it or not.

For instance, you wouldn't buy a car unless it met certain criteria. I don't know exactly which criteria you use because everyone has a slightly different perspective (which is why there are so many types of cars on the road). But I do know that your criteria probably include things like attractiveness of design, comfort, how well it drives, price, reliability, safety, color, and size. Since I know people generally look at criteria like these, I can fairly easily put myself in your shoes as a car buyer and empathize with your view of a car.

And I can therefore understand that if you have three young children and a spouse, you will want a car with at least five seats, one with a good safety record, and (because three children demand much of your attention and funds) you will value moderate price and trouble-free maintenance. And the vehicle ought to drive decently and look okay, too. Knowing this, I should be able to guess why you buy one kind of car and not another. A station wagon or a sturdy minivan are obvious choices, whereas a sports car isn't. (Too bad. Guess you'll have to wait until you get those orthodontist bills and college tuitions paid off!)

When it comes to that biggest of motivational questions, "*Do They Buy In?*", you need to understand employees' evaluative criteria. What makes them feel that the job is okay and worth their throwing themselves into? What sours them to it and leads them to withhold their highest levels of commitment from their work?

When you ask people to be motivated, to commit themselves to your objective and work hard toward it, you are in a sense asking them to buy it. But does it fit their needs? Does it match their criteria? You don't know, I bet, because nobody bothers to ask this question in most workplaces today.

As a result, we are managing the way Henry Ford used to sell cars. He's the one who is quoted as saying, "They can have it any color they like, as long as it's black." But when Ford's competitors recognized that color was important, Ford had to start offering choices, too. He could no longer ignore this important evaluative criterion.

Don't forget that your employees are always keenly aware of choices and options. Even if they aren't ready to hand in their resignations and apply for other jobs, the possibility is always in the back of their minds. They quite naturally compare their situation with other options. You need to be at least as good as, and preferably significantly better than, the typical choices if you want employees to be better than average, too!

So let's make sure we fully understand your employees' evaluative criteria before you try to get buy-in from them. Here are some of the most important criteria employees use to evaluate their supervisor, work environment, compensation, and rewards:

If you want better-than-average employees, offer them above-average jobs!

CRITERION	EXPLANATION
Open communication	Do I have access to the information I need?
Security	Am I safe from threats and risks?
Management commitment	Are managers committed to a course of action?
Fairness	Am I treated fairly?
Respect	Am I respected as an individual?
Development opportunities	Can I achieve something meaningful here?

If employees don't see problems in these areas, they are generally able to focus on their performances and your aspirations for them. You will find it fairly easy to get them motivated. In fact, their self-motivation will be fairly strong to start with, and you won't have too much trouble tapping into it.

But if employees see a problem in any of these areas, it will color their whole viewpoint. They will feel that there is unfinished business between them and you, or between them and the organization.

Employees rank good communication as their #1 priority, but managers don't.

Motivating them will be like trying to borrow money from a bank again after defaulting on your first loan. You keep trying to steer the conversation to what you need the loan for and why it is such a safe investment. But the loan officer just can't seem to stop talking about that old loan. The only way to change the focus to your topic of choice is to take care of the lingering problems first. Pay off the old loan before you apply for a new one!

To help you appreciate each of these important employee criteria, I'm going to tell you a little more about each one. And because there are so many to consider, I'm going to divide this effort into two chapters. In the rest of this chapter, we will tackle the one that employees often treat as most important–open communication. Then we'll look at the rest of them in Chapter 4.

Open Communication

The most important criterion for many employees is whether they feel there is open communication or not. Now, open communication implies a two-way street, with employees being able to speak their minds to managers and managers being open and honest with employees. But I'm going to focus in this discussion on what I regard as the most important direction: the communication from managers to employees. I don't mean to imply that listening isn't important, too, but I know that we'll be working on listening in the context of later chapters. So let's focus right now on how open management communicates important information to employees.

According to the Families and Work Institute, 65 percent of employees consider open communication to be very important (and it at least ranks as important to somewhat important for all employees). And David Carr, of consulting firm Coopers & Lybrand, found in studies of successful leaders and change managers that communication was one of the critical issues, too. For instance, in order to get buy-in for a new direction, leaders must "communicate the critical need for change, the change vision, what change will 'cost' in human terms, and results as they occur" (Hiam, *The Portable Conference on Change Management*, HRD Press, p. 191).

Based on Carr's studies of leadership needs during change events, I developed a planning template in which managers set specific goals, then think of and try out various actions to help them achieve their goals. Here are some actions for the goal of achieving more open communications (*The Portable Conference on Change Management,* p. 198):

> *Goal*: To communicate.
>
> *Actions*: Start by assessing the ways I communicate with the organization right now. How many ways do my employees hear from me? How many messages do they receive from me in a week or month? Do these messages focus on important issues or trivia? Are they consistent or conflicting? Find out if my answers to these questions are different from employees' answers (do a quick-and-dirty survey?). Write a list of the things I need to communicate in order to make the desired change happen. Figure out what channels to use, and how often, in order to reach all the key people with these messages.

It took me only a little while to brainstorm that list of possible actions, and there are probably many additional actions you could consider as well. Do your own brainstorming to see what you might do to find out whether you really provide the open communication employees desire. And seek new ways of communicating with them to make sure they have plenty of information and don't feel as if you are keeping secrets from them that they really ought to know. (Yes, I know you don't think you "keep secrets" from your employees. But they think you do! See the next section.)

Do employees suspect you are keeping secrets from them?

Open Communication or Secrets?

It is fascinating to me that most employees accuse their managers of keeping secrets and "keeping them in the dark" about important information, events, and decisions. But if you talk to the managers in the same workplace, you will find that they believe they are very open and informative. Managers often feel that they spend too much time communicating, and wish they could spend less time writing memos and running meetings, and spend more time "working" instead.

What's at the root of these very different attitudes? Well, for one thing, managers who complain that communicating with employees takes vital time away from their work are managers who don't realize that communicating with employees *is* their work.

Communicating *Is* Your Job

Management is all about communication.

Since managing is a personal process in which one person works on building commitment and competence in others, management is all about communication. Communication is often the most important work you can do. So the employees are right when they place the communication criterion at the top of their list. Their work goes better when they have open communication. They can accomplish more and get more out of their work when communication is open and clear than when they are kept in the dark. Take a hint from your employees on this one and put communication higher on your personal list.

What's your job as a supervisor or manager? What do you do all day? When someone asks you a question like this, I bet "communicate" is not the first word out of your mouth. Or even the second, third, fourth, or fifth. So the fact is, you do not think about and work on open communication on an hourly and daily basis. *And if it isn't on your mind, then you aren't doing it as well as you could.* Don't tell me you are!

Open Communication About *What*?

So one good reason why employees complain about a lack of open communication is that it's a priority for them, but not for their managers. That's easily fixed when you realize what's going on and make communication the top priority for you, too.

But there is another very good reason for employees' complaints, this one requiring a little bit different approach to fix. The problem is that employees are interested in *different* information than their managers. So when you communicate the information you care about, they are not likely to be satisfied. In fact, they will probably be more frustrated than ever. They may feel you are holding back on them, when in fact you've told them everything you thought they might want to know.

Time to think again.

Basically, the information of interest to employees falls into one simple, clear category:

They want to know about any changes affecting them.

If it's not a change, they don't care. If it doesn't affect them, they don't care. Why should they?

In addition, they are not very interested in your side of these change stories. At least not at first. For instance, if you communicate in detail the process whereby you hired consultants, developed alternatives, then finally selected a particular performance review system, they will not find that information of any use. They will fail to appreciate what you see as incredible openness and honesty. Instead, they will feel you are withholding (or worse, simply don't care enough to know) the absolutely vital information about this new system: *how it will affect them, personally.*

If it's not a change, they don't care. If it doesn't affect them, they don't care. Why should they?

So we can extend the first point, that employees want to know about any changes affecting them, as follows:

They want to know exactly how those changes affect *them.*

Yet we often communicate other information to our employees first: why the change is good for the organization, for example. To help managers see the employees' information needs more clearly, Blanchard Training & Development uses the following model. It portrays the employees' information needs as moving through six stages, starting with a general need for clarification of what's going on, then moving to an interpretation of how it will affect them personally, and only gradually evolving into a perspective similar to the manager's.

MOTIVATION IDEA 5

Writing a Communications Plan

Sometimes the best way to get communications right is to develop a plan in advance. Your plan needs to identify who will be affected by a change, and it needs to analyze the impact on them in order to craft appropriate messages for them. Every change in the workplace has two potential kinds of impact on employees: negative and positive. Often, the impact is mixed. Some effects are seen as good, others bad. When you inform them of the changes and tell them how they will be affected, it helps to have thought through both the negative and positive impacts from their perspective. That's where your planning comes into play.

THE SIX STAGES OF CONCERN IN THE CHANGE PROCESS

STAGE	EMPLOYEE THOUGHTS
1. Information	"What's going on?"
2. Personal	"How will it affect me?"
3. Management	"What do I need to do?"
4. Consequences	"How will it affect our organization?"
5. Collaboration	"What more can I do to help implement change?"
6. Refocus/refinement	"What else can we change to get even more benefits?"

Most supervisors' natural tendency is to start communicating at level 4, which doesn't do employees a bit of good. Until they satisfy the other levels of need in sequence, employees can't really process level 4 information. And when you give them level 4 (or anything but level 1) information, they feel you are keeping secrets because they sense the lack of starting-level information and are frustrated that they cannot move through their stages of concern in a natural manner.

This hierarchical model of employee concerns gives you a simple game plan for getting communication right. Whenever you anticipate or require a change that affects employees, make sure you provide open information in sequence, matched to employees' hierarchy of concerns.

If that sounds a bit abstract and hard to remember when in the heat of battle, here's a simpler way to do it. Simply *answer each of the questions* in the table (under Employee Thoughts) in order. Make sure you give plenty of information on "What's going on?" before informing them about how it will affect them. And make sure they know how it will affect them before giving them information about what they need to do. And so forth, right through the list, checking that they really have gotten it at each level before communicating at the next level.

Your knowledge of the six stages of concern allows you to determine what information needs your people will have and to speak to those needs. They may not be able to explain their information needs to you (few of us are that analytical about ourselves), but when you address those needs, they will feel that you are giving them more open and useful information than most managers do. And that will help you motivate them by eliminating a common employee concern that often distracts them from the motivation effort.

Well, now you know a lot more than most managers do about employee communications, and you should be able to satisfy the employee's natural urge for open communications in the workplace. At least, you are farther along on the road to that goal than 99 percent of managers are if you follow these simple rules and procedures.

But like anything, there are always additional layers of complexity. I'll introduce you to many other communication tools, including a number that help you listen better to your employees. You probably noticed that the approach I took focused on what information you communicate to them, not the other way around. But two-way communication is, of course, important, too. Much of what this book covers has to do with this vital issue of open communication in the workplace because open communication sets the stage for high motivation.

If you aren't sure how to analyze and plan employee communications, don't despair! All you have to do is use The Manager's Communications Plan at the end of this chapter. It leads you through a simple seven-step process to make sure you get those vital employee communications right. Follow its directions to design the right informative messages for each employee when you are introducing any new directions or initiatives.

Parting Shots

In this chapter, we've taken a look at ourselves in the mirror to see if anything is "off" and threatens to distract employees from our efforts

MOTIVATION IDEA 6

Maximize Overlap

In many organizations, open communication is unlikely because managers and employees simply don't interact on a daily basis. There is nothing like getting people together at the same time and place to foster good communications! To maximize employee–management overlap, think about ways of bringing them together in either time or space. For instance, if you can organize your facilities so that employees and managers are involved in informal activities like lunch and coffee breaks at the same time and place, they will tend to communicate far more than otherwise.

Scheduling can also help create healthy communications, as Jim Lundbergh of RF Micro Devices in Greensboro, N.C., realized when he contributed the following thoughts: "We're building a new semiconductor plant and will be going to a 2-3-2 schedule when it's completed. We're thinking there are advantages of going from 10 A.M. to 10 P.M., such as less traffic, more personal time for errands and better overlap with managers, who work from 8 A.M. to 5 P.M." (*Workforce*, January 1998, p. 11). Facilities that run night shifts without any overlap have lots of employees who never even see, let alone talk to, their management. Creative scheduling can help solve that communications problem.

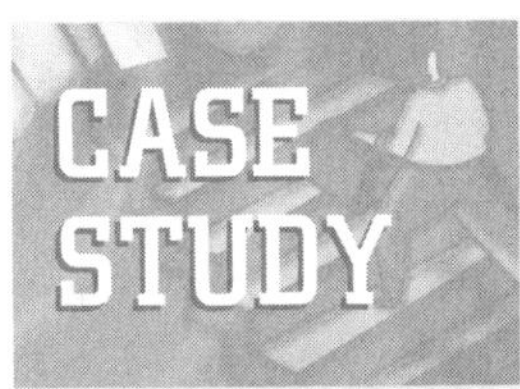

Cashing in on Good Health at Search Resources, Inc.

The three Minnesota offices of this placement and temp firm handle many positions such as machinists, welders, log peelers, and construction workers where safety is a key issue. To help drive home the message that safety is important, the company introduced the In Search of Safety incentive program in which each employee who is injury free with no lost time in a month is entered into a drawing. Winners are chosen from each of the firm's offices, and the winners receive an extra $100 in their paychecks.

Analysis. This kind of program can be effective if it is presented in an informative way. For instance, you could calculate the average cost of injuries to the company, and give away a prize equivalent to that amount as a way to build awareness of the cost of injuries and the reason for the company's concern with them. Even better, you could make the prize vary inversely with an index of overall injury time to add feedback to employees about their overall progress toward 100 percent safety. But as long as the incentive is tied to a well-measured goal, it has the potential to inform employees about their performance and therefore to help motivate them to perform better.

This kind of program is also effective for another reason. It provides public recognition and acknowledgment of the individual employee's successful safety record. Like many incentive programs, it publicizes good work so as to inform the group about the individual's accomplishment. Public recognition of this type works because it increases the positive feedback from good performances. But only if it is timely and accurate and fair, so make sure your program measures and rewards good performances well and quickly, or the recognition will appear arbitrary to many employees. Arbitrary recognition is demotivating, whereas appropriate recognition is motivating, so there is a fine line here that program designers need to be aware of.

Even if you recognize safety accurately and quickly, the rewards will seem arbitrary if employees feel that accidents are out of their control. And employees sometimes do feel this way, especially if they lack training in industrial safety and accident prevention. They may feel, for instance, that an accident was just bad luck. And rewards for good luck (and thus punishments for bad luck) are not at all motivating.

So train them to understand how their own behavior affects their safety and to practice good prevention. Knowledge-based training coupled with a safety incentive program increases the effectiveness of the program by giving employees the know-how they need to feel in control of their own safety.

A final concern in analyzing this type of incentive program is that the employers (remember Search Resources places people at many companies) will not do their part. Their part is to provide a safe working environment. For instance, an employee

(*continued on following page*)

who finds himself working with equipment that lacks proper safeguards or is poorly maintained will feel that he has little control over his own safety, even if he has personal knowledge and incentives. So a safety incentive program needs to be accompanied by a safety audit of the work environment, and perhaps training of supervisors and an employee safety suggestion system for reporting unsafe working conditions, too.

This analysis is a whole lot more complex than the program. I hope you stuck with me for it because it is really vital to understand the dynamics behind any incentive program. If you ignore the reasons behind a behavior and simply try to change it with rewards, you are like the doctor who treats only symptoms. Make sure your incentives are accompanied by an appropriate course of treatment, or you'll just make the disease worse!

Is It the Right Reward? I Don't Care Until I Know the *Information* Is Right! This analysis differs from the kind of analysis you might get from many experts in the incentive field because I ignored the issue of whether the cash rewards are the "right" awards or not. Most people look at the reward first. One of the classic debates in the employee motivation area is whether to use cash incentives or not, and I'll address this issue elsewhere. Would it be more effective to hand out trophies to those who achieve perfect safety records? Or certificates? How much less safety would you get if you just applauded them at a monthly banquet? Or put their names on the wall? Or what if you entered their names in a monthly drawing in which one of them has a chance to win $1,000? Or a trip to Hawaii? And so forth. Whole books have been written just about the many possibilities.

It is fun to devise creative new rewards, and I don't want to discourage you from that pursuit. I'll give you as many fresh ideas as I can in this book. *But* please remember that this is probably the least important question to ask. Why? Because with rewards we're designing the Band-Aid, and no Band-Aid will work if it isn't accompanied by proper understanding and treatment of the condition. Band-Aids treat symptoms instead of causes. Sure, kids love it if you give them colorful new Band-Aid designs. But they still won't get better unless you clean their scratch and put the Band-Aid on it. And anything more than a minor scratch will require a lot more than that Band-Aid, so you have to be prepared to go a lot deeper than "Band-Aid motivation" usually does.

Rewards are a lot like Band-Aids. Get the diagnosis right, prescribe the right antibiotic, and even a deep problem will heal itself fairly quickly. Stick a Band-Aid on it to make sure everyone feels good about the treatment and to let them know you care. Band-Aids can even be used to remind someone not to use that sore finger until it has healed, so they serve an informative role, too. *But they aren't the cure.* And nor are rewards.

to motivate them. To put ourselves in their shoes, we looked at the criteria that they often use to decide whether their jobs are acceptable or not.

The first priority among these criteria is often open communication. Employees feel that they are being left out of the loop much of the time. They need more and different information, more quickly, in order to feel that management communicates openly with them.

> I'm open, honest and up front. As soon as I get information, employees get information.
>
> —NANCY SINGER, PRESIDENT, FIRST OF AMERICA BANK

In the next chapter, I'll explore a number of additional employee concerns, although not in as much detail as I gave to the issue of open communication. (Since, after all, the communications issue is top priority for employees.) But before I leave the subject of communications, I want to give you a tool to help you actually plan and design employee communications. It should help keep you out of trouble by ensuring that your employees see your communications as open, honest, and informative. Here it is.

PLANNING TOOL

The Manager's Communications Plan

To design your motivational communications, or any communications with employees about new initiatives, goals, programs, rewards, or other changes, follow each of these steps carefully. And sharpen your pencil. You will need to make some notes as you work through the planning process.

Step 1. Identify the changes.

Be sure you identify all the changes clearly right now. No last-minute surprises please! And be sure to follow the KISS rule (keep it simple, stupid) by developing a single-sentence version of this change story to use as the lead-off message in all communications. Example: "I've redesigned the incentive system to eliminate cash bonuses, introduce merchandise coupons as rewards, and make the selection of winners more fair and accurate." That's a simple, clear explanation of what is going to change. You owe it to your people to give them something as clear as that.

Step 2. Identify the stakeholders.

Stakeholders are people who have a personal interest in the change. They are the ones you need to communicate it to. If they don't buy into it, it won't work. Yet it is easy to overlook key stakeholders by accident. For instance, when you introduce a new reward system, it is obvious that eligible employees need to be motivated to participate in it. But what about others who will need to be involved in making it happen, like the employees' supervisors? A communications plan needs to include them, too.

And in addition, you need to recognize that some of these stakeholders may view the change as beneficial to themselves, whereas others will resent it. For instance, any employees who have the old system "wired" and get lots of bonuses will feel threatened by a replacement system. They are a different kind of stakeholder, needing different communications, from the employees who think their chances of getting rewards will increase.

Here are four types of stakeholders you will probably need to consider:

- Implementers, the people whose actions will be essential to making the change.
- Losers, the people who stand to lose something as a result of the change.
- Winners, the people who stand to gain something from the change.
- 0Influencers, the people who control or influence communications to any of the other groups. You may need to motivate them to help you motivate the others!

These four groups are your audience. Generalized messages about the change must reach all four groups effectively and consistently. And you will probably need to communicate specifically with each individual group, too, because they have different interests and concerns.

Step 3. Decide what you want each stakeholder group to do.

You need to define some clear behavioral goals for each group. For instance, you might decide that you want employees (the key implementers of your new reward system) to nominate each other for rewards based on observations of exceptional behavior. So you will need to encourage them to learn about and look for specific behaviors, and to nominate other employees who engage in the desired behaviors. You also want to discourage them from unhelpful behaviors. For instance, you don't want them to subvert your system by nominating only their best friends, so you will need to communicate the seriousness and importance of their role.

Make one list of desirable actions for each group of stakeholders, and another list of undesirable actions. Your communications task for each group is defined by these lists, which you can develop using a worksheet such as the worksheet on the next page:

STAKEHOLDER ACTIONS WORKSHEET

STAKEHOLDER GROUP	DESIRED ACTIONS	UNWANTED ACTIONS
Implementers		
Losers		
Winners		
Influencers		

You must develop a message that encourages desirable actions and discourages undesirable ones, but to do that effectively requires an additional step.

Step 4. Figure out what's in it for them.

Once you know what you want each stakeholder to do, the tempting thing is to just tell them to do it. But motivation is rarely that simple! To help develop a simple, focused message that really motivates each stakeholder group, think about what is in it for them. Use a worksheet such as the following to list positive and negative impacts of the change:

STAKEHOLDER IMPACT WORKSHEET

STAKEHOLDER GROUP	POSITIVE IMPACTS	NEGATIVE IMPACTS
Implementers		
Losers		
Winners		
Influencers		

This worksheet is the key to how stakeholders will perceive the change, and it will help you make sure they see it in as positive a light as possible.

Your first task as a communicator is to make sure all stakeholders get enough information to see these positive and negative impacts clearly. Otherwise, you will be communicating to them on the basis of false assumptions about what they know and think. Your second task as a communicator is to make sure you craft a message for each group that will generate the desired behavior given the stake they have in the change–which is indicated by the Impact Worksheet. To do this, you must put your communications into the context of this impact. Otherwise, you are not really communicating to them on the level they care about.

Step 5. Decide what you need to communicate to each stakeholder group. You have done some basic preparatory work. You've defined the changes clearly, figured out who cares about them, defined the actions you want those people to take, and thought about what is in it for them. That research doesn't take very long–usually just a little time thinking about it before you try to write. But I guarantee it will make your communications more open, helpful, and motivational!

After you research the situation, you know who you need to communicate to, what they need to do, and how they will perceive the change. You are now ready to craft a simple, clear message to communicate with each stakeholder group. It should be action oriented, and it should state both desirable actions and undesirable actions.

A generic format for the action part of the communication is as follows: *to bring about the needed change, you will have to do X and Y; some of you have asked if you can do Z, but this will only lengthen the process and make it more difficult.* You get the idea, right?

You should also plan to add (usually at the end) some *invitational elements*. That's what I call them, anyway, and they are invitations to provide you with feedback. If you respect your employees, you have to respect their reactions and opinions. And a great way to show that respect is to end any communication, even an announcement about a decision they weren't privy to, by inviting their feedback.

Note that one message, including both an action statement and an impact statement, is needed for each of the four stakeholder groups. For instance, you might craft the following message for employees whom you want to participate in your new recognition program:

Dear Employees:

I've redesigned the incentive system to eliminate cash bonuses, introduce merchandise coupons as rewards, and make the selection of winners more fair and accurate. In the new system, employees will nominate each other for rewards by filling out a nomination form and dropping it in a box or by sending me an e-mail.

Most of you will find that you receive more rapid, accurate feedback from this system, and I think you are going to love the new merchandise you'll get to buy using your reward points. You can store up reward points until you have enough to buy the products or trips of your choice. Some employees may miss the cash bonuses, especially those who seemed to have figured out how to get them every month under the old system. But I hope they will find the new rewards even more appealing and valuable.

It is possible that some people will ask you to nominate them in the hope of accumulating more points than they deserve. Of course, I discourage this because it will take the fun out of the system for the rest of us, and I don't think it will be practical anyway because the nomination forms need to include a good explanation of why the person deserves a reward.

Systems like this have recently been introduced at the X and Y companies, and I hear from their employees that they are very popular. I hope this one will be a big success for us, and look forward to hearing what you think about it.

Please stop me in the hall, send me an e-mail, or visit my office if you have any questions or suggestions.

Sincerely,

Your Manager

Now, you might have noticed that the communication designed using the planning process turned out to be fairly detailed. There were a lot of things to cover. The planning process uncovers lots of important points you will want to put into your communication.

But it's okay to go into detail when communicating about something as important as a new reward program. Employees want to know all the things this memo contains. They want to know whom it will affect, what they are expected to do, what the pros and cons are, and even what not to do. This information qualifies as "open communication" from management, and is therefore motivational. It's what employees say they want in survey after survey, so let's give it to them!

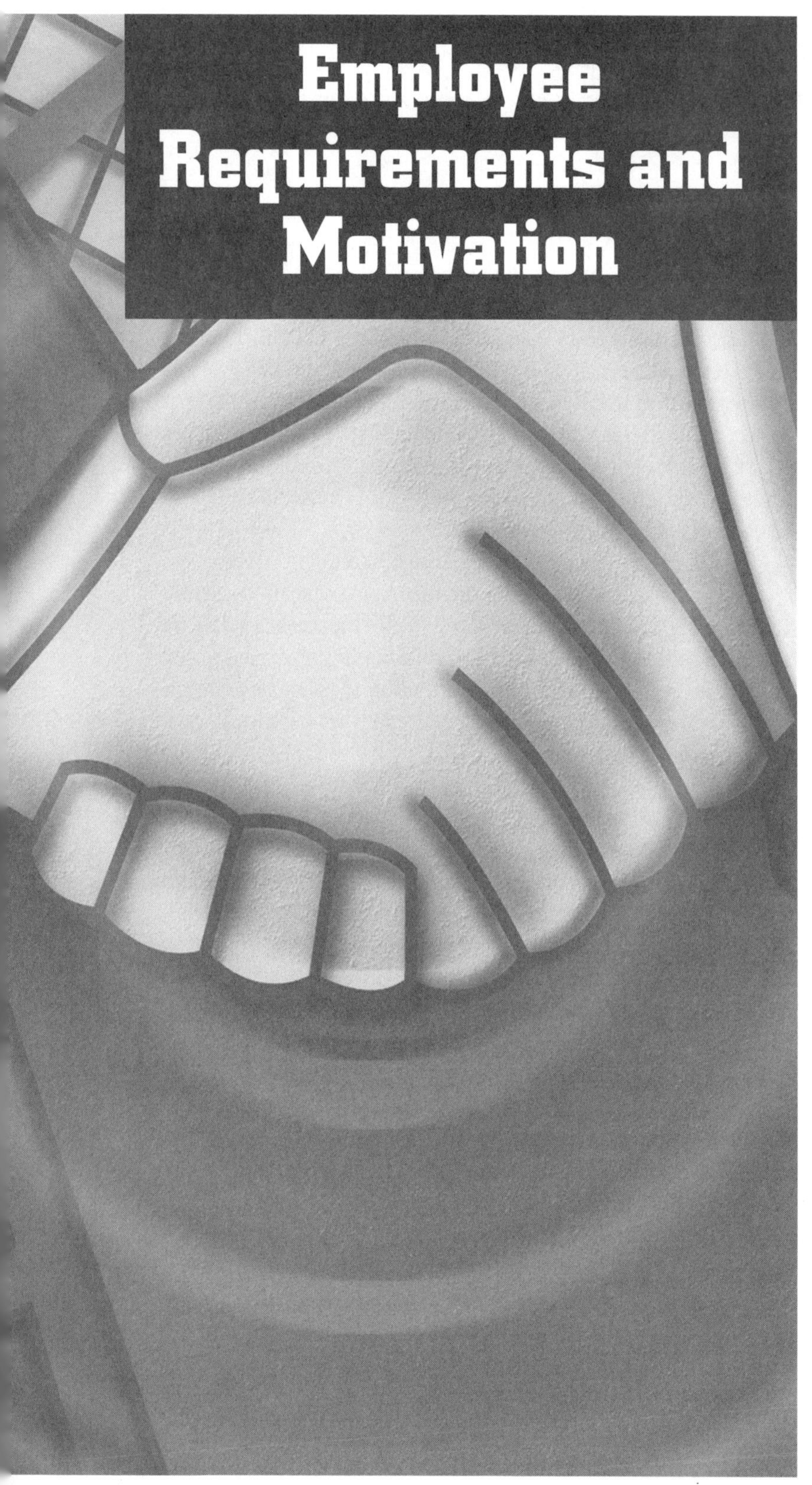

Employee Requirements and Motivation

Chapter 4

> Any time you make people feel better about themselves, you are building strong motivation.
> —REBECCA BOYLE, EMPIRE OF AMERICA FEDERAL SAVINGS BANK

In the previous chapter, we "checked the mirror" to see how your employees view you and their jobs. Are they happy enough with the general situation to be able to pay attention to your efforts to motivate them?

If not, if they are distracted, then motivational efforts won't make a bit of difference. They will appear to be immune to incentives and rewards. You won't be able to generate any significant commitment to work. That's why you need to understand employees' evaluative criteria, the criteria that they think about, consciously or unconsciously, and that determine whether they buy in to their jobs and your efforts to motivate them.

As we saw in Chapter 3, one of the biggest concerns for employees is that managers provide open communication, giving employees the information they need on the topics that interest them. By recognizing and fixing any information problems, you can help create the kind of open communication that employees say is their top priority. But if you allow communications issues to distract your employees, your communication problem will become a motivation problem, too.

Quite a few issues can work in a similar manner. If employees feel job insecurity or feel threatened with loss of status, for example, they will be concerned about this issue and not easy to engage in motivational efforts. Here are the evaluative criteria of concern to employees that we explore in this book:

1. Open communication (Chapter 3)
2. Security (this chapter)
3. Commitment (this chapter)
4. Fairness (this chapter)
5. Respect (this chapter)
6. Development opportunities (this chapter)

In this chapter, I'll take you through the rest of these employee criteria to help you see the situation the way your employees do. You need to consider each of these criteria when "checking the mirror" to see what factors could be interfering with your efforts to motivate your people. Often, one or more of these is an issue in employees' minds, and you simply have to fix it before you can turn your attention to moving them up their personal motivation curves.

Security

It's hard to focus on a task when you feel as though there are serious threats that affect your safety. For example, do you think you could concentrate on reading this book if you had just been told a tornado was in your area and could be coming your way?

Yet there are often security issues in employees' minds that loom as large as the threat of an earthquake or storm. And some managers are viewed as unpredictable and dangerous–the workplace equivalent of a drunk with a knife. You just want to steer clear of them. You certainly wouldn't want to let them get you into a conversation.

What makes a workplace unsafe? One of the biggest factors these days is the risk of a downsizing or cutback that eliminates jobs. Whether it actually cuts your job or not, it greatly increases the perception that your job is not safe.

If you think about the widespread nature of layoffs and cutbacks, combined with the clearly visible trend to replace full-time people with temps, you can make an educated guess that the majority of employees feel some insecurity from this direction. And that insecurity can easily get in the way of their buying into motivational efforts.

The problem is strikingly visible in two statistics from a survey of workplaces by consulting firm Arthur D. Little. First, they found that 60 percent of organizations are introducing major changes designed to "improve employee satisfaction" and boost motivation and performance levels. But, second, they also reported that more than 80 percent of organizations consider "overhead reductions and streamlining the organization" as a key objective of change. So a large majority of employees will see continued threats to their jobs, even as they experience those new incentives and rewards. What do you think the net result on employee attitudes will be? (I don't think the lambs will be very sleepy.)

> The lion and the lamb shall lie down together, but the lamb will not be very sleepy.
>
> —WOODY ALLEN (IN THE MOVIE *LOVE AND DEATH*)

The now-prevalent approach of introducing major, threatening changes along with new incentives and rewards is the workplace equivalent of saying, "I brought you a good book to read. And by the way, there's a tornado headed this way." If you expect someone to give that book their rapt attention, you're in for a disappointment.

Other safety concerns work on a smaller scale, but can be equally distracting. From the employee viewpoint, many management efforts to link rewards and other consequences with performance are seen as threat-based management. "If you don't do this, I'll do _____ to you." Or, in the case of "positive" incentives and rewards, "If you don't do this, you won't earn the reward." Either way, such efforts to motivate can degenerate into threats in the employee's eyes. Then there are the intended threats, as when a supervisor gets mad and punishes or threatens to punish an employee.

> Whenever our people hear the word "reengineering" they run for cover.
>
> —A manager with a major telecommunications firm

I have to backpedal a bit here because I know I'm at risk of losing you. You probably don't agree that employees feel threatened by their bosses, even though I did my best to convince you back in Chapter 1. At least *your* employees certainly don't feel threatened by *you*, right? But I've done a lot of surveys of employees in which I've been able to document fears and anxieties that indicate employees do feel threatened by their managers. And *they do not feel safe in their jobs*. You're going to have to trust me on this one.

It's not just that they might lose their jobs. After all, most supervisors cannot be blamed for a company's decision to downsize. And even though downsizings are traumatic events, they don't occur every month or even (at most companies) every year. (On average, employees in the United States run a one in thirty chance of losing their jobs according to my analysis of government statistics.) Why don't employees feel secure in the short term and in their direct relationships with their supervisors?

Because there are lots of *little injuries* they experience or anticipate. Industrial psychologist Andrew DuBrin divides these fears and concerns into seven broad categories:

1. *Financial concerns.* Will the supervisor or the organization as a whole do something that takes money out of the employee's pocket? Bottom-line financial worries are a serious threat for

many employees, since the supervisor and the organization control the "purse strings." For instance, a bad write-up or performance review by you could prevent your employee from qualifying for the raise he or she is counting on. We're talking about a serious threat here. See what I mean?

2. *Fear of the unknown.* Uncertainty about what the supervisor or company will do or how it might affect the employee creates risk. And risk means trouble. If you aren't sure what will happen, you can feel out of control of your fate. And that is very threatening indeed.
3. *Erosion of power and influence.* Supervisors often fail to appreciate the importance of status and power issues to employees. If you introduce a change in procedures that takes someone out of the loop in order to make a work process flow more smoothly, that individual will probably resent the change and feel that his or her power and influence are threatened. Oops!
4. *Difficulty breaking old habits.* It's a hassle to relearn something in order to accommodate the supervisor's latest bright idea. Sure, you meant only to be helpful when you said, "I've been thinking. Why don't you do it this way instead of that way?" Your goal is improved performance. But they may feel you are threatening them by forcing them to relearn their job. When they follow their habit, they are competent and the work is easy. When they have to do it *your* way, they are forced to be incompetent. Will they ever be as good at the new method as the old? Probably, but at first it doesn't seem that way, so the change is viewed as a personal threat to their competency.
5. *Inconvenience.* Then there is the added trouble of a transition. Even if they have the confidence to try it a new way, and believe they can learn new habits to replace the old, they still have to *do* it. Every time you have a bright idea, or you have to implement someone else's bright idea, you make your employees' work more difficult. Inconvenience is perhaps too mild a word for someone who barges in and makes your work more difficult for no good reason. That's a serious threat to your sanity if you are like most employees!

Your goal is improved performance. But they may feel you are threatening them by forcing them to relearn their job.

6. *Prior negative experiences with change.* Some people are naturally very open to change and thrive on variety. Others are afraid of change. Those who fear changes typically have had some bad experiences with them in the past. Even though your change may not be harmful, they remember that old conditioning and feel threatened because of it. The worst part of this problem is that any change experiences, on the job or off, can create a negative attitude toward your proposed change. DuBrin gives this example:

   Parents may have told a child that geographic relocation would be a wonderful experience. In reality, the child felt lonely and friendless in the new location. Later in life an executive tells that same person that she will enjoy relocation to another company division. Childhood memories predispose the person to balk at relocation.

   It's easy to create a sense of threat by pushing these hidden emotional buttons. You have to be a good listener to surface such concerns and deal with them effectively.

It's awfully hard to know what the right thing to do is, and sometimes employees can see the flaws before you do.

7. *Legitimate concerns about proposed change.* To put this point in employee-speak, *managers are often wrong.* "They say we have to do such-and-such, and that it will produce great results. But they don't know the half of it. When we do it that way, all hell is going to break lose."

   Well, it's true. Sometimes your ideas or the ideas of your superiors are just plain wrong. They have some flaws that management has overlooked. It's awfully hard to know what the right thing to do is, and sometimes employees can see the flaws before you do. And when they feel they are being forced to implement a bad plan, they feel threatened by their *anticipation* of what will go wrong. They fear they will be blamed for the bad consequences they can't prevent. And that is also a significant threat. (Not only that, but it touches on respect and trust criteria, too.)

When you look at the workplace through your employees' eyes, it *does* look like a threatening place. Threats include the occasional "perfect storm" of a downsizing, rightsizing, merger, acquisition, reorganization, or reengineering initiative. And they include routine personal concerns such as those raised by the day-to-day decisions and actions of management.

Unless you tune your ear to the employees' concern for threats to security, you won't be able to prevent them from contaminating the motivation process. *There are two practical steps you can take to reduce the threats employees feel:*

- *Don't make unnecessary threats.* Often, employees fear the worst when a more optimistic view could be justified. When you know they may sense a threat, counter that tendency by explaining why it isn't really very threatening to them. Often, the threats are more imagined than real. Workplace threats usually have a far worse bark than bite. So you can defuse them simply by talking about them and showing employees that they will be okay.
- *Help them cope with legitimate threats.* A threatened downsizing is a real deal, and employees are justified in feeling threatened. You can't argue it away unless you are willing to lie (forget it–they'll learn the truth later and never trust you again!). So you have to help them cope with legitimate threats by giving them what support and aid you can. Whenever you sense a threatening side to actions you or the organization take, you need to acknowledge the threat. You need to provide some reassurances. You need to help employees feel strong and resilient enough to cope with the threats. Your sympathy and support will help them feel stronger. And if you can give them control over other things in their work lives to compensate for their lack of control over the threat, that also goes a long way toward reviving their spirits. (Also check out the reassure leadership style in Chapter 11, where I'll teach you about the commitment-based leadership methodology.)

The best antidote for lack of control in one area is increased control in another.

The worse the news, the more effort should go into communicating it.
—ANDREW S. GROVE, CHAIRMAN, INTEL CORP.

Commitment

Are you committed to whatever direction you are asking your employees to go? Many managers appear to be as changeable as the wind. From week to week and even day to day, their priorities seem to shift and reshuffle. Even major, long-term initiatives like reengineering, total quality control, and customer service excellence seem to come and go over time with little explanation.

Of course, there are always good reasons for these changes of heart. A supervisor is committed to whatever priorities the senior managers demand of him or her. And senior managers react to changes in the status of the organization or the world in which it must compete, so their priorities may change, too. But in spite of there being good reasons for many of the changes in direction, they look to employees like, well, like continuous changes in direction!

As a result, it seems as though management can't make up their minds about what they want to do next. They collectively seem to act like squirrels caught in the headlights of an oncoming car. First they dash one way, then another, then back again. And with each new dash, they expect perfect commitment from their employees.

Ever asked employees how smart they think their managers are? I have, and it's a real eye opener. Usually, they rate their immediate supervisors as moderately smart, but not as smart as they are. And they rate the next level of managers as even dumber, and so on up the hierarchy. The top executives are typically viewed as *completely out to lunch*! If employees encountered a squirrel in the road with as much intelligence as they attribute to their CEO, many of them would feel no compunctions about running it down. This is such a little-known but vital point that I feel a strong urge to break into large lettering to emphasize it (you might consider enlarging this and *posting it by your desk* to avoid making this common mistake).

How can you expect employees to respect you when you constantly seem to be flip-flopping?

* * *

Each change of direction strengthens the view that you have no idea where you are or where you are going.

* * *

Unless you share your view of the situation, they are perfectly justified in assuming you can't see a thing.

Why should they throw themselves into the latest project as if it were a life-or-death matter when they figure you'll probably forget all about it in a little while?

To employees, most managers seem to lack commitment. The constant shifts of direction and reshuffling of priorities send an unintended signal that today's priority will be forgotten tomorrow (and it often is, after all!). Some employees learn to "wait it out" when they get an unpalatable instruction, knowing that the boss will probably forget all about it when some new problem catches his or her eye.

The problem, and it's a whopper, is that you as a supervisor are asking employees to give you a level of commitment that you do not seem to display in your own behavior. Why should they throw themselves into the latest project as if it were a life-or-death matter when they figure you'll probably forget all about it in a little while?

So *your* apparent level of commitment needs to be high. When you look at yourself in the mirror, ask yourself how committed to your own goals you seem to be from the employees' perspective. In many cases, managers may appear to be going in a new direction to their employees, when they are actually trying a new approach to an existing direction. It is common to pursue a single goal in multiple ways until you find the one that works best. But if you are experimenting, you better tell your employees so and ask them to help you on your quest. Otherwise, they'll just think you can't figure out how to get out of the road before the next car comes along.

Instead of sharing their journeys of discovery, most managers feel that they need to act as if they always know what's best. That precludes learning or experimenting, of course. So they don't like to admit to uncertainty. But by pretending they know what's best, they end up presenting each new approach as if it is the ultimate solution. Which sends the unintended signal that they can't make up their mind about what to do next. It undermines their commitment to their course of action (or to any course of action) in the eyes of their employees.

> Employees' doubts about being treated fairly in the workplace are growing.
> —STEVE BOOKBINDER, TOWERS PERRIN

Fairness

Fairness is an important criterion for many employees, and if they feel the workplace is not fair, this will definitely interfere with your efforts to motivate them.

Employees are keenly aware that their managers have more authority than they do, and worry that they will not be treated fairly as a result. Lacking the power to stick up for themselves, they are quick to perceive unfairness in the treatment they receive from those who do hold power. Unfortunately, most employees feel that unfair treatment is commonplace in their organizations. That puts you and other managers at a disadvantage when it comes to motivating employees because you must work against this perception of unfairness.

You need to be aware that employees are quick to judge your actions on the fairness scale, and because of previous injustices, they may see unfair treatment where none was intended. Minor issues from your perspective will be major to them, so keep your antennae up when it comes to questions of fairness.

Here are some statistics I derived from a major employee survey conducted by the consulting firm Towers Perrin to explore the issue of perceived fairness in the workplace.

PERCENT OF EMPLOYEES BELIEVING THAT	
Promotions are unfair	65%
Companies don't consider employees' interests in decisions affecting them	69%
Job openings aren't filled with the most qualified candidates	51%
Top performers aren't rewarded with higher pay	66%

The fairness issue arises whenever raises, perks, promotions, rewards, recognition, and other benefits are handed out (also when assignments are given out). Some get them, some don't. What if everyone who doesn't get a reward feels he or she has been treated unfairly? Usually rewards are given to a minority of employees, so the trust issue could turn rewards into *de*motivators for the majority who don't get them! (It's amazing how easy it is for well-intentioned efforts to backfire.)

So it is important for supervisors to think about fairness whenever they make a decision that affects individual employees *differently*. And many decisions do. Perhaps certain desks or offices are considered better than others. Or certain vacation times are most desirable. I know of one case in which the head nurse in a hospital ward did not give much thought to the issue of allocating vacation periods. Knowing this, one of the other nurses signed up for prime periods, holidays and peak summer weeks, for several years in a row. All the other nurses were stuck with less desirable slots because they got to the signup sheet later.

Confronted with what the nurses felt was a serious injustice, the head nurse threw up his hands and said it was up to them to solve the problem. As a result, his ability to motivate and manage them was undermined for the rest of his tenure. One little case of unfairness is all it took to sabotage his leadership ability. Don't let that happen to you!

Another common fairness problem arises from what I term a *structural unfairness*. That's when employees feel that the basic terms of their employment are unjust because others are getting a better deal than they are. For instance, if you find out that people who do your job at a competing company receive a higher salary and better benefits, then you will feel that there is a fundamental unfairness in the terms of your employment. Such structural unfairness undermines any positive attitudes and destroys motivation.

No amount of motivational methods, rewards, and incentives can undo a structural unfairness. It simply must be remedied before you can go on to performance motivation. Which means you need to give some thought to fairness issues when you define the structure of a job, especially in the areas of compensation, benefits, and hours.

Motivation Idea 7

Sticky Praise

To make sure your employees know you notice when they do well, and to reaffirm their personal interpretation that their performance was good, you need to praise them briefly but frequently. In other words, you need to stick to it. So why not use a medium for your praise that also sticks to it?

Post-it or competing brands of sticky notes are great for giving quick, handwritten affirmations of good performances. (And 3M is not underwriting this book, in case you're suspicious as to whether I really mean it.) We all have pads of this sticky note paper around the office, but nobody ever thinks to use it for communicating praise. Why don't you select a color nobody uses for anything else in the office, and make it your Praisings Pad. Keep some around your desk or in your briefcase or daily calendar—somewhere you will see them frequently during the work day. And whenever you see a pad in your color, ask yourself who might deserve a quick praising.

Oh, and keep it informative and positive. Not negative. Not controlling. If you want to tell

(continued on next page)

MOTIVATION IDEA 7

(continued from previous page)

somebody, "Good try but you need to improve X, Y, and Z," tell them in person. Don't contaminate your sacred fuchsia Praise Pad, or they'll worry when they see the next note instead of feeling good.

Stick quick notes like "Juan, thanks for handling that customer problem so well. I appreciate it.—Julia" where the employee will see it in the normal course of his or her work.

Don't overuse your Praise Pad, but don't forget about it either. If an employee is properly managed and is given an appropriate level of challenge, he or she will naturally tend to do something notably superior or clever at least once a week. Once a day would be great, but I doubt you'll start there so if you are writing notes to each employee every hour, you are overpraising, and it will come across as controlling. Which will lead to "learned helplessness" and lower commitment, not higher. Wow. Nothing's simple, huh? But the Praise Pad is certainly one of the simplest motivation tools around. Go check the supply closet or stationery store to find "your" color right now!

Try to be at or above the average so employees will be pleased by what they learn of others' treatment. They have no objections to being treated unfairly if they are treated unfairly *well* instead of unfairly poorly.

It is a good idea to check on what benefits are offered at other companies like yours so that you can anticipate the impact such information might have on employees' perceptions of fairness. Or you can consult the following table, which I compiled from U.S. Bureau of Labor Statistics surveys.

BENEFITS BENCHMARKS

	BIG COMPANIES (MORE THAN 100 WORKERS)	SMALL COMPANIES (FEWER THAN 100 WORKERS)
Paid Time Off	**Percentage of Employees**	
Paid vacations	**97**	**88**
Paid holidays	**91**	**82**
Sick leave	**65**	50
Personal leave	21	13
Maternity/family leave	3	2
Unpaid Time Off		
Maternity/family leave	**60**	47
Paternity leave	**53**	–
Insurance		
Life insurance	**91**	**61**
Medical care	**82**	**66**
Dental care	**62**	28
Vision care	26	10
Long-term disability insurance	41	20

	BIG COMPANIES (MORE THAN 100 WORKERS)	SMALL COMPANIES (FEWER THAN 100 WORKERS)
Additional Benefits		
Retirement plans	**78**	42
Education	**72**	37
Employee assistance programs	**62**	15
Travel accident insurance	44	13
Nonproduction bonuses	38	47
Wellness programs	37	6
Recreational facilities	26	5
Child care	7	1
Employee stock ownership	3	–

Bold numbers indicate benefits available to more than half of employees in your company's size category. Employees can reasonably expect these benefits at better employers. Other benefits are reasonably viewed as "extras."

If you find it is impractical to remedy a structural unfairness at the moment, then you will need to compensate for it. Greater flexibility is a good compensation for fewer benefits, for example. With a little imagination (yours and perhaps your employees' as well), you can often find a way to make it seem fair without requiring you to spend more money on costly benefits or raises. But one way or another, you need to fix any structural unfairness that threatens to contaminate the motivation environment.

For example, one nonprofit human rights organization offers its employees three weeks paid vacation plus the option of another three weeks unpaid leave each year, starting in the first year of employment. This is obviously a far better vacation plan than they could get at higher-paying for-profit jobs, and it helps the organization hire and motivate top employees in spite of somewhat lower pay levels.

Motivation Idea 8

Use Praise to Reaffirm Direction

As long as you are writing quick, informative notes from your Praise Pad of sticky paper (see Motivation Idea 7), why not use them to reaffirm your commitment to an important goal, strategy, or initiative? It's easy. Just select performances to praise that are somehow relevant to the direction in which you are trying to get everyone to go. Then design your praising to inform them of the relevance between the specific action they took and the big-picture goal you want everyone to accomplish.

For instance, you might write, "Juan, thanks for handling that customer problem so well. It moves us one step closer to our Transform Customer Service goal.—Julia" instead of a more generic message like "Juan, thanks for handling that customer problem so well. I appreciate it.—Julia." (Of course this approach works equally well with verbal praise, e-mail praise, or any other form of positive feedback, too.)

The link in your message between a specific behavior and the end goal reinforces the goal, and helps the employee see which behaviors are relevant to accomplishing that goal and how they are relevant. So you can build task-related motivation and also broader commitment to cause at the same time. Good work!

> The biggest lie told by most corporations, and they tell it proudly, is that "people are our most important assets." Total fabrication. They treat people like raw material. If you're serious about treating people as an asset, we're looking at a dramatic increase in investment in them.
>
> —MICHAEL HAMMER

Respect

Do you respect employees? Only if they feel that you take them seriously. And if you don't display an obvious interest in and respect for their ideas and their work, then they won't think you take them seriously.

When you take someone seriously, you care about their needs and desires, not only what they produce. You care about what they feel and what they can become. You care about their inner life so they can, too. And that helps them on their journey of self-awareness.

What is self-awareness, what does it have to do with job motivation, and why am I talking about it in the context of respect? I thought you'd never ask!

Billie Jean King once said, "I think self-awareness is probably the most important thing towards being a champion." If you aren't attending to your own performance and to the thoughts and feelings that shape it, you can't improve it. And to attend to yourself, to be sufficiently self-aware to manage your own development, you have to respect yourself. You have to feel that your thoughts and feelings and the performances they produce are valuable enough to be worthy of your undivided attention.

So self-respect is a prerequisite for self-awareness. And supervisors who treat employees without respect hurt their self-respect. Which gets in the way of attention to self. It makes them feel unworthy. It keeps them from becoming champions. So it is important to affirm people's importance in your attitude toward them. It is important to affirm their importance in ways you might not have expected. Your respect builds their own self-respect, which helps them gain the self-awareness needed to develop into champions. Wow! You never know what you are messing with when you start messing around with people's feelings.

> I don't want to take myself seriously, but I want others to.
>
> —NINA TSAO

Another aspect of respect is that it leads you to have a genuine concern for each employee's concerns and desires. *What they want is important* if you respect them. That doesn't mean you will necessarily give them what they want, but by respecting their right to have wants, you will at least dignify their desires with a respectful level of

What Your Employees Are Really Doing on the Internet

Here's a funny message someone wrote and circulated on the Internet. I'm pretty sure it has made its way to every Web-connected employee in every English-speaking office everywhere in the world by now. But I don't know if *you've* seen it since you're one of "them."

Prison vs. Work

In prison you spend the majority of your time in an 8×10 cell. At work you spend most of your time in a 6×8 cubicle.

In prison you get three meals a day. At work you only get a break for one meal and you have to pay for it yourself.

In prison you get time off for good behavior. At work you get rewarded for good behavior with more work.

In prison a guard locks and unlocks all the doors for you. At work you must carry around a security card and unlock all the doors for yourself.

In prison you can watch TV and play games. At work you can get fired for watching TV and playing games.

In prison you get your own toilet. At work you have to share.

In prison all expenses are paid by taxpayers with no work required. At work you get to pay all the expenses to go to work and they deduct taxes from your salary to pay for prisoners.

In prison you spend most of your life looking through bars inside, wanting to get out. At work you spend most of your time wanting to get out and go inside bars.

In prison there are wardens who are often sadistic. At work they are called managers.

It goes to show that there are many ways to look at the workplace. Until you are able to appreciate your employees' perspective, you don't really know *how* they see it. Are you a supportive, helpful supervisor . . . or just another warden?

Food for thought.

"It's as if I'm not in the room," many employees say when describing their interactions with their managers.

interest and attention. They will therefore feel that it is more likely they will be able to get what they want eventually, in one way or another. And that sets them up for a high level of self-motivation.

Many employees feel that their supervisor has no appreciation for or interest in what they want. People describe their experiences with their supervisors as if they are dealing with creatures from another planet who just don't "get it." Aliens in human bodies who seem to be perfectly normal, but are strangely unable to listen to employee concerns and respect employee requests. "It's as if I'm not in the room," many employees say when describing their interactions with their managers.

The reason managers have trouble "hearing" what employees want is that they don't respect them enough to care. If you think someone isn't important, then you won't find their needs to be important either. And they will respond to this disrespect by withdrawing emotionally. They may still do their work perfectly well because they respect *themselves* enough to feel bad if they didn't. But they will be completely immune to the motivational efforts of any manager who does not respect them.

Many women in business feel that male supervisors disrespect them by assuming they are motivated by family concerns, not career goals. There are many cases in which women get fed up and quit because their supervisors thwarted their career goals. But the supervisors typically don't realize what they've done. They just didn't respect their employees enough to really listen and find out what they wanted. If they had, in many cases, they would have been able to find a way to give them what they wanted and thus keep them engaged and motivated in the work of the company. That is what a study by consulting firm Catalyst revealed. The following case illustrates the respect problem particularly well (from *The Wall Street Journal*, November 11, 1997, p. B1):

> **What drove her to leave the bank was the fact that she was turned down when she requested a transfer from mutual-fund services to investment management and, later, did not get the raise she thought she deserved. At**

her exit interview, the bank's human-resources manager said "You're leaving for lifestyle reasons, right?"

If you respect your employees, you don't make mistakes like that. You certainly don't ignore obvious signs of a desire to try something new and make some progress. The employee described in the quote was highly motivated to develop in her career, but *nobody paid any attention to her desire to accomplish and achieve*. It is highly disrespectful to ignore such requests. Even if she couldn't be given the opportunities she asked for, she could certainly have been given *some* opportunities to grow and develop, and in time, those might have led to or even replaced the opportunities she sought.

Which leads us to the next important criterion by which employees evaluate their supervisor and workplace—the desire for developmental opportunities. It is closely related to respect because the workplace that respects its employees believes in them and wants them to grow and develop. The company or supervisor who does not seem to respect employees is also likely to take no interest in their need for personal development. And if your employees think you have these attitudes, they will certainly treat all of your efforts to motivate them with scorn. *You don't respect someone's desires if they don't respect yours.*

The workplace that respects its employees believes in them and wants them to grow and develop.

Development Opportunities

People have a very natural and healthy urge to accomplish things, both in the short term and in the long term. As a result, they wish to grow and develop so that they are able to accomplish more and more as time goes by. Sometimes their desires seem to be at odds with the goals of the organization, as when employees desire raises and promotions and companies want to minimize payroll costs. But you can't expect the same people to do the same work the same way, year after year, and still have a healthy, motivated work force. Everyone needs opportunities to grow.

MOTIVATION IDEA 9

Subsidized Dining Room

Here's a good one on the free lunch theme. Create a dining room or (if that's not economical) hire a caterer to prepare and bring in lunches. Start doing it one day a week, and if it pays off, expand to more days. The key is to offer good food for free or at least well below market rates to all employees. It's not as expensive as you might think, and people really like being treated to a good meal.

Benefits. It shortens lunch hours by reducing the travel time, shows great respect for your people (if you really value their work, why not make sure they are well fed and contented while working?), and it encourages mingling and sharing of information, ideas, and solutions since your employees will tend to eat with each other a great deal more than they used to. A lot of good work gets done, or at least planned, in the corporate dining rooms at Coca-Cola's headquarters, for example. And the food's pretty darn good, too!

William J. O'Brien, the former head of the Hanover Insurance companies, believes that "People are reaching for self-respect and self-actualization. Those things happen through engagement with family or work–so the key to motivation is designing organizations congruent with those needs."

This is a powerful statement, well worth the time it takes to think through exactly what he's getting at. As I read it, he seems to be calling for us to line up business goals with personal goals. For instance, if the business has a growth goal to bring in more revenues, then how might this be implemented so as to give the maximum number of employees an opportunity to pursue their career development goals? The most obvious solutions involve sharing the wealth, but cash isn't always the most motivating reward.

Let's take a look at one of the classic studies of employee motivation, by Frederick Herzberg. He studied thousands of workers back in the 1950s to find out what factors contributed to their motivation. Approaching the question with an open mind, he looked at a long list of possible sources of motivation. Some of the items on his list turned out to be important when he analyzed his data, and others didn't. The interesting thing, at the time and still a dramatic finding, was that development-related factors popped up to the top of the list. They were highly motivational.

The things people usually work with in their efforts to motivate employees, including salaries, were not as important. They didn't explain as much of the variation in people's motivation.

Here is a summary of his findings:

Very high impact	Achievement
	Recognition
High impact	The work itself
	Responsibility
Medium impact	Advancement
	Growth
	Salary

Low impact	Company policy and administration
	Supervision
	Relationship with supervisor
	Work conditions
	Relationship with peers
	Personal life
	Relationship with subordinates
	Status
	Security

At the top of this list are achievement and recognition for that achievement. Employees find that the opportunity to achieve something important makes their work meaningful. And that is the most motivating thing of all. The need for meaning in work is what drives some people to seek adventure careers, and so many others to feel trapped in their jobs and to fantasize about doing something more exciting.

Nobody goes to work to *work*. They go to work to accomplish something they can feel proud of.

Yet most jobs are built around the lower-impact factors from Herzberg's list. Although these are important and need to be present in order for motivation to be present, they don't create high motivation. They simply set the stage, making it possible for the right development opportunities to come along. When people develop in their work, learning to accomplish important things and receiving recognition for their accomplishments, that's the real drama. It takes place on a stage formed by the job description and compensation, so you can't eliminate salaries or other expected components. But it's the opportunities to accomplish something meaningful that produce exceptional levels of motivation.

Based on his findings, Herzberg developed the concept of *job enrichment* to increase motivation. It involves redesigning work to create more opportunities for accomplishment and recognition. And though there continues to be study and debate, the concept has

Employees find that the opportunity to achieve something important makes their work meaningful. And that is the most motivating thing of all.

proved successful in a wide variety of tests. You enrich jobs, according to this theory, by "vertical job loading," which uses seven different principles to enrich an employee's job. I'm going to review and explain each of these principles because they are such powerful motivational tools. (My review follows Herzberg's article in *Harvard Business Review,* Sept.-Oct. 1987.)

Switch from tracking a department's overall productivity to tracking the productivity of each individual in the department.

Principle: *Remove some controls while retaining accountability.* For example, you might stop tracking certain measures of the employee's performance, but to make sure he or she is still accountable, you could put the employee in charge of making the same measurements. This principle engages two strong motivators: personal achievement and responsibility.

Principle: *Give the employee a complete, natural unit of work.* For example, you might redesign a line of workers who hand off work, organizing it into cells with teams of workers, and having each cell do a chunk of work that produced an important component. This principle engages achievement, recognition, and responsibility.

Principle: *Increase the accountability of individuals for their own work.* For example, you might switch from tracking a department's overall productivity to tracking the productivity of each individual in the department so each can be held accountable for his or her contribution to production. This principle engages responsibility and recognition.

Principle: *Give employees more job freedom to make sure they feel they have authority in their own work.* For example, you might "put employees in charge of their own work" by asking them to submit plans for redesigning it in order to achieve quality or efficiency improvements. This principle engages the motivating power of achievement, recognition, and responsibility.

Principle: *Make management information available to employees directly, not just to their supervisors.* For example, you might try some of the new "open book management"

Give Them a Break at MTV

At MTV's headquarters in New York, employees are permitted to leave at 1:00 P.M. on summer days. And if they work the full day instead, they can take the next Friday off.

This benevolent policy indicates a healthy understanding of and respect for employees. On a hot summer day, even the most dedicated are more enthusiastic about recreation than work. By permitting, even encouraging, employees to get out of the office and "get a life," MTV improves the atmosphere in its offices. Employees don't have to pretend they are hard at work and highly motivated on a sunny Friday afternoon. The policy encourages employees to work hard and play hard, too. And notice the increased control over time the employees gain. They can shift work around so as to accommodate personal plans for long weekends. Control is a powerful motivator.

techniques, like posting weekly financials and other management indicators on all the employee bulletin boards. This approach engages the motivating power of achievement, responsibility, and recognition.

Principle: *Introduce new challenges by making tasks more complex or adding tasks.* For example, an employee who has been responsible only for answering incoming telephone calls could be put in charge of learning about the telephone system's various options and training other employees in how to use it better. This principle offers opportunities for achievement through growth and learning.

Principle: *Encourage the development of expertise.* For example, you might assign people specialized tasks. The prior example, in which a telephone operator becomes the expert on the phone system, also illustrates this principle. It taps into the power of responsibility, growth, and learning.

In horizontal job loading, you just pile up more of the same kind of work on the employee's desk or back. And that's not at all motivating.

When you use one or more of these principles to alter an employee's job, even in small, easy-to-do ways, you are increasing the motivating power of that job. And what these principles have in common is that they lead to new opportunities to develop and grow. They encourage employee development.

If you try them, be careful to avoid a common mistake: horizontal job loading. That's Herzberg's term, and it's the opposite of the vertical job loading he recommends. I find it easiest to distinguish between the two approaches by saying that you can either increase the opportunities to grow and develop through work or increase the amount of work.

In horizontal job loading, you just pile up more of the same kind of work on the employee's desk or back. And that's not at all motivating because it does not provide any development opportunities.

Both approaches often lead to more work, but more work doesn't seem bad when it is the result of more opportunity. So the distinction is critical. Just remember:

From the employee's perspective, more work is bad. But more opportunity is good, even if you have to do more work to get it.

Parting Shots

We've examined six important criteria by which employees decide whether their jobs are on the level or not. Any one of these criteria can derail your efforts to motivate employees if it isn't right. So make sure you check each criterion out before you ask for buy-in. Otherwise, you've lost the motivation game before you even got started.

We started (in the previous chapter) with the employees' desire for open communication from management. Make sure that's covered. And we ended with another really big issue, employee development opportunities. Is there room for them to spread their wings and fly? Are you giving them opportunities to grow and develop? Can they accomplish things that make them feel proud and give them a sense of, you guessed it, accomplishment? If not, back to the drawing board.

Can they accomplish things that make them feel proud and give them a sense of accomplishment? If not, back to the drawing board.

One of the factors we addressed in this chapter is security. Now, I know you can't offer anyone lifetime employment, and it might be a mistake to do so even if you could. But the kind of security people need to be effective and productive in their workplaces is far short of that ideal. They need to feel relatively safe from arbitrary bad events, so give them enough control over their daily lives and surroundings to balance the threat of occasional random no-nos like downsizings. And *they need to feel safe from you*, so try to clean up your interpersonal act and treat employees in a fair and supportive manner. (How? Reread this chapter whenever you forget, please! And also make sure you read later chapters, especially Chapter 9 on interpersonal intelligence. It's truly hard to reprogram habits we all have relied on for years.)

Before I end this chapter, I want to give you a tool to help you measure the level of threat employees feel in the workplace. It is a twenty-question assessment that takes only a few minutes at most to fill in. It is designed to be photocopied and distributed to employees

> The trees that are slow to grow bear the best fruit.
> —Molière

to find out what they feel. I've used it to predict the amount of employee resistance to change in organizations, since the level of perceived threats to security is a good predictor of how much employees will resist. And I added eight questions to the usual group of twelve security-related questions in order to make it a good indicator of problems with any of the other job criteria I covered in this chapter and the last. You can use the survey to find out whether employees have any basic buy-in issues you need to address.

Hand it out for anonymous completion by a big enough group of employees so that they won't think they may get in trouble for what they say on the assessment. That way you'll get more objective answers. And consider giving the same assessment to employees again after a few months and every six months thereafter. That way, you have an ongoing measure of their level of security or insecurity and can work on raising their average score over time.

ASSESSMENT

Please complete this as honestly as you can. Other employees are filling it in, too, and the results will be averaged.

Circle one:

yes no I worry that I may make less money as a result of changes. (a)
yes no I worry that my job is at risk. (b)
yes no I worry that my job may change but I don't know exactly how. (c)
yes no I'm afraid there may be some negative impact on me from upcoming events. (d)
yes no It's possible I will lose some of my power and authority. (e)
yes no I'm worried that my work methods and habits will be forced to change because of what's going on around me. (f)
yes no I'm currently being asked to do things that are highly inconvenient for me. (g)
yes no I'm currently being asked to do things that are highly disruptive to my regular work. (h)
yes no I have to work with new people who are difficult to handle. (i)
yes no I have to work with new people who don't pull their own weight. (j)
yes no I have to work with new people who are unhelpful and don't care about my problems or needs. (k)
yes no I worry that our organization is heading toward some serious challenges it hasn't anticipated fully. (l)
yes no I feel that individuals are treated fairly in this organization. (m)
yes no I feel that people are treated at least as well by this organization as they are by any similar organization. (n)
yes no I feel that managers are firmly committed to a course of action. (o)
yes no I feel that managers are committed to an appropriate and wise course of action. (p)
yes no I feel that employees are respected by their supervisors in this organization. (q)
yes no I feel that employees are given plenty of opportunities to grow, develop, and achieve their potential in this organization. (r)
yes no I feel that information is shared freely within this organization. (s)
yes no I am always well informed about how any changes will affect me and my work. (t)

With these twenty questions you should get a pretty good indication of how well your organization is doing on basic employee criteria. Ideally, you will get a run of no answers for the first twelve questions, the ones labeled (a) through (l). These measure different sources of threats often felt by employees. If you get some yes answers on questions (a) through (l), you've uncovered some feelings of threat that will make people resistant to supporting current initiatives. Try to remove the threats or reassure and support those who must cope with the threats.

You also want to see a run of yes answers for the last eight questions, the ones labeled (m) through (t). These are straightforward tests of the fairness, opportunity, communication, commitment, and respect criteria (the first twelve concern the security criterion since it's a more complex one to measure). If you get any no answers on questions (m) through (t), you've uncovered possible problems you will want to explore. Look for the roots of these problems in the policies and procedures of your organization or the interactions between supervisors and employees. There is something in the Us column of your Us/Them table that needs attention (see Chapter 3 if you need a review of how to use that powerful tool).

Now it's time to take a long, hard look at your employees.

Okay, that's enough. You can stop looking at yourself in the mirror. Now it's time to take a long, hard look at your employees. It's time to look at them with enough care to see beyond how they look to how they actually *feel.* Because your employees' feelings are the next stop on your quest for high employee motivation.

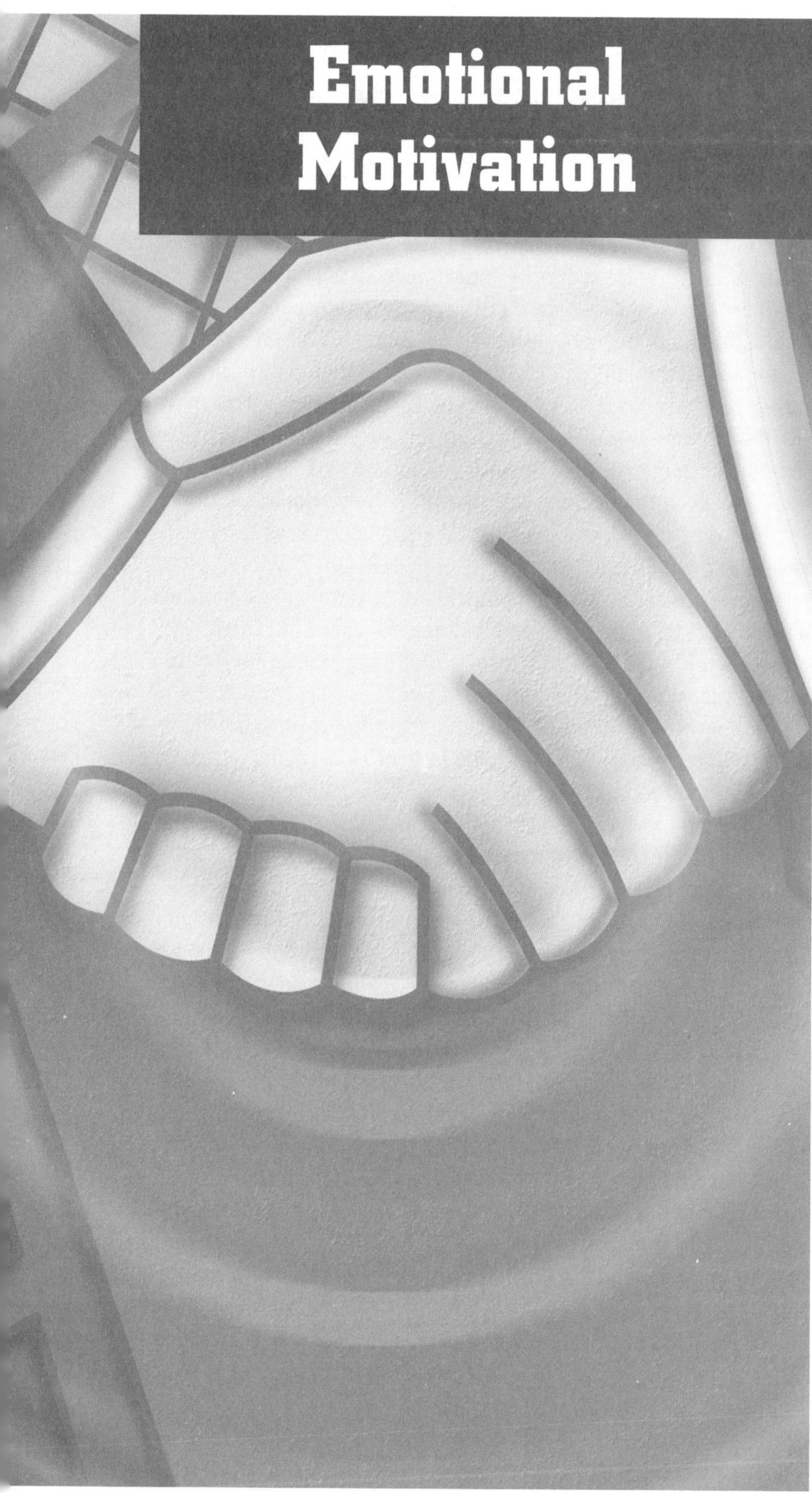

Emotional Motivation

Chapter 5

You need to make sure employees *feel good enough to get motivated.*

I originally called this chapter "Building the Emotional Foundations of Motivation." And that's what I will teach you to do in it. But I realized as I talked to managers and motivation consultants that most people (1) didn't know you needed an emotional foundation for motivation, and (2) weren't clear on what, if any, foundations might be necessary for motivation. So I decided a more in-your-face title was needed to make sure these well-meaning skeptics got what I was driving at from the very beginning. I was left with no choice but to come up with a descriptive name for the foundation you need to build and maintain true motivation.

Put most simply, you need to make sure employees *feel good enough to get motivated.*

I guess this is a radical approach to motivation, since most managers don't realize their job requires them to make sure their employees feel good. And as a result, most employees don't feel all that great most of the time they are at work.

So I've bowed to reality. I have to admit the approach you are about to learn is in fact a radical one in the field of management in spite of its solid foundations in psychology and common sense. I guess we might as well call it *emotional motivation,* on the theory that the simplest term is best. But I also think you'll agree by the end of this chapter that it is more than another new buzz word. I really don't care *what* you call it, as long as you *do* it. Because the fact is that emotional motivation is a very important complement to the more traditional rational approach to designing incentive and reward systems. Without an emotional approach, these systematic approaches are doomed.

I was intrigued to discover that so many people have so little idea about what the foundations of motivation really are. But with hindsight, I guess it makes sense, since after all most employees are not very motivated right now. Like a building's foundation, which we never actually see, there is a vital emotional foundation to motivation. And it turns out nobody looks at it very often or has much of an idea what it's made of. It's just down there somewhere. Or is it?

Unfortunately, this foundation isn't as permanent as the cement foundation beneath your home or apartment. In fact, it can be

MOTIVATION IDEA 10

Developing Positive Emotional Habits

The idea behind this method is stunningly simple: that people will *get* better at and *do* better at their jobs if you encourage them to *develop the habit of getting good at things.* Now, think about this for a moment.

It means that you don't have to focus on better job performances if that seems difficult. Just pick something, anything, and get them interested in mastering it. It can be something totally irrelevant to work or, more likely, something relevant but relatively trivial. Like getting the office plants to look healthier or even getting any plants at all to live in the office if you have none now. You might think that asking an employee to develop a green thumb doesn't do anything for his or her ability to perform complex computer programming (or whatever the employee's key value-added work assignment is). But the wonderful thing is that it does! Here's why, in the words of Daniel Goleman, Harvard-trained psychologist and best-selling author of *Emotional Intelligence*:

> Optimism and hope—like helplessness and despair—can be learned. Underlying both is an outlook psychologists call self-efficacy, the belief that one has mastery over the events of one's life and can meet challenges as they come up. Developing a competency of any kind strengthens the sense of self-efficacy, making a person more willing to take risks and seek out more demanding challenges. And surmounting those challenges in turn increases the sense of self-efficacy. This attitude makes people more likely to make the best use of whatever skills they may have—or to do what it takes to develop them.

In other words, the emotional foundation of the motivation path is really a *habit* of thought. Get people feeling good about anything—even something as goofy as putting on a good Friday afternoon barbecue for the office—and you help them develop a habit of thought that will carry over to their work and boost their motivation and performance in all they do.

I so often have to tell you that motivation is more complicated than you thought. But here's one approach that is far more simple than most people realize. *Any* opportunities to succeed will do. So simply *start small. Start with anything at all.* And *let it build naturally from there.*

assembled or destroyed in minutes, and most managers don't even notice the change.

You have a huge impact over how your people *feel.*

Do You Take Responsibility for How Your Employees Feel?

If you think long enough about your own behavior as a supervisor or leader, one of the realizations you will eventually arrive at is that you have a huge impact over how your people *feel.* Most of the links between the Us reasons for employee problems and the more obvious Them reasons are emotional links, for example. (I'm referring to the Us/Them table and analysis I introduced in Chapter 3.) And the daily mood swings of a manager affect the moods of his or her employees to an amazing extent.

Yet we all grew up in a rational management tradition. Management is taught and practiced *as if it were a science, not an interpersonal skill.* (In reality, it's probably 90 percent interpersonal skills and 10 percent science.) But our scientific management baggage leads us to overlook the many powerful emotional links between our behavior as managers and the feelings of our employees.

You aren't an engineer running a machine, you are a person trying to get other people to perform up to their potential. If you really want to take ownership of the motivation problem, *you've got to take responsibility for how you make your people feel.* Why? Because:

1. You have a surprisingly large impact on how your employees feel.
2. How they feel has a surprisingly large impact on how they perform.

Yet these simple points are not on most of our minds when we interact with our employees. They certainly don't receive much attention when people talk about employee motivation and reward programs. And that is a fatal error.

Nobody can be motivated unless they feel good about themselves and their day. That's the basic starting point for all motivation. It takes a positive frame of mind to get motivated. Let's put that in **bold** type, too, to make sure we never, ever forget it:

It takes a positive frame of mind to get motivated!

This, like much of what I've told you so far, is a simple, commonsense truth. But we often fail to follow our own commonsense judgment on the job because other beliefs and traditions steer us off course.

As a result of the almost universal tendency to focus on the rational side of management instead of the emotional side, we create a pattern of employee attitudes that guarantees mediocre performance and wavering commitment. And then we wonder why performance is suboptimal and struggle unsuccessfully with our employee motivation problems.

Even when we study the problem carefully to identify the Us reasons along with the Them reasons (using the Us/Them table in Chapter 3), it can still be maddeningly difficult to fix the problem. Even when we eliminate gross structural problems that make the workplace seem insecure, unfair, or unrewarding, as we discussed in Chapters 3 and 4, motivation may still refuse to blossom. Even when you think you've put your finger on the right cause and tried to eliminate it, you can still have trouble turning employee attitudes around. (In other words, there is *even more* to motivation than I told you about in earlier chapters. Figures, doesn't it?)

> Whatever the reasons, we do not pursue emotional development with the same intensity with which we pursue intellectual development. This is all the more unfortunate because full emotional development offers the greatest degree of leverage in attaining our full potential.
>
> —BILL O'BRIEN

A (Very) Difficult Case

For example, take the supervisor of a data entry department who was frustrated that employees kept taking extra long breaks and coming in to work late. Her first instinct was to scold them and remind them of the company policies. But after a few months of this negative approach, she realized that threats and punishments weren't very

> It takes a positive frame of mind to get motivated.
>
> —The basic tenet of Emotional Motivation

effective. They did take shorter breaks–when they thought she was looking. But they did their best to avoid her and, whenever she wasn't checking, fell back into the old habits right away.

Realizing that her approach was negative and threat based, she decided to try positive incentives. She designed a sign-in and sign-out system using a big board just outside her office, and rearranged the cubicles so that the only way to enter or exit the office was by her door. Then she announced a program of cash rewards for the employees who missed the least amount of work time each week. Now she got even better compliance, and felt that she had at last solved the problem of employees shirking work.

But she continued to have a broader motivation problem and was still not satisfied. Employees worked an average of forty-five minutes longer each week than they used to, but she was startled to find they were actually less productive in spite of their longer hours. She tried adding rewards and incentives for productivity, too, but this didn't seem to fix the problem. It helped at first, but then she noticed that errors were increasing in the work. And employee turnover began to rise, forcing her to replace several seasoned people with new, less productive employees. On the advice of a consultant, she changed the rewards and increased their value, and also added incentives for quality of work. But the problems persisted.

At this point, her frustrations with "their" motivation problem higher than ever, she tried to diagnose it using the Us/Them table. And after much thought and observation, and what little listening to their side she was able to do (she often heard stray comments when she walked past the break area), she decided that the employees' perspective was indeed very different from hers. She listed a number of Us reasons, things that employees felt about her and the rest of the management team that might be at the roots of their poor motivation and performance:

- They think we are too controlling and don't trust them.
- They think we don't care about them as individuals, only "getting the work done."
- They think I'm a tough manager who is always trying to "catch them doing something wrong."

Satisfied that she had really dug deep to uncover possibly unpleasant but real attitudes, she hoped she would be able to redefine the problem in a productive manner and finally fix it for good. But when she studied her list, she was still not sure what to do. If she defined it as a "trust problem," for example, it would require her to stop tracking employees' work time, to reconfigure the office again so she couldn't see them come and go, and perhaps to "empower" them to be in charge of tracking and controlling their own hours worked. But she was very hesitant to take such steps because she was 90 percent sure the employees would abuse such displays of trust and backslide to old patterns of abuse or worse.

She had the same problem with the toughness issue. The idea of switching from "catching them doing something wrong" to "catching them doing something right" appealed to her because it would help her switch to using positive instead of negative reinforcements. In fact, she felt that she'd started to implement that idea already by offering rewards and incentives instead of just threats and punishments. But to go any further didn't sound realistic. If she stopped policing their behavior entirely, she was pretty sure they would take advantage of her and do even less and worse work.

In short, she felt as though everything she tried was like pushing down on one part of a big balloon. The problem just seemed to "pop up" somewhere else. It was impossible to burst the balloon and eliminate the problem.

And she was right, of course. No amount of fiddling is going to change the basic outlook of her employees in that data entry department because they are *on the wrong path* to start with. They are locked in a negative, us-and-them framework in which they feel that *management's role is to force them to do unpleasant things.*

And in the current framework, *their role is to avoid doing these unpleasant things called "work"* as much as possible without actually getting fired.

That is a *resistance-based* pathway, and you can't do much to boost motivation on it regardless of what steps you take. You have to go deeper than the dynamics of any specific problem to "pop the balloon." So the manager in this case just isn't at a point where she can start building motivation and performance. She has to get to an appro-

MOTIVATION IDEA 11

Fresh Flowers

Have a local florist deliver fresh flowers early each Monday morning in a bucket. Stock the supply cabinet with an assortment of simple vases. Encourage employees to select and arrange flowers for their desks. Also consider introducing a weekly or monthly contest in which employees cast ballots to decide which arrangement is the most beautiful if you want to add another dimension to this idea.

Benefits. Sets an "up" tone for the week. Gives them a reason to get in early. Shows them you appreciate them. Permits individual expression and greater control over work space. Encourages mastery of a simple but rewarding art, and the pursuit of mastery in one area tends to spill over into other areas, so encouraging them to arrange flowers nicely helps create the emotional foundations for better job performance, too.

priate starting point first. But not realizing this, she feels as though nothing works. She feels as though she has run into the limits of management. She, like many managers, is truly at her wits' end.

When Nothing Seems to Work

> Our team is well balanced. We have problems everywhere.
> —TOMMY PROTHRO, AMERICAN FOOTBALL COACH

The employee motivation problem often seems to defy rational analysis, for the simple reason that we overlook the emotional foundations of it. When you analyze and fix only what's above ground, you can't always solve motivation problems.

What you get in many situations is what I call the *performance puzzle,* as Figure 5-1 illustrates. And when you get a performance puzzle such as the one in the preceding case, you know it is time to turn your attention to the emotional foundations of motivation.

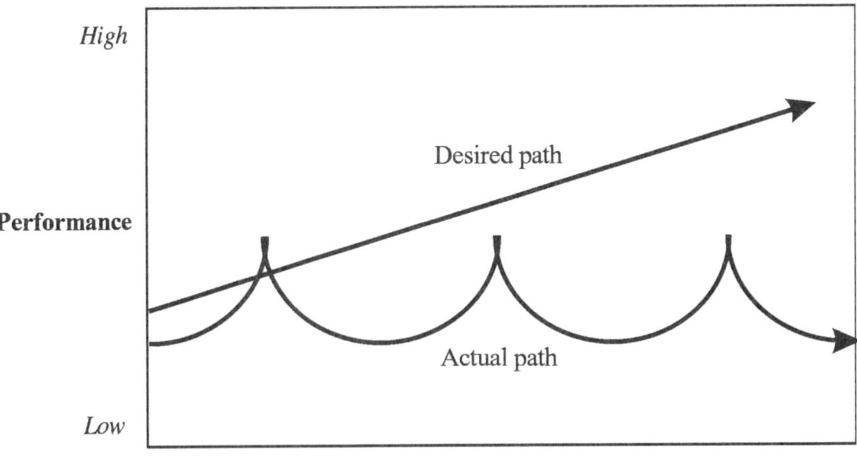

Figure 5-1

In the performance puzzle, employee performance initially responds to management pressures to improve. But it peaks prematurely, then slides back to virtually the same level at which you started. Managers conclude the "program" was flawed and seek another approach, perhaps a new incentive or reward program.

But the new program follows a similar course, with initially promising results, followed by a disappointingly premature peak and a gradual slide back to status quo. It's great for consultants and others who want to peddle yet another "solution" to motivation and performance problems because each new peak is always followed by a new trough. But it's rough sailing for the people involved, and after a while we all tire of it.

Which Path Are They On?

The reason many employees never seem to get where you want them to go is that they're on the wrong path to start with. They're on the wrong path because we got them started on the quest for higher performance without thinking about their emotional state. But emotional state has a striking impact on motivation and ultimately on performance. It forms the foundation, and depending upon the shape it takes, you can get true motivation or a false compliance that soon leads to resistance and backsliding. I bet you recognize this phenomenon and can think of many occasions where you've seen it occur.

> If you assign people duties without granting them any rights, you must pay them well.
> —GOETHE

What Emotional State Should Motivation Be Based Upon?

Here are a few interesting facts from classic psychological studies that highlight the importance of emotional state:

- Hopefulness is a better predictor of college grades than SAT scores.
- Optimistic athletes win more medals.
- And optimistic athletes are especially good at coming back from a disappointment to win anyway.

- Optimistic insurance agents outsell better-qualified pessimists by 57 percent.
- Hopeful people motivate themselves.
- Optimists are more resourceful problem solvers.

As these results illustrate so powerfully, feelings drive motivation by determining which path employees take. Get them started on the right path, the path based on optimism and hopefulness, and your motivation efforts move them toward ever higher levels of performance. But start on the wrong path and the exact same efforts will produce only disappointment. (That's why incentives that work in one case will often fail in another. Ever wonder why programs that work in one company or setting so often bomb in another? Wrong emotional foundation in all likelihood.)

The desired path, the motivation path, starts with an optimistic, positive attitude.

So how do you know when you have them going in the right direction? Is it just random chance? No, thank goodness. It's actually quite simple. Figure 5-2 shows *how* feelings drive performance. It shows two paths, and it shows how emotional frame of mind determines which path employees take in response to your efforts to motivate them.

The desired path, the motivation path, starts with an optimistic, positive attitude. You have to feel good to get this journey started. Optimism boosts confidence, which sets the stage for personal development. Success breeds success, and employees experience the exhilaration of accomplishing new and challenging goals. This is the path any highly motivated individual is on, and it's a gas.

Unfortunately, the motivation path is rare in the traditional workplace for all but the senior managers, who have enough control over their environment to make it happen for themselves (although they don't always have enough sense to do so, but that's a problem for *their* supervisors, not us).

I call the other path the resistance path. It's not nearly as much fun. It starts with a neutral or negative attitude, and deteriorates from there. If you aren't feeling really good, challenges and changes look like trouble to you. You get frustrated easily. You run through the gamut of negative emotions, feeling angry, depressed, jealous, hurt–but certainly not good about your experience.

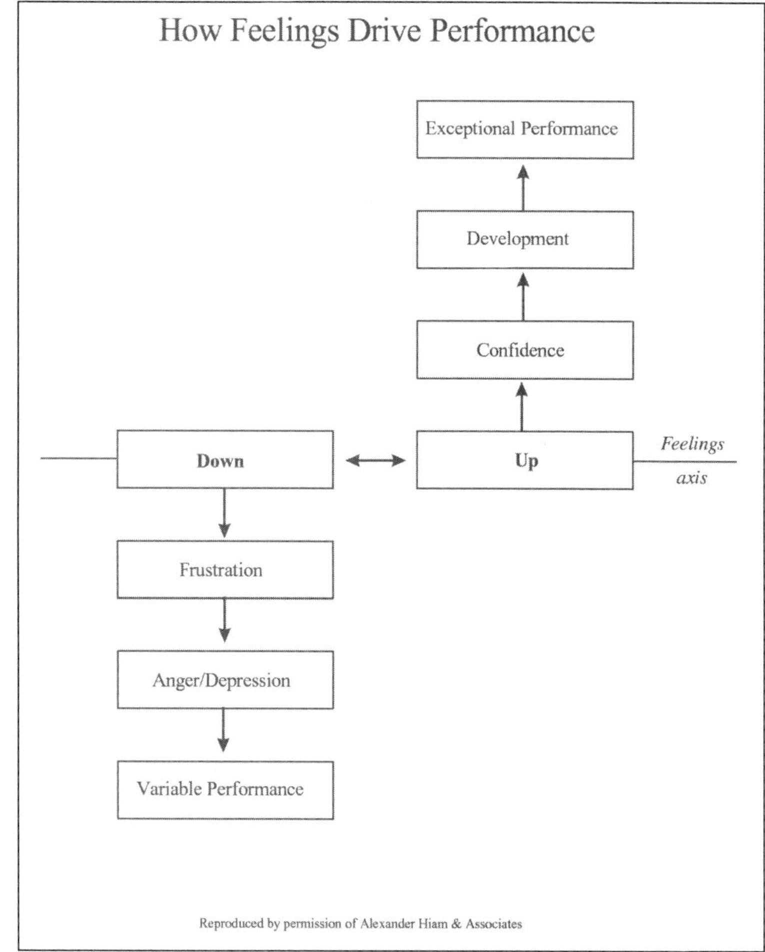

Figure 5-2

If managers push hard enough, they can generally achieve some success on the resistance path. But since the resistance path runs naturally downhill, you do have to push people pretty hard to get them to go up. Any performance peaks come as a result of managers' hard efforts. You really need to rock the boat to get any waves going. That's why successes peak early and performance falls back to suboptimal levels so often, as Figure 5-1 illustrated. The resistance path produces the performance puzzle pattern,

> The resistance path produces frequent "performance waves" instead of a rising tide of performance improvement.

with frequent "performance waves" instead of a rising tide of performance improvement.

But the fact is that the majority of workplaces are on the resistance path, not the motivation path. That's why external "push" motivation is by far the most common approach to employee motivation in workplaces today. When people are on the resistance path, they need lots of pushing to keep them moving along. So the manager's role becomes one of pushing, pushing, pushing for performance. And the more you push, the more dependent they become on your pushing. Push a little to get a result, and soon you will find you have to push a lot to get the same result.

Is your organization hooked on external motivations?

We consultants often advise organizations to replace external (or extrinsic) motivations and rewards with internal (intrinsic) ones. That's what you do when you offer the opportunities that drive peak performers such as the ones you met in Chapter 1. But when employees are on the resistance path, it can't be done. They ignore opportunities and seem to have no internal motivation of their own.

The organization is *hooked on external motivations.* Whenever the pressure is let up, performance slides down into another trough. To break this pattern is a difficult thing. It's like overcoming any unhealthy addiction. And it requires a serious commitment to change on the part of the individual manager or supervisor. You don't take care of a drinking problem by drinking a little less. You can't quit smoking by cutting back. And you can't get off the resistance path by doing a little less external motivating and controlling. You have to actually go back to the very beginning of that path, to the baseline attitudes and feelings prevailing in the workplace, and change those in order to build a new set of behavior patterns in yourself and your people.

The resistance path is the key to the second most common of all management complaints:

"They seemed to be making good progress, but they backslide whenever I let up the pressure."

(The most common complaint is "My employees aren't motivated." We explored that one in the first few chapters, and I hope we replaced it forever with the more realistic and helpful version, "I'm not motivating my employees, so I better think about how to change my behavior." Now we're going to focus on one really key part of your behavior: how you make people feel.)

The backsliding problem requires constant leadership effort. It leads to complaints such as this one, from a manager in charge of getting his company certified as a supplier under International Standards Organization (ISO) quality standards (Don Peck, ISO Update, in *IVID Herald,* Dec. 1997):

> **As the ISO guru, I believed that it was my job to plan, organize, command, coordinate, and control the ISO activity. In other words (to use author James Belasco's terminology), I believed that the ISO project should function like a herd of buffalo. Eventually, the project didn't work as well as I'd like. The buffalo stood around and waited for the leader to show them what to do. I found it was very hard work being the head buffalo. Giving the orders, doing all the "important" work took 12–14 hours a day.**

This manager's comments appeared in an employee newsletter, in which he told employees he'd rather see them behave like a flock of geese than a herd of buffalo: "What I really want is a group of responsible, independent workers similar to a flock of geese. I see the geese flying in their 'V' formation, the leadership changing frequently, with different geese taking the lead. I see every goose being responsible for getting itself where the gaggle is going."

What I really want is a group of responsible, independent workers similar to a flock of geese.

What great images to express the difference between the resistance and motivation paths. (Although I wouldn't use these images with your employees. Most people take offense at being compared to a buffalo, goose, or almost any other animal. It shows a lack of respect, which, as we saw in the previous chapter, is something most employees are highly sensitive to.)

With our growing knowledge of the emotional foundations of motivation, we can readily see that the "herd of buffalo" employees are on the resistance path. It's no wonder the manager says he's working too hard! The alternative he presents—that self-motivated

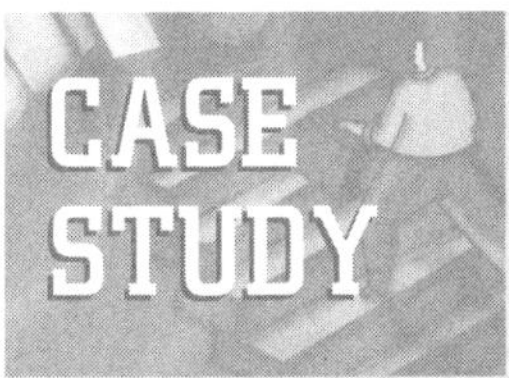

Gift Certificates from America's Body Company

Sometimes it just feels right to give your employees a gift. To celebrate a record quarter or acknowledge a successful transition to a new system or mark the company's birt-hday, for example. But what to give them? It's always hard to know what to give people, which is why gift certificates are so often a choice. And if you choose gift certificates from a well-known and popular catalog retailer, then the odds are employees will find something they really like. That's what America's Body Company did, for example (the "body" in their name refers to truck bodies, by the way). The president sent a letter and $100 Lands' End gift certificate to each of their 300-plus employees on the company's 20th birthday, and he reports that "I've never had a finer response from employees."

Benefits. If you want to acknowledge your gratitude and appreciation for employees, a fine gift is always a good option. Just make sure you communicate clearly why you are recognizing them. For instance, in the example described above, the gift certificates said on them, "Thanks for your contribution to a great 20 years. Let's make the next 20 even better!" Then the gift is linked appropriately to performance in the receiver's mind. And the obvious benefit of a gift certificate is that it increases the odds of each employee actually liking their gift. But there is another important benefit, too. A gift certificate gives the employee more control over the gift. And control is a great motivator. It encourages a sense of personal responsibility that can carry over to job attitude and performance as well. Whenever you can push choices out to employees instead of making them yourself, you are aiding their development of intrinsic motivation.

flock of geese–represents employees on the motivation path. If their leader sleeps in, then they'll just get the flock underway without him or her. But how do you transform a buffalo mentality into a goose mentality? How do you get off the resistance path and onto the motivation path?

Taking the "How Are You?" Question Seriously

The first step on the motivation path is a sincere concern for your people. It's not enough to say that, in some abstract sense, employees are your most important asset. You have to actually treat each employee interaction as the most important thing on your mind. And you won't do that unless it really is! (Is it? Yes, *if* you remember that employee performance is driven by employee motivation, and that motivation rests on an emotional foundation. After all, motivation is a feeling.)

But it's easy to agree with me while you are sitting back in a comfortable chair with your feet up. It's a little harder when you get back to workplace routines.

Why should some cranky employee whom you happen to bump into on the way to your office be the most important thing on your mind? Come on. You've got work to do, and so does he or she. In the "real" world, all you have time for is a quick "Good morning" or "How are you?" and a dash for the safety of your office.

On the other hand, in that real world, your employees are not exactly performing at their peak potential. Maybe it's time for you to introduce a new reality.

We all deliver lines like "How are you?" and "How's it going?" thoughtlessly, without expecting people to actually *tell* us how they feel. But anyone who wants to motivate others needs to treat these questions about ten times as seriously as usual. (In other words, give them ten times as much of your time, right?) Take the time to find out how your people are actually doing, and to improve their attitude if the answer isn't a positive one. That's your number-one responsibility as a motivational manager.

> Make people who work for you feel important. If you honor and serve them, they'll honor and serve you.
>
> —MARY KAY ASH, MARY KAY COSMETICS

> Good moods, while they last, enhance the ability to think flexibly and with more complexity, thus making it easier to find solutions to problems.
> —DANIEL GOLEMAN (IN *EMOTIONAL INTELLIGENCE*, BANTAM, 1995, P. 85.)

Fixing the Emotional Frame

In the opening chapter, I illustrated motivation as the result of opportunity. And it is–*if* the emotional foundations are in place. But the reality is that nobody will rise to an opportunity unless they are in a receptive frame of mind. So we need to expand our motivation model slightly to reflect the need for an appropriate emotional frame for that opportunity. And you as a leader need to provide that emotional frame, as illustrated in Figure 5-3.

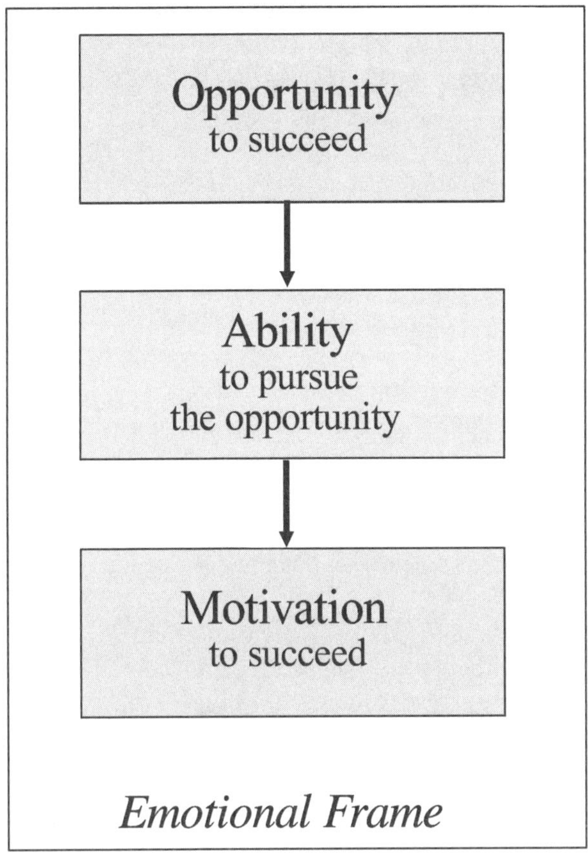

Figure 5.3

Unless you make sure an employee is in the right frame of mind, the things you think of as opportunities will look like problems to them.

Fortunately, the opposite is also true. When they are in the right frame of mind, your problems will look like opportunities to them. They'll be as eager to solve your problems as you are to let them.

How do you know if an individual is in the right emotional frame or not? You'll know. It's a matter of simple common sense. You'll know if you stop to ask yourself instead of brushing them off to get to something "more important" (like redesigning your so-called incentive program, right?). It's just that none of us are in the habit of checking on employees' emotional frames.

You'll know. It's a matter of simple common sense.

Figure 5-4 is a simple mental checklist you can use if you wish to make sure your people are in the right frame of mind for self-motivated development and performance improvement. It's a simple checklist because it's a simple task to find out what their frame is. You can easily tell when employees are not "up" for the motivation path. And if they aren't–if they score anything but yes answers on the checklist–then *you have to fix their emotional frame before you can motivate them!*

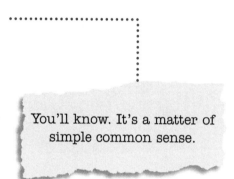

IS THE EMOTIONAL FRAME RIGHT?

DOES THIS PERSON	YES	NO
1. Feel optimistic?		
2. Believe in himself or herself?		
3. Feel excited about current opportunities?		
4. Believe he or she will be able to solve personal problems and accomplish personal goals?		

Figure 5.4

> Optimism and hope—like helplessness and despair—can be learned.
>
> —DANIEL GOLEMAN

Stimulating Positive Emotions

Perhaps you've already noticed that I'm asking you to rethink your role as a manager and leader in some fundamental ways. I'm asking you to start seeing your role as *stimulating positive emotions* in your people in order to get and keep them on the motivation path.

To do this, you need to be up yourself. You need to bring your natural enthusiasm and optimism to bear. You need to take a hopeful approach to your people–which means focusing on their greatest strengths, not their greatest weaknesses.

We've all heard the old story about the experiments proving that students whom teachers expect to succeed do, even if they are "worse" students based on intelligence tests and past performance. High expectations lead you to seek out and focus on each individual's strengths. Low expectations lead you to focus on their weaknesses. Focusing on weaknesses leads down the resistance path. Focusing on strengths leads up the motivation path. But unfortunately, our habits of management lead us to focus on weaknesses over strengths, usually without realizing it.

When we worry about the people we supervise, we are thinking about the many ways they might *fail.* Most managers view preventing failure as their number-one priority. Well, that's the precise opposite of what you need to do to get people on the motivation path. If the only time you think about your people is when you worry about them, then you are focusing only on their weaknesses.

The alternative is to focus on potential to *succeed* instead of potential to fail. Everyone has some strengths. You (or somebody else) hired each employee for a good reason. What was it? If you remind yourself of each employee's strengths instead of his or her weaknesses, you will automatically become more hopeful and enthusiastic about your employee. Your enthusiasm will automatically spill over to him or her as well.

Let's just do a little experiment based on that well-worn classic of management decision making, the pros-and-cons analysis. This time, though, we are going to use it to describe one of your employees by listing his or her weaknesses and then his or her strengths. Use the table that follows or draw one like it on a piece of scrap paper.

Which employee should you analyze? Please pick someone who is "giving you some trouble" right now, someone whose performance definitely needs improvement and who seems to have a motivation problem. (Keep your employee in mind, but don't write his or her name down here. You don't really want this sort of exercise to fall into the wrong hands and embarrass you later.)

What makes this an experiment? Ah, I knew you'd ask. Here's what I want you to do. I want you to *time yourself* with a watch or clock that has a second hand. I want you to time how many seconds it takes you to *list five weaknesses* of the employee. And then time how many seconds it takes you to *list five strengths*. Ready? Here you go:

Is it easier to think of an employee's weaknesses or strengths?

Employee's Greatest Weaknesses

1. ____

2. ____

3. ____

4. ____

5. ____

It took me ______ seconds to write this list.

Employee's Greatest Strengths

1. ____

2. ____

3. ____

4. ____

5. ____

It took me ______ seconds to write this list.

We all tend to focus on employees' weaknesses, especially when we think they have a motivation problem.

Now let's analyze the results of your experiment. My hypothesis is that it took you considerably less time to list the employee's weaknesses. I expect that these weaknesses are in the forefront of your mind. And that the employee's strengths are in the back of your mind and needed some dredging to bring up. Am I right?

I hope so because I hate to stick my neck out and get it chopped off. But I'm willing to take the risk in this case because we all tend to focus on employees' weaknesses, especially when we think they have a motivation problem. Yet, as we saw in the first half of this chapter, it is especially important to focus on strengths and take an optimistic attitude toward an employee when there is a motivation problem. That's when you need to focus hardest on their strengths because that's when you need to be building an emotional foundation of optimism and belief in themselves.

Now, if your results are an exception to this general rule and it was easy for you to list their strengths, then you are going to find emotional motivation an easy technique to master. You have a natural instinct to see the best in people. You believe in your people already, and you've probably been nodding your head throughout this chapter and saying, "Well, of course. It's about time some management author figured this one out." Great. I'm proud of you, and I want you to recognize that you have a rare gift that you should nurture and prize. You are a natural leader.

But the rest of us can acquire your talent, too, if we work at it, so in the long run I'm not worried about the result of our little experiment. Either way, we've now got the list of strengths for that "problem" employee. Let's copy it onto a clean sheet and post it at your desk, and I'll bet you turn that employee's performance around in a week or two.

Employees on the Run at IVID

A number of companies encourage employee fitness, and at IVID Communications, the emphasis is on running. The company sponsors 10K runs for employees and also has offered employee clinics on running form and style. For instance, a recent July 4 was celebrated with an invitation to participate in an IVID 10K run around the lake at Scripps Ranch, a scenic San Diego picnic spot. Though not every employee likes to run, this sport provides a touch-point for enthusiasts that brings together employees from different functions and levels of the company. It is healthy for employee attitudes to have the senior managers running for fun along with lots of other employees. And the IVID announcement for the July 4 run mentioned other options, too, such as rowing and fishing on the lake with your kids, so all employees could feel welcome to attend.

Thanks to IVID Communications, Inc., a training program developer in San Diego, Calif., for this case. See their monthly employee newsletter, the *IVID Herald*, for more information at www.orientxpress.com/news.

Analysis. There is a corny saying that the family that plays together, stays together. Well, it can apply to organizations, too. If managers or other employees of a company have an enthusiasm for a sport, it is a great idea to find ways to share that enthusiasm by organizing sports events through the company. You want to be careful, however, not to let them become obligatory in the eyes of employees. If you feel, for instance, that you "have" to play golf in order to advance in a company, then golf becomes an obstacle to opportunities rather than a healthy way to get involved in the company's social life. It's also important to think about safety issues. Many people injure themselves in running as they get older, for instance, and it's easy for anyone to sprain an ankle in a pickup volleyball, soccer, or basketball game. So encourage caution and don't create events that push people into sports they have not trained for. IVID's approach of offering a clinic on running is a good model of a safety-conscious approach. Education and training are important to most sports.

Perhaps because of the risks, learning a new sport or improving your skill in an old sport is a wonderful experience for employees. It proves you can "do it" despite your age or condition, a lesson that often carries over to the workplace in the form of greater confidence and willingness to try new things. So programs that make it safe and fun for employees to develop a sport are generally good for motivation and performance levels. You don't have to put them on an expensive custom ropes course; you can just get them out on a golf course or tennis court!

Parting Shots

I want to emphasize the importance of managing the emotional foundations of motivation. Too often, we ignore this issue and carry on with our analyses and programs as if everyone were feeling just fine. Sorry but there are lots of times when people feel down or lack self-confidence. And you need to know how your people are feeling about their work before you try to motivate them to do it better.

I hope you noticed that I confined my focus to *how people feel at work*. It is entirely possible that the people whom you supervise have lots of extraneous distractions that give them plenty to feel bad about. People get divorced. Loved ones die. Relationships hit rocky times. Health problems arise. We are all mortal, after all, and there are plenty of downs for even the most optimistic of us. I'm not telling you that you have to take responsibility for making sure everything is always great for each of your employees. Face it, you can't do that, not even for yourself, so don't even try.

Working with you should be a renewing experience, not a draining one.

But what you can do is make your work and theirs a cause for and source of optimism and self-affirmation. Working with you should be a renewing experience, not a draining one. When people have problems, you will of course feel bad for them, and I trust you will have the good sense to let your empathy and sympathy come forward in a genuine manner. But you don't have to solve those problems for your employees. You simply have to encourage them to feel good about what you and they *can* control–their work and their development through the pursuit of excellence in their work.

If you do this, you'll feel better about your people and your performance as a manager. They will feel better about their performances as employees. And they may even feel better about the uncontrollable injuries and losses that are an occasional but necessary part of any life fully lived. Emotional motivation is a powerful innoculant against life's downs as well as a great way to maximize the ups.

Chapter 6

Overcoming Challenges to Emotional Motivation

Emotional motivation, as we saw in the previous chapter, builds the positive frame of mind needed to put someone on the motivation path and keep him or her off the resistance path. Without this positive frame of mind toward work, nobody can attain or sustain a high level of motivation. When you as a manager accept this simple rule of human nature, you begin to redefine your role as the keeper of your people's attitudes and feelings toward work. And this gives you a simpler and far more powerful lever with which to build their motivation than any of the traditional systems and programs. In fact, without this emotional foundation, no system or program will work. Instead of building motivation, your incentives will be greeted with resistance and scorn. They will make employees laugh, cry, or whisper behind your back, but they won't make them work any harder.

> All over the country, in every group I've worked with—governmental agencies, Fortune 500 companies, small and medium-sized businesses, banks, hospitals, school districts, community organizations—I have observed the same habitual responses to criticism. No matter where or who, people set up the same roadblocks to good communication and feedback. Individuals lose self-esteem, intimate relationships flounder, organizations become inefficient and unwieldy. But it doesn't have to be that way.
>
> —Mary Lynne Heldmann, consultant and author of *When Words Hurt*

It's a healthy thing to get in touch with the real feelings of employees toward incentive systems when the emotional foundations for them are lacking. Not pleasant, perhaps, but healthy. It reminds us just how terribly our efforts to motivate can flop. So I think it is therapeutic at this point to let my favorite cynic, Scott Adams, share some of the e-mailed feedback he's gotten from employees who just had to vent their feelings about their managers' efforts to motivate them:

> **Scott,**
>
> **The stupidest thing my boss ever did for our group was institute a point system. We all had checklists, and we checked off what we did during the day, and we got points.**
>
> **Not a bright guy.**

Maybe not, but no doubt a well-intentioned guy. I bet he got that idea from one of the many experts or books on the subject. And he's probably still wondering what went wrong. Too bad he didn't take a look at the foundation before he tried to build an elaborate incentive structure on it. Or how about this one:

Scott,

True story. When we were down in the dumps one year, our newish CEO decided that we needed a motivational meeting, complete with professional corporate motivation video. The video featured the "try again until success" attitude of balloonist Maxie Anderson and was coordinated with a personal letter from the famed balloonist.

Maxie had been killed three years earlier in a ballooning accident.

I don't know what to say about this one, except the obvious point that you can't delegate responsibility for how your employees feel to someone else. Especially if that someone happens to be dead.

Then there is this one, destined to become a true classic in the literature of management:

You can't delegate responsibility for how your employees feel to someone else.

A "Work-Out" was called to address the morale problem. (I think they're a little worried that people are starting to leave without being laid off first.) Alternatives discussed at the Work-Out included:

- **Recognizing and rewarding technical expertise.**
- **Getting a pay scale close to market value.**
- **Communicating outsourcing plans.**

After all those alternatives and many more were discussed, the outcome of lengthy deliberation was . . . The Fun Team!!!

Employee morale is low. We need more picnics and bowling. If we just socialize more, all our problems will go away.

I think I detect a faint note of cynicism in that one. How about you?

On the other hand, you're probably thinking, hey, isn't this guy telling me that ideas like a Fun Team are good? Well, not quite. What I'm saying is that a genuine (that's a pretty serious word) concern for how your people feel is a prerequisite for motivating them. Emotional management can't be delegated to a Fun Team any more than it can be handled by a dead balloonist. You need to take care of it yourself, one to one with your employees.

You better face the fact that most employees are starting out with a pretty cynical Dilbert-style attitude toward their managers

And that means getting to know them considerably better than many managers bother to do. If you don't know your people well enough to know whether *they* are sending e-mails about *you* to Scott Adams, then you have some more work to do. In this chapter, I'm going to explore the challenge of emotional motivation in order to give you additional insights and techniques. More ammunition, if you will. Because you better face the fact that most employees are starting out with a pretty cynical Dilbert-style attitude toward their managers. Even if you are genuinely concerned about them, it's going to take a while to convince them you aren't just another goon like all the others who've come and gone.

Focus on Strengths, Plus...

Focusing on your people's strengths is really the key to creating a positive emotional frame for the motivation process, as I argued in Chapter 5. And it's a remarkably simple and rewarding formula. It *will* give you renewed optimism and energy, and you *will* communicate your enthusiasm to your people. It's that simple.

The wisdom of the ages:

"Where there's a will, there's a way."
"Look on the bright side."
"You can't keep a good man or woman down."

Yet though focusing on the positives is in theory quite simple, it can seem difficult when you are trying to break old habits and learn new ones. Especially if your employees are cynical to start with and need to change their habits as well. Then you may need to try some more structured and specific techniques. You may need to fall back on additional approaches just to keep your own spirits up when you run into initial setbacks or discouragements. Because you will, I guarantee it. Even if you don't find yourself the butt of a joke in the next Dilbert strip, you may find yourself lampooned in the bathroom graffiti or ribbed by your fellow managers. Emotional motivation is, as I warned you in the previous chapter, a pretty radical concept. It'll take persistence and resourcefulness to make it stick.

Fortunately, there are plenty of things you can do to create the right attitude for high motivation. In this chapter, I'll show you some additional techniques that may help you get over the "hump" of adopting a new attitude in your approach to your people. You may well find you need these options in order to gain the confidence to make this fundamental change in your habits of thought and your interpersonal style.

You're Up Against Some Tough Opposition

One reason why you may need more ammunition in your quiver in order to make emotional motivation work is that more and more managers are trying to make employees (including your employees) feel *bad* about their work. Life in the workplace is increasingly like a Dilbert cartoon. And many managers, including ones who view you as a competitor for the next big promotion, want to make your people miserable and are eager to see you fail. So someone else may actually be putting a sincere effort into making your people feel like sh*t.

You need to know what's going on out there in the increasingly Machiavellian world of cut-throat management.

I'm not kidding! If you don't believe me, you are pleasantly naive. But you need to know what's going on out there in the increasingly Machiavellian world of cut-throat management. Here's some interesting advice from Blaine Pardoe, a successful consultant and author who says it's now a "hypercompetitive workplace." The following is a quote from his book, *Cubicle Warfare*:

Sabotage happens more often than people will admit. Given the advances in technology there are numerous ways to slow up progress, screw up meetings, or simply make projects a living hell for those working on them.

(Hold on a minute. I want you to understand that this is now a *serious treatise* from someone who consults at places like Ford and GM. I know it *sounds* just like a Dilbert strip, but that's the point, isn't it? Okay, let's get back to the quote.)

> Trust everybody, but cut the cards.
>
> —FINLEY PETER DUNNE

Some of the more common methods of sabotage include:

- **Removing projection panels or overhead projector light bulbs—enough to end many meetings.**
- **Stealing all the erasable markers from white boards (or switching them with permanent markers).**
- **Damaging network cables to ruin connectivity. The same can be done with fax machine phone lines and so on.**
- **Hiding or stealing all the toner from a copier, or shipping all the paper to another location.**
- **Damaging a key computer hard drive on a project. (A magnet and a PC simply do not mix.)**
- **Stealing, shredding, or hiding key documentation such as purchase orders or requisitions, requests for supplies, and so on.**

Pardoe's book also covers nifty little techniques like finding job ads in the paper that offer higher salaries than employees currently receive and putting the clippings where they are sure to be found. That always cheers the other managers' employees right up, I'm sure!

Face it, the reality is some of your fellow managers and maybe even your employees are reading *his* book instead of this one. *And it is a hell of a lot easier to ruin someone's day than to make it.* So you have to be persistent in the face of such marvelously creative negativity in order to really build a positive foundation for motivation in your people.

Feeling good is powerful medicine, but in today's workplaces it often requires you and your people to swim against the current.

Is that true in your workplace? Are others likely to contaminate your people with their negative attitudes, or worse, to actively sabotage your efforts to create a positive climate? If so, don't despair.

But do *isolate*. Do what you can to create a "skunk works" environment in which you reduce access to your space and your people, so as to keep unfriendly forces away. Lobby for a separate office space in your own wing, floor, or block of cubicles. Physical separation from "the enemy" is sometimes your only defense, at least until you have built strong enough foundations that your people are ready to spread their good attitude to other parts of the organization and stamp out negative practices such as those Pardoe documents.

And whether you can achieve isolation or not, remember that you can have a powerful influence over how your people feel *if you choose*. And that influence is largely exercised in natural, one-on-one interactions, not by goofy programs or Fun Teams. In fact, you better have pretty solid emotional foundations before you stick your neck out with any new incentive programs.

How to Keep Up the Momentum

There are a variety of specific techniques that you can try if "the bastards" begin to wear you down and your faith in your people and ability to buoy their feelings slips. After all, if you aren't feeling up, it's pretty hard to raise anyone else's spirits. So when sabotage or fatigue begin to wear you down, you can turn to any of the techniques I'm about to give you in this chapter. Each of them will do wonders to renew your enthusiasm and build positive foundations for your employees as well.

If you aren't feeling up, it's pretty hard to raise anyone else's spirits.

Each of these techniques can be used one on one to build optimism, even when dealing with someone who is feeling negative. I recommend taking them in turn, from 1 to 5, but I don't insist on it if you think you've got a good reason for trying one out of turn.

1. *Clear your head of your own frustration and stresses when you listen to your employees.* Research shows conclusively that you can't empathize with others if you are angry or upset. Your own strong emotions block your ability to sense how the other person feels. (That's why people are so insensitive and bad at listening when they get into a heated argument.) If you can't shake your own negative emotions in order to empathize with an employee, explain that to him or her and ask the employee to give you a little while to deal with your own problems before you listen to his or hers. But make sure you get back to the employee as quickly as possible after promising to listen to him or her later on. That's a promise you cannot break.
2. *Mirror their feelings.* Try to penetrate the surface of the conversation by adopting their stance and expression long enough to sense the feelings behind them. And ask follow-up questions to probe for information about "how they're doing" and "how it's going." Then tell them what you think they are feeling and ask if you have it right. (Your interactive listening skills apply here.) These techniques help you get beyond the typical casual encounter to find out how people really feel. And when they realize you actually care how they feel and take a personal interest in their feelings, they will start feeling more up. Even if you can't think of anything to say or do to "make" them feel better, you will have a positive impact just by sharing your interest and concern.

You will have a positive impact just by sharing your interest and concern.

3. *Use praise to create optimism.* For instance, take the comment, "I know you're having a rough time with that project right now, but I can see you've already done some good things and I'm confident in your ability to see it through. In fact, I recall that you've solved even harder problems in the past." This is not very specific as feedback goes, which might make you think it is poor feedback. It doesn't instruct the employee in what to do, so it runs counter to much of the advice you'll hear on feedback. But it is actually great feed-

back because it does something essential. It empowers the employee to figure out what to do by sharing your optimism and confidence in him or her. It is *positive emotional feedback*, a powerful lever for improving someone's emotional frame. When people are in danger of going down the resistance path instead of up the motivation path, they don't need task-specific feedback. Don't tell them what they did right or wrong. Give them positive emotional feedback instead. Tell them things or remind them of things that will make them feel more optimistic and hopeful.

4. *Ask them about relevant strengths.* When you encounter pessimism or frustration, you can probe to surface positives they aren't focusing on. Try questions such as, "I know you are frustrated right now, but are there any reasons for optimism?" or "It sounds like a tough situation, but on the other hand, aren't you pretty good at ______________________?" (Pick a relevant skill.) Then follow up to draw them into discussing strengths and resources that they might be able to apply in the situation. This exercise always helps build optimism. And there *is* always a positive side to be found, even in the worst situations. Sayings like "Every cloud has a silver lining" and "It's always darkest before dawn" hold for those who seek the light.
5. *Increase their sense of personal control.* Many employees feel they have very little control over their situation when at work. They can't decide where they work, how they decorate the office, whom they work with, when they work, or what they do. Nor can they decide how best to do it since in many cases specific procedures are taught and required. And when you top off these daily inabilities to control the circumstances of work with the inability to control the occasional "bad event" like a reduction in staffing that forces them to do someone else's job along with their own, you have a situation in which almost anyone would conclude they aren't in control.

Positive emotional feedback is a powerful lever for improving someone's emotional frame.
—A basic tenet of Emotional Motivation

> Control is such an important psychological process that it affects our very brain chemistry.
>
> —PETERSON, MAIER AND SELIGMAN, *LEARNED HELPLESSNESS*, OXFORD UNIVERSITY PRESS, 1993

Let's Explore This Control Issue a Little More

Why should we give employees more control? Isn't control one of the basic *management* tasks? (It is according to most textbooks on management.) So the way things work in the typical workplace is that managers control, and employees are controlled. But the problem with that setup is that a lack of control makes people feel helpless and resigned. It pushes them onto the resistance path and off the motivation path.

It's truly amazing to me that the concept of *learned helplessness* is not taught in any business schools. Learned helplessness is the "helpless, hopeless, and depressed" state people fall into when they "are faced with repeated traumatic events over which they have no control," according to psychologist David G. Meyers (*Psychology*, Worth Publishers, 1995, p. 490). (According to Scott Adams's Dilbert strip, work *is* basically a series of traumatic events over which we have no control!)

(DILBERT reprinted by permission of United Feature Syncicate, Inc.)

At its greatest extremes, learned helplessness leaves people so down and debilitated that they won't save themselves from dangers even when they have the opportunity. And there are lots of classic psychological experiments in which laboratory animals are conditioned into learned helplessness, for example, by receiving unpredictable electric shocks. Then when their cages are opened so that they can escape the shocks, they don't. They just sit there and take it. And so do people after they've experienced too much bad management. (The same syndrome is behind the terrible phenomenon of battered women and children who seem unable or unwilling to escape their abusers.) The worst thing about learned helplessness is that it destroys the motivational power of opportunities. It saps the will to achieve and succeed. *Learned helplessness prevents people from taking advantage of opportunities*, and as I pointed out in the first chapter of this book, opportunities are the key to high motivation and excellent performances. So learned helplessness is the worst enemy of motivation.

I wouldn't really worry about employee cynicism as you try to bring about a new emotional climate. At least it demonstrates they've got some fight left in 'em! If they just sit there and stare at you passively, then you know you've got a far more serious problem. And you can expect to spend many months working on rebuilding a healthy emotional foundation.

The average workplace does not dish up enough severely traumatic events to create extreme forms of learned helplessness. But it does create mild cases on a routine basis. And even a mild case prevents people from getting onto the motivation path. So you have to counter this broad tendency toward learned helplessness by giving employees as much control as you can.

You have to counter this broad tendency toward learned helplessness by giving employees as much control as you can.

The Difference Between Giving Control and Giving Up Control

Now, I know you are unwilling to give up your control as a manager, at least until you have seen a developing pattern of self-motivation and are confident your people will shoulder responsibilities well. So how do you give control without feeling that you are giving *up* control?

MOTIVATION IDEA 12

Open Questions

The art of finding out how someone really feels or what he or she really thinks is the art of the open question. Open questions get the other person talking while you listen and encourage him or her to talk. Here are some words and phrases that make for great open questions. Use these as your building blocks:

"Why?"
"How?"
"Tell me about...?"
"What do you mean by...?"
"Can you explain that to me?"
"What's the matter?"
"How do you feel?"
"How does that make you feel?"

Notice the difference between "How does that make you feel?" and the more common "Do you feel all right?" The latter is a closed question because it does not invite a detailed or honest answer. It is a yes-or-no question, and 99 percent of people answer it with a yes 99 percent of the time because that's what they assume you want to hear unless they are actually bleeding to death. Almost all managers use closed questions when talking to their employees. If you start using open questions, you will be amazed at how different your relationship with employees becomes. You will find yourself becoming a so-called motivational manager who seems to get the best out of people. And others will think there is something mysterious and special about you. Which is true in a way since you know the secret of the open question.

The trick is to recognize all the many little ways in which you can give control of working conditions, the work environment, and the ways in which work is done. There are lots of little things that have great symbolic value and impart a real sense of control, but don't go so far as to put your results at risk. Let people decorate or rearrange their work spaces. When assembling project groups or teams, select the one or two core people, and let them pick the rest.

Even when you have to set policy or announce a decision, you can increase their sense of control by giving them choices instead of a single option. And introduce elections whenever they are appropriate. Why not let the office decide which brand of coffee to use in the coffee maker? Or what time everyone should come in to work? Or (if that's nonnegotiable for now), what time the staff meeting should be? Or how about asking them what order to tackle the items on the agenda for the meeting?

By the way, I recommend Thursdays for such requests in which employees have to discuss options and make collective decisions. According to recent research, people are usually more productive and ready to get along on Thursdays than on other days of the week if they work on a Monday-to-Friday schedule. If you ask them earlier in the week, they will waste a lot more time dickering over the details or whispering about you behind your back before they can reach consensus.

Once you turn your imagination to the task, it is easy to find a thousand ways to give employees more control. And when you do, you will be fighting against learned helplessness and encouraging the positive, in-control frame of mind they need to walk the motivation path.

As you try out these five methods, or develop methods of your own, keep in mind the value of the "open question," any question that invites the other person to open up and provide you with more insight into his or her situation. Check out Motivation Idea 12 to learn how to use open questions more effectively.

Motivation Idea 13

Pizza Party

According to a friend of mine who used to be the editor-in-chief of a weekly newspaper called *The Advocate*, pizzas can be a great feel-good motivator: "The Classified Ad Department was always ordering pizzas, whenever they made their goals. They'd eat them right at their desks. And it did seem to be motivational for them. I think it worked because it made them feel good."

One of the reasons these pizza parties worked is that they were under the employees' *control*. Try giving employees a budget for pizza deliveries, and allowing *them* to pick the time and place. The only rule: It has to be a reward for some identifiable accomplishment!

How Do You Handle Pessimism and Depression?

Employees with a truly bad attitude provide another form of sabotage that is extremely destructive to your emotional motivation initiative even though they don't mean to. There are simply some employees who are downers. They absolutely radiate negative feelings. And they have an amazing ability to suck you dry of enthusiasm and empathy.

The first type you need to be prepared to deal with is the died-in-the-wool pessimist. These people seem to have been born with a negative attitude. Ask them how they are doing, and they will tell you they are doing terribly. They will tell you they are doing terribly in a pretty convincing manner. They may even go into considerable detail about how badly they are doing.

Ask pessimists how a project is going, and you'll really see them come into their own. They can and will identify an amazingly creative range of possible problems and pitfalls. And they'll also put any minor glitches into the absolutely worst possible light, presenting them as deadly roadblocks that are destined to kill the project in as painful and torturous a manner as possible.

If you have true pessimists in your group, you will soon learn to be wary of asking them how things are going. You will dread their response, and you will realize (quite rightly) that you cannot overcome their negative attitude with your positive attitude. They are amazingly immune to positive thinking.

Modify your one-on-one strategy for extreme pessimists

So you need to modify your one-on-one strategy for extreme pessimists. First, don't focus on what they say. They are so used to forecasting gloom and doom that they always do. Focus instead on what they *do*. Then draw your own conclusions about how they are doing and how their projects are going. If in your judgment things are pretty good, then tell them that. Don't ask them, tell them. They are wrong, you are right.

If, on the other hand, you see that there are valid, objective reasons for them to be down and out, point that out to them, too. Identify the problem as best you can, asking specific, factual questions to find out more about it. Then tell them how you feel about the problem rather than asking them how they feel. You *know* how they feel since they always feel bad. So that's not useful input for you.

For example, let's say you have observed a pessimist for some weeks, and given her feedback about how you think things are going that is basically pretty up. You've said things like, "Looks like your work is coming along nicely. I'm feeling optimistic about it." (You tell rather than ask because you realize her judgment of whether things are good or bad is flawed.) But then one day you see that she is looking even more down than usual. And when you inquire, you discover that something has gone wrong with her project and she has a fairly serious problem to overcome.

Now you need to once again tell her rather than ask her how she feels. But this time, you need to acknowledge the problem and model an appropriately negative response rather than the "end of the world" response a pessimist is likely to have. For instance, you might say, "I'm sorry to see that the _________ is late and I understand it's because something went wrong with the _________ system. I'm discouraged by that and you must be, too." (She'll probably acknowledge feeling discouraged. That's an easy point to get agreement on when dealing with a pessimist!) Then you can go on to frame the problem in a positive emotional manner, for instance, with a comment like, "On the other hand, I've seen you fix problems much worse than this. And I also know that if you get really stuck you can get some help from _____ and _______ since they dealt with similar problems last year, right?"

In other words, you need to *lead* pessimists through more appropriate emotional reactions than they are likely to produce on their own. After a while (probably a long while!), this constant modeling of a more balanced, optimistic approach will begin to rub off.

The other thing you can do with pessimists is to give them more and easier opportunities to succeed. Even the most stubborn pessimist has to bow to overwhelming evidence that things are going well. So make sure things go overwhelmingly well. That's not as hard as it seems because you always have a range of assignments, from simple to hard, and you can make a mental note to throw a string of simple, success-oriented projects at your pessimist. Some people are

> There is nothing better at building your own confidence and optimism than a successful "turnaround" of a hard-core pessimist.

actually born pessimists, but on the other hand, we also know that optimism can be acquired over time. So don't despair! If you are stuck with a pessimist, you are admittedly in for a long bout. But it ought to be winnable if you persist. And you know what? There is nothing better at building your own confidence and optimism than a successful "turnaround" of a hard-core pessimist.

Serious depression is another story although it has some of the same chapters. Depressed people are people who, though not always pessimistic, are currently in a very down stage and don't feel good about themselves or life in general. In fact, they probably feel dreadful. You will feel sympathetic toward a depressed employee, in contrast to the exasperation you are likely to feel toward a pessimistic person. If you feel worried about them, you should. Trust your instincts. Depression is a serious malady, and people struggle and suffer terribly from it.

I recommend you use the same prescriptions I gave for dealing with pessimists since you don't want to let the depressed person's pessimistic viewpoint contaminate your emotional motivation. And your efforts to provide opportunities for success may help the depressed employee overcome his or her depression, too. But on the other hand, you are not qualified or prepared to cure depression. And the tools I offered earlier, though helpful, are probably inadequate when you must deal with someone who is seriously depressed. *Depressed employees may need additional help and treatment.*

However, I must warn you it's likely to be a bit tricky going about getting depressed employees some treatment or convincing them to seek it themselves. Sometimes organizations provide or subsidize counseling and/or medication. Sometimes they don't. In general, even when they do, there are stigmas associated with a diagnosis of depression so employees may rightfully fear that acknowledging the problem could hurt their careers. (On the other hand, not treating the problem definitely will hurt their careers.) They may resent your well-intentioned efforts to refer them for diagnosis or treatment. Some employees see such management initiatives as harassment and even go so far as to sue their employers and name supervisors (like you!) in their suits. So

MOTIVATION IDEA 14

Logo Art

Many companies give out pins, mugs, and other objects bearing the corporate logo or trademark. Boring! Why not put some excitement into your company's visual symbol by holding contests for artists with cash prizes. Rules: any nonoffensive, relatively permanent, and easy-to-display artwork that features the company logo in some way. Have a contest in the community and let all the employees cast votes for the winner. Also consider adding an employee art category for which members of the public who visit the exhibit can cast votes.

Benefits. Adds new life and excitement to your logo and image, which employees are probably tired of by now since they see it constantly. Creates a fun, engaging event. Gives employees a good feeling that they are supporting the community in a fun way. Everyone likes to be part of a great event. And the good feelings from their participation in this event will tend to color their perception of work, improving employee attitudes and satisfaction levels.

depression is a tough problem and requires thoughtful and cautious handling.

I can tell you only one thing for sure. If you supervise a seriously depressed employee, you'll probably need more support and help than I can offer in this book. At a minimum, seek advice from your boss and/or the director of human resources or personnel. Maybe your firm's legal advisors, too. Because it may be difficult to come up with a good way to intervene. However, on the other hand, I hope you *do* try to intervene if it is at all practical because depression can have serious consequences for the employee and for the morale of those who must work with him or her.

And whatever you do, don't forget that nobody can fault you for being sympathetic and genuine in your concern for your employees. Or for believing in them and emphasizing their strengths instead of their weaknesses. Even the most difficult employees generally respond favorably to favorable treatment. You may not be able to work miracles with everyone, but you certainly can improve everyone's motivation at least a little. And that is miracle enough for me.

Parting Shots

Accounting tracks bottom-line variables. But managers need to control "top-line" variables to produce a good bottom line. They need to look where the ship is headed, not just to study its wake. What am I talking about? Hang on and I'll explain.

As we've seen in this chapter and the last, the top-line variable that determines whether your people get and stay on the motivation path is how they feel. Employees who feel good about themselves and their day will do good work and seek new challenges. They are ready for the motivation path and likely to be self-motivated to develop and improve. Optimism and a positive frame of mind are extremely strong predictors of good performance. And even where there are no major problems to prevent people from being motivated (such as we examined in Chapters 3 and 4), you may still see low motivation until you get the emotional foundations just right. Yet

> That happy people are helpful people is one of the most consistent findings in all psychology. No matter how people are cheered—whether by being made to feel successful and intelligent, by thinking happy thoughts, by finding money, or even by receiving a posthypnotic suggestion—they become more generous and more eager to help.
>
> —David G. Meyers

1,001 Rewards at MCDOT

MCDOT stands for Maricopa County Dept. of Transportation, and now it also stands for a nurturing, supportive place to work. At least that's the goal of one of the most extensive rewards programs ever devised, which MCDOT's director announced with a "call to become a nurturing community." The program includes an informal component, in which employees are trained to use peer-to-peer recognition. Ideas include sending someone a thank-you e-mail message and hints like, "Buy her a morning cup of coffee if she's done extra work for you."

The formal program includes a Superior Achievement Award, whose purpose is to "recognize the one-time contribution of an individual employee, team, or work crew that results in a definite improvement in carrying out the department's mission of providing a quality transportation system." Any employee may submit nominations, and a committee selects winners whenever appropriate. The award takes the form of a certificate presented by the director at the Quarterly Awards Ceremony.

But that's just the beginning. Employees who help implement a quality improvement team process are eligible for QIT Awards, which take the form of letters of appreciation and a simple gift. They are presented annually by the director. Then there are Employee Service Awards based on years of service. And an Extra Mile Award to recognize anyone who puts extra effort into a project, also presented at the Quarterly Awards Ceremony.

And that's still just the beginning. Here are the titles of other awards used in this organization: Excellence in County Government awards, Divisional Employee/Team or Crew of the Quarter, Departmental Employee/Team or Crew of the Quarter, Employee Team or Crew of the Year, Customer Service Excellence Award, Employee Retirement Award, Outstanding Attendance Award, Inter-Departmental Cooperation Award, Team/Crew Achievement Award, Employee Advancement Recognition, Volunteer Appreciation Recognition, Yard Lost Time Award, Safety Awards, Community Service Award, and Internship and Summer Student Awards. It would be hard to find another organization that takes awards as seriously as this one does!

Quotes from MCDOT Online (http://nova.mcdot.maricopa.gov/mcdot/admin).

Analysis. When you see an organization with as many rewards as this one has, it is tempting to dismiss it as overkill. Most experts would say, "Cut the number by half and focus on a few really important goals." Well, perhaps. But on the other hand, think about the director's stated goal for a moment. He didn't say his goal was to improve any specific behavior. Instead, his goal is to "become a nurturing community at MCDOT." In other words, he's focusing on the feelings axis, not the performance axis. He wants to make sure that people feel needed and appreciated. He wants to create a positive emotional climate in which everyone tries to support each other. So institutionalizing praise is a very sensible thing to do. And although it is no doubt true that the impact of any single award will be diluted by adding many others, the overall impact of this program on employee attitude should far outweigh the dilution effect. I'd say when it comes to saying thank you for a job well done, the more the merrier!

One small note of concern to keep in mind if you go down this road. *No* amount of positive feedback, formal or informal, can counter fundamental issues of unfairness or anxiety. So make sure your program has a clear runway before you try to introduce anything as extensive as this. You can't expect to create a nurturing environment if, for example, employees feel your organization is "cheap" because it doesn't offer as many benefits as similar organizations do. Nor can you expect a program like this to counter the effects of a brutal layoff. Make sure you deal with any major problems that can lead to negative feelings before you introduce a program designed to generate positive feelings. First things first.

most managers fail to define their job as making sure their people feel good about their work.

It might be a problem that employee feelings have such a dramatic impact on their motivation and performance–except that it also turns out supervisors can and do have a far bigger impact on employee feelings than they realize.

Fortunately, you can and do have a large impact on how your employees feel. If you take ownership of the motivation problem, it will lead you to the realization that your own behavior can "fix" most employee problems by simply developing and sharing an optimistic view of their potential. *Make them feel better, and they will be more motivated.*

And you will know you are accomplishing this important goal if you keep track of their emotional frame. You need to begin keeping track of the emotional score.

To make sure your people avoid the resistance path, why don't you do some simple *emotional accounting*?

Here's an easy way to track emotional frame over time. Each day, make a point of checking on each employee's emotional frame. A brief conversation is enough to find out how they feel.

You probably "go through the motions" already. (Don't you already make a point of saying "Hello, how are you?" to all of your direct reports?) Just follow up a bit more than usual. Try some of the techniques in this chapter to see how your people *really* are. Then track their moods in a ledger. (Or a table in the back of your appointment book, or a spreadsheet, or a poster on the back of your door. You can even create an *emotion control chart*. Whatever works for you.) The simplest systems are usually the best since they take little time to maintain. All you really need to do is enter a + or – in a ledger for each person each day.

Whenever your ledger shows a pattern of – scores for an individual, you are reminded that you have to take responsibility for improving his or her state of mind. And when you see a pattern dominated by + marks, then you know your people are ready to climb the motivation path. (Pluses should outweigh minuses by at least four to one.) If so, then your people are ready to self-motivate. And you are ready for *your* next challenge, too, so let's go on to the next chapter.

To make sure your people avoid the resistance path, why don't you do some simple *emotional accounting*?

Motivating with Positive and Negative Feedback

Chapter 7

> Feedback is the Breakfast of Champions.
>
> —Ken Blanchard

"How Am I Doing?"

This question is at the heart of motivation. If you don't get clear feedback, you aren't going to be motivated. Period. So one of the best things any manager can do to boost motivation is to improve feedback.

In fact, some experts argue that feedback is at the root of motivation issues and explains why people are often more motivated away from work than on the job. For example, listen to this story Ken Blanchard told when asked by a manager how to motivate employees ("A Personal Approach to Change," in Hiam, *The Portable Conference on Change Management*):

> *Manager's question*: I'm a manager who likes to play my cards close to the vest. My employees complain that I don't tell them enough about what's going on. Is it necessary to loosen up with information?
>
> *Blanchard's answer*: Let me answer your question with the results of a study I learned about from Scott Meyers. He assumed that people who are unmotivated at work would be equally unmotivated away from work. To test this theory, he watched a man who went bowling after work. This guy was considered a poor performer on the job, but when he threw the ball down the alley he jumped up and down with excitement. He was a different person and highly motivated. Why the difference between work and play? Simple. The fellow was getting feedback and results. He could see the pins go down. At the office he never knew how he was doing. Remember, the number one motivator for people is feedback.

Ken Blanchard is fond of saying that "feedback is the breakfast of champions," and in fact, his famous *One Minute Manager* methods are based on feedback. For example, the one-minute manager methodology emphasizes the use of positive feedback on the theory that you help people reach their potential by "catching them doing something right." More specifically, positive feedback should be provided according to the following plan:

1. Observe employees' actions very closely to make sure you know when their performance is good.
2. Insist that employees keep track of their own progress and send you their records periodically so you know that they are taking note of accomplishments, too.
3. Take a moment to praise the employee for what he or she did right, using a genuine, personal, one-on-one approach.
4. When you praise them, tell them precisely what they did right and tell them how good you feel about what they did.
5. Continue to request that employees track their own performance and teach them to note accomplishments and pat themselves on the back for a job well done. In the long run, you want them to be less dependent upon your praisings and better able to provide their *own* positive feedback.

(I'm basing my version of this method on a reading of Blanchard and Johnson, *The One Minute Manager*, Berkley Books, 1982, especially pp. 39–42, and on past discussions with Ken Blanchard about the subject.)

This is pretty good advice. If you build up feedback on a foundation of positive, personal feedback that is timely, accurate, and appropriate to the employee's work, then you will have a solid foundation for other forms of feedback as well.

And compare this approach with what we usually see in business. Because managers are concerned with what might go wrong and eager to avert disasters, they naturally tend to look for errors and mistakes. As a result, they inadvertently spend their time "catching someone doing something wrong" instead of catching him or her doing something right.

Because managers are concerned with what might go wrong and eager to avert disasters, they naturally tend to look for errors and mistakes.

Thus the most basic form of feedback in the typical workplace, the feedback that forms the foundations of any additional feedback or motivation efforts, is negative personal feedback: what you did wrong. And that's not a very good foundation upon which to build motivation.

An emphasis on correcting mess-ups gives employees the feeling that *you are looking over their shoulder because you don't trust them.* It leaves them feeling as if they don't have any control or responsibility, which is discouraging and makes your job seem meaningless and dull.

In contrast, an emphasis on noticing and praising good work gives employees the feeling that *you are looking over their shoulder because you do trust them.* You must trust them to do something good, or you wouldn't bother looking for good behavior. So that is a positive foundation for your feedback, one that is consistent with the motivation path instead of the resistance path.

> A poor or weak self-image makes criticism difficult, sometimes impossible, to deal with.
>
> —Mary Lynne Heldmann (in her book, *When Words Hurt*)

How Do Rewards and Incentives Fit into One-Minute Management?

Note that small *incentives and rewards,* including symbolic ones like candy bars, certificates of accomplishment, and thank-you notes, are particularly useful in implementing the one-minute manager's approach to positive feedback. They help you demonstrate your positive feelings about the good behavior you've witnessed or seen records of in the employee's log. But don't postpone giving them or wait for a formal, group setting. Keep it informal, spontaneous, and one to one. And don't forget that in this method, your personal praise and thanks are the most important reward. Other rewards can be used to vary the diet or make note of an especially important employee accomplishment, but you don't need to hand out gifts each time you see good behavior.

Is Negative Feedback Off Limits?

Negative feedback is off limits as a *foundation* for employee feedback. If in employees' eyes, their managers spend most of their time trying to catch employee errors, then you have a weak foundation that will not support any progress on the motivation path.

But negative feedback may still play an important role. After all, sometimes people will mess up even when they have learned how to do their work well. *You can't ignore bad performances entirely or you will encourage them.*

In the one-minute management methodology, the supervisor waits until he or she is sure that the positive praisings have taught the employee to recognize what good behavior looks like. No criticism until the person definitely knows what is expected of him or her. Otherwise, the criticism feels unfair.

In addition, reprimands are given as quickly as possible so as to provide immediate feedback. (Again, the method presumes you start out by supervising someone quite closely.) This emphasis on fast feedback is important. It prevents managers from doing what they naturally do, storing up a bunch of criticisms for an opportunity when they unload them on the poor employee. When you do this, the employee feels picked on and isn't likely to listen to each individual complaint in an open-minded manner. So please remember:

> **Only by dealing with one behavior at a time can you ensure the employee focuses on understanding and improving that behavior.**

The final point about Blanchard and Johnson's approach to discipline is that they encourage supervisors to talk only about the *behavior* they observed and what is wrong with it. This is quite different from attacking the individual. The rule is, "never attack a person's worth or value as a person." In fact, they recommend saying something *supportive of the person* at the end of the reprimand, after your criticism of the person's behavior.

> The deepest principle in human nature is the craving to be appreciated.
>
> —WILLIAM JAMES

When the New Employee Messes Up for the First Time

For example, let's say you have been training an employee for several weeks, using directive supervision and supportive, positive feedback. The employee knows how to do the basics of his job right by now. But one day he takes an extra-long lunch break, then comes back smelling like beer and proceeds to make a bunch of obvious mistakes. You might well decide it is appropriate to reprimand him about this behavior.

As soon as you can, say, when he comes in the next morning, call him into your office, describe the problems with how he did his work, and tell him you are disappointed with his behavior. You keep it short and clear to avoid it feeling as though you are venting your anger at him. You end with a supportive comment. For example, you might tell him how pleased you are with the speed with which he has learned the job and that you are positive he is going to be a great employee. You try to communicate your positive feelings about him and your high expectations based on his high value as a person.

> It's very uncomfortable for me to be a disciplinarian because it feels like I'm undoing my efforts to empower them.
>
> —MANAGER SEEKING ADVICE ON HOW TO REPRIMAND

This positive ending helps employees turn the criticism of their behavior into a learning lesson. It helps motivate them to correct the behavior and rise to your expectations. By communicating positive expectations with the negative information about their behavior, you make it more likely that they will be motivated by the negative feedback. To counter the naturally depressing and demotivating nature of bad news, you need to combine it with good news about their potential. One way to think of it is to say that:

When it comes to feedback, make sure every story you tell has a happy ending!

Expectations do have a powerful effect on motivation. And criticism can easily communicate negative expectations if you don't watch out. Are your employees hearing that you think "they've messed up again" when you roll your eyes and say, "Oh no, hear we go again. I can't believe I'm still seeing these errors!" A comment like that is really for your benefit, not theirs. It expresses your frustrations.

Venting your frustrations may make you feel better (at the expense of employee feelings). But you'd feel even better if you took a deep breath and designed a more productive, thoughtful feedback statement designed to correct the behavior instead of attacking the people.

If you want even more ideas about how to design your verbal feedback, look for "I messages" and "we messages" in the chapter on interpersonal intelligence (Chapter 10, coming up soon!). The more you learn about and practice feedback skills, the easier it is to give productive feedback.

Is Negative Feedback Destructive to Your Relationship?

Most managers are uncomfortable about giving negative feedback to their employees. It puts them in the role of the "heavy" and seems to create barriers between them and their people. For example, take the case of Susan, a woman who recently became manager of an office with a dozen people working for her. She likes to think of these employees as her colleagues, and encourages them to take "ownership" of their work and responsibility for what they do. In fact, she says her goal is for them each to *act like entrepreneurs, not employees*. But she was frustrated that they didn't seem to care as much about the quality of their work as she did. If they were truly entrepreneurs, most of them would go out of business with quality like that.

She asked me for advice about how to handle mistakes by her staff, explaining that:

> **I want to count on them to think about what's best and make the right decision, without always having to ask me. And I've hired the best people I can. So it frustrates me when they act like low-level employees and wait for me to tell them what to do and to catch their errors. I don't think I should play that role. I can't develop a colleague-to-colleague relationship with each of them if I then have to treat them like children and reprimand them whenever they mess up. It's very uncomfortable for me to be a disciplinarian because it feels like I'm**

> Encouragement after censure is as the sun after a shower.
> —Johann Wolfgang von Goethe

MOTIVATION IDEA 15

Winning the Sport of Life

This idea aims at the child within. Here's what you do to make a memorable impact when you want to recognize exceptional individual or team achievement. You open your Yellow Pages phone directory and look up "trophies." Call around until you find one of the many companies that specializes in sports trophies, serving the athletic teams in your area or nationally. Get hold of their catalog and design the most incredible, flashy, absurd skyscraper of a trophy. Put a gold figure of "Lady Victory" (wings spread, wreath held high) or some such non-sport-specific symbol at the top of a tiered trophy with marble or varnished wood bases and gold pillars. Add gold eagles with their wings spread on each level. Toss a few miniature victory wreaths or gold urns wherever they may fit. Go all the way to make this the biggest, gaudiest, splashiest trophy anyone's ever seen. You'll find that the components are surprisingly inexpensive and that the salespeople you speak with are happy to help you design a show-stopper. Add an engraved brass plaque at the bottom with the employee's name, what the trophy is for, and the date (add team name if appropriate).

Benefits. Let's be honest. Trophies are a little goofy, but everyone wants them. I guarantee any trophy you give will be displayed with pride (even if with tongue in cheek) for years to come. You get a lot of recognition bang for your buck with a two-plus-foot-high trophy festooned with do-das and personally engraved. It says "great performance" all over it, in a pretty loud voice. So if you want to make a special point of recognizing and thanking employees for great performance, why not try the mother of all rewards, the traditional sports trophy?

(I've done satisfactory business with a company called Dinn Bros., which you can reach at 800-628-9657 or on the Web at sales@dinntrophy.com as of my publication date.)

undoing my efforts to empower them. When I can, I try to push the responsibility for catching and correcting errors down to a lower level.

My advice took several forms, as follows:

- First, I pointed out that she could not really avoid giving some negative feedback along with the positive since there were some negative performances along with the positive. Giving negative feedback just comes with the territory. It's a tough job, but it can't be avoided.
- Second, I warned her that she needed to avoid a sudden shift from positive to negative or her employees would say, "What's gotten into her?" instead of appreciating that she is working on improving both her own and their behavior. A transition in which she makes sure she keeps a balance by giving more positive feedback than negative is important.
- Third, I suggested she make her feedback be timely, focused on a single behavior (not stored up), and about the behavior, not the person. This formula (which applies to positive as well as negative feedback) helps keep it from "getting personal" and ruining the relationship.
- Fourth, I suggested that she not try to model her relationship with her employees on the equal-colleague ideal and that she not try to apply the rules of friendship either. Neither of these types of relationships actually applied in her situation. She isn't their best friend. And she isn't an equal colleague. She has additional responsibilities these people don't have. (And the same applies to you.) Instead, she needs to create a comfortable and productive employer–employee relationship, one that fits her friendly personality but also permits her to pursue her aspirations for her employees. *And the foundation of this employer–employee relationship is open discussions of performance, based on both positive and negative feedback.* After a while, it will become easy and comfortable to talk to them about their on-the-job behavior.

Love your neighbor; yet don't pull down your hedge.
—BENJAMIN FRANKLIN

It is easy to fall back on the habits we've developed for other types of relationships, such as friendships and parent–child relationships, instead of facing the fact that we have to develop relationships specific to our roles as supervisors. But when we face this fact and begin to develop positive management roles for ourselves, we are able to try different behaviors until we find the ones that feel right and get results, too!

I have yet to find the man, however exalted his station, who did not do better work and put forth greater effort under a spirit of approval than under a spirit of criticism.

—CHARLES SCHWAB

Getting Negative and Positive Feedback Sorted Out

As the preceding example illustrates, your role as a supervisor requires you to provide both negative and positive feedback to employees. But remember to maintain a foundation of catching people doing something right so they will maintain a positive attitude toward their work.

> **If their mistakes outweigh their good performances, then you've got to give them instruction or simpler tasks in order to maintain the positive foundation.**

In general, you should strive for situations in which employees succeed more than they fail since a high level of failure is discouraging and reduces motivation. Excessive failure leads to pessimism about future performances, which pushes employees toward the resistance path and away from the motivation path. So successes are important, but on the other hand, you don't want 100 percent success either, or employees will get bored. You need to give them those developmental "stretch" goals we talked about earlier, goals that encourage them to try harder and improve their performances so as to keep their work inherently meaningful and rewarding. Nobody feels a sense of accomplishment from doing something so simple it's impossible to do it wrong.

Add these reasons up and you realize that some failure and a lot of success is about the right mix. So if your feedback is accurate (it better be!), you will be giving them some negative feedback and a lot of positive feedback. Ratios of one negative to three, four, or five positives are about right, depending upon the individual's natural level of optimism and determination. And over time, resilience will rise if you are providing positive emotional motivation, and their ability to handle a "leaner mix" of negative and positive feedback will increase.

The more resilient people are, the tougher you can be with them. They can maintain a positive, optimistic attitude in the face of less success and more failure. And that means you can push them along their motivation path toward higher levels of competence and higher performances. People who can handle more negative feedback can be developed more quickly. But everyone can handle some negative feedback, so everyone can develop if you work at it.

Which brings us back to the initial point: that you will need to give both negative and positive feedback to your employees in order to get and keep them motivated. But it's not enough to dole out the right ratio of negative and positive feedback. You have to apply the feedback appropriately. You have to avoid feedback that appears to be randomly negative or positive. Otherwise, you will make employees feel they don't have any control over when you give them negative feedback and when you give them positive feedback.

And if they think they can't control the feedback based on their performances, then the feedback pushes them down the resistance path in a hurry. Arbitrary feedback leads to learned helplessness and erases any intrinsic motivation with amazing effectiveness. Avoid it like the plague!

> Many managers seem to praise or reprimand their people depending on how they themselves feel on a given day, regardless of anyone's performance. If they are feeling good, they pat everyone on the back, and if they are in a bad mood, they yell at everyone.
> —"The One Minute Manager" (in Blanchard and Lorber, *Putting the One Minute Manager to Work*, p. 29.)

The Mystery of the Motivated Salespeople

Let me tell you a little story that has intrigued me for years (in fact, I wrote about it in my very first book). It involves a team of researchers at Harvard Business School who were studying salesperson performance at a selection of companies in different industries. Like most of us, they assumed that the use of incentive-based compensation probably made the most difference in salesperson performance. People who get bigger commissions ought to sell more, right?

MOTIVATION IDEA 16

An Apple on Every Desk

Contract with a local produce distributor to supply your office with fresh fruit—apples and peaches, pears or plums when in season. Place them in big bowls in lobbies or corridors for easy access by employees. A fruit snack is a nice treat and is a healthy and energy-boosting alternative to typical coffee-break foods. (If you are worried about the cost, start with a once-a-week program and move to every day when you see how happy everyone is with the program!)

Benefits. Helps employees feel they are special and they work in a special place. Allows them to treat themselves when they feel they need it (gives them control). Shows them you value and trust them.

They also figured that the right personality profile ought to be a good predictor of sales success. People with the classical salesperson's profile, lots of confidence and a drive to succeed, ought to be the top sellers, right?

Wrong. In the companies they studied, these two factors did not explain the variation in performance particularly well. There were high-performing salespeople who did *not* have the right personality profile and who were *not* receiving big commissions. What motivated these people? Why were they doing so well? (And others who had it all did not seem to be producing as well as they should. Why weren't these people busting *ss to earn their potentially huge commissions?)

After considerable sleuthing, the researchers identified an entirely different issue that had a far greater impact on motivation and performance than the others. They called it *task clarity,* and defined it as:

1. *Personal impact.* The potential to bring about results through your own efforts.
2. *Fast feedback.* Rapid feedback as to whether your efforts worked or not.
3. *Accurate feedback.* Truthful feedback reflecting your personal impact on the results.

The mysteriously high-performing salespeople were the ones who were able, through their personal efforts, to accomplish their goals (see 1). They had the power on their own to bring about sales. Those who couldn't see the links between their efforts and the end results were far less motivated by their work. That's the personal impact part of task clarity, and it helps make your task clearer, which is motivational.

The mysteriously high-performing salespeople also received relatively fast feedback about their results (see 2). They knew *right away* whether they had "won" or "lost." In contrast, low-motivation salespeople weren't sure of the score, which made the game far less compelling. That's why fast feedback is an important part of task clarity.

The mysteriously high-performing salespeople also received accurate, truthful, and fair feedback about their work (see 3). They got credit where credit was due. In contrast, other salespeople were not always recognized for good work or penalized for bad work. And that takes the challenge out of work, making you feel as though it doesn't matter whether you do it well or poorly. (Learned helplessness, here we come!) So the accuracy component of task clarity is also very important.

It turned out that the nature of the task and feedback determined who was highly motivated and who wasn't. These task and feedback issues, termed task clarity by the researchers, were far more important than compensation in motivating people. Yet sales managers always look at compensation and other incentives first when they address the motivation issue. Many ignore the three key components of task clarity. Many fail to ensure that the positive and/or negative feedback is related to individual performances, plus quick and accurate feedback. (This story is based on the work of Benson Shapiro and Stephen Doyle. See Hiam, *The Vest-Pocket CEO*, Prentice Hall, 1990, pp. 314–316, for details.)

Why Clear Feedback Is More Powerful Than Money

Even the most generous financial incentives and rewards cannot motivate people to excel if the task and feedback are wrong. But make the task clear to them, and it becomes inherently motivating. It becomes a game you want to win simply because you see *how* to win it. Which means that *a little investment in task clarity can save you a lot of expense on incentive pay and rewards*. Don't you like mysteries? They so often reveal useful new insights into how to do our jobs.

> He who praises everybody praises nobody.
>
> —SAMUEL JOHNSON

Raising Task Clarity to Boost Motivation

Great story, but what does it mean for you and your people? First, let's clarify its relevance to any and all employees. In my own research and consulting in the decade-plus since I first came across this concept, I've found it works with all sorts of employees, and with children and athletes as well. It isn't just about salespeople by any means although it certainly helps motivate them, too.

Second, let's clarify the two practical points you must master to use this concept for building employee motivation. They are how to *diagnose* a task clarity problem and how to *remedy* it. Naming problems isn't enough, after all. You're a manager, so you have to solve problems. (Business seems so much simpler from the vantage of a tenured professorship, I bet!)

There are three components of task clarity, so your diagnosis needs to look for problems in each of these areas. And you need to be prepared to *fix* problems in any of these areas as well. Here's how.

Ask yourself or your employees if the connections between individual performances and end results are obvious. "Why" questions reveal a lack of clarity about personal impact on results quite quickly.

Diagnosing and Remedying Disconnects Between Effort and Results

Ask yourself or your employees if the connections between individual performances and end results are obvious. Do employees know what happens when they do their work one way rather than another? Often they don't seem to be aware of these connections or to take a strong interest in them. You'll know it's a problem if they seem vague about why certain results happened. "Why" questions reveal a lack of clarity about personal impact on results quite quickly.

To remedy this problem, first check to see if they receive enough information about what the end results of their work *are*. Sometimes a desired end result, like a new sale or the production of a product, is many steps downstream from the employee. In that case, flow-charting the process to show the employee where he or she "fits in" can boost clarity about personal impact.

You can also try using an "internal customer" system in which you identify who "consumes" the work of each employee, and teach employees to talk to their internal customers and find out what they think of the work. For example, a janitor might not see any links between his or her work and the company's ability to find and keep customers. Yet there must be some or why would you need a janitor? If you identify the people who work in the janitor's area as his or her *internal customers,* then have the janitor ask them what they need in order to be better at finding and serving customers, the janitor will be able to see the links in the business system more clearly. You can even have the janitor and his or her internal customers develop a list of the most important things from the internal customer's perspective, so the janitor can keep these in mind. (Make sure the janitor knows why they are important in terms of their bottom-line impact. Lists such as these should describe the what *and* the why!)

But often the simplest approach works best. It is to teach the employee how his or her work fits and what its impact is, then to provide relevant information to make that impact visible. Knowledge is the best antidote to unclear connections between effort and results, especially in the complex business systems you see in many workplaces today. You need to know a lot more about the company and its work than most employees do before you can see all the connections between your work and the company's important results.

That means training and information about the company and how it works is highly motivational. At least that is the theory, and I've seen some real successes from implementing that theory. For instance, I was involved some years ago in an initiative at Mass Mutual, a large insurance company, to train office workers in the basics of finance.

Training and information about the company and how it works is highly motivational.

The rational for this large-scale training program was that nobody could really understand the work of a company that operates in the financial services sector without understanding the principles of finance. And employees hired to do word processing, filing, billing, and other functions rarely had much training in finance. *Employees knew their work, but not the company's work.* Teaching them about the company's work made them better able to see how their work related to it. And this boosted their task clarity and job motivation levels. Knowledge is a very powerful motivator!

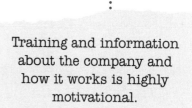

Diagnosing and Remedying Feedback Lags

Do your employees receive rapid feedback on whether their efforts worked or not? If you rely on a quarterly or annual performance review system for personal feedback, then the answer is a

From the employee's perspective, much of the work disappears without a splash, like a rock dropped into a bottomless hole.

loud no. Or even if your people get more frequent feedback, it still may not be fast enough. For instance, take the case of an employee who works hard on one component of a project or product. When the project is completed or the product finished, any quality problems or errors ought to surface. And at that point, there is usually an effort to track down the perpetrators of any problems.

So if your employee messed up, he or she will eventually get the blame, at least some of the time. Is that good enough? Definitely not! From the employee's perspective, much of the work disappears without a splash, like a rock dropped into a bottomless hole. An occasional, muffled splash in the distance does little to make the bottom of that hole more visible.

What your employees need is routine, immediate, or almost immediate feedback. Like when you roll a ball down a lane and see how many of the pins fall over. If pins fell over on a variable, delayed schedule, you'd never know which of your balls produced which results. You wouldn't be able to improve with that kind of feedback. You wouldn't even want to play for very long. Might as well go pull the handle of some slot machine instead. At least you have the chance of a jackpot. Why gamble when there isn't anything to win?

There are many ways to make feedback more frequent and immediate. If you are handing work off to the next person in a process, he or she can provide the immediate feedback. Add a simple checklist or survey for them to fill in to tell you what they liked and disliked about the job you did. Presto! Instant feedback.

Perhaps the best way to provide fast feedback is to:

Teach employees to evaluate their own work as they do it.

That way, they can provide their own feedback. For example, if there are five important things you look for in your employees' work, teach them to identify these things and give them a process and a form for tracking them. For example, they might stop and evaluate every fifth or tenth job they do using their checklist or survey. This is the same method used in manufacturing under the name of statistical process control except that employees are often using measurement instruments and plotting their results on a control chart. If that's preferable in your work area, create a control chart instead of a checklist. However, a simple checklist based on employee judgment is often fine outside of complex manufacturing applications.

But either way, *make sure employees know how to evaluate their own work*, and make sure they know they're responsible for doing so. That way they are guaranteed all the feedback they need as frequently as they need it.

Make sure employees know how to evaluate their own work, and make sure they know they're responsible for doing so. That way they are guaranteed all the feedback they need as frequently as they need it.

Diagnosing and Remedying Feedback Inaccuracies

Does the employee receive accurate feedback? Is the feedback fair and truthful? Feedback in the form of supervisor or customer comments is often seen as inaccurate by employees, so be alert to this possibility. After all, you can easily make a mistake. You don't watch people all the time. Sometimes you guess what happened or think you can tell what happened but end up blaming the wrong person, therefore:

> **Be careful to ask employees what happened, rather than tell them what happened, unless you were actually the eyewitness with the best view!**

That way, you'll avoid mistakes that employees will easily see and resent. Whether you give positive or negative feedback, make sure it is as accurate as possible. (This touches on that critical fairness criterion employees care so much about, as we saw in Chapter 4.)

That's the personal level of accuracy, but there is a structural level, too. It's the institutionalized forms of feedback, and they can be inaccurate to say the least. I call the problem *structural feedback inaccuracies* since that's what they are.

For example, take the case of a company that awarded most valuable employee medals and cash prizes to the employees from each department and team that contributed the most during each quarter of the year. Employees were nominated by their individual supervisors, then finalists were selected by vote of all the supervisors. As a result, departments that had the most supervisors also had the largest number of most valuable employees. And employees were

MOTIVATION IDEA 17

The Thinking Sabbatical

If an employee has shown an ability to improve performance significantly by mastering skills or by making clever modifications to the work process, make sure you recognize and reward the fact! One way to do so is to ask the employee if he or she would like to take a Thinking Sabbatical. Structure it with rules such as the following: You take a day "off" from your normal work to do some thinking about how to improve work performance at the company. Before you go, we give you an (attractive) blank notebook and a (fancy) pen. When you return the next day, you should have written down or sketched some ideas to share with your associates concerning how to improve the way we work. You will then have an opportunity to present your ideas to an appropriate group of employees in a staff meeting the next day.

Benefit. The real reward in this plan is not the day off (since employees may actually spend much of the day thinking and worrying about their assignment). It is the recognition for their ingenuity and accomplishment. It recognizes those who develop and grow in their own work and encourages them to share their good attitude with peers by making them peer leaders.

Suggestion Systems. The Thinking Sabbatical can also be combined with most suggestion systems by giving contributors of accepted ideas a chance to take a sabbatical to prepare a report on their suggestion, then giving them an opportunity to present their ideas to peers.

Parting Shot. How often do you complain that your employees just don't seem to be thinking? Well, why should they? You don't recognize or reward them for thinking. Here's a way to start!

aware of this bias and viewed the program as inaccurate. It didn't motivate anyone as a result.

The way to fix structural feedback inaccuracies is to *fix the structures that cause them.* When that company switched over to team-based work, managers took advantage of the transition to introduce a new structure for selecting most valuable employees. Now the teams each select one of their employees, and he or she receives an award. In addition, teams write up their reasons and a rotating committee of employees votes on which one should receive the company-wide MVE award (with any same-team members abstaining). This system is more fair and accurate since it lacks any obvious source of bias and since the coworkers who know the employee's work best make the nominations. It is far more motivating as a result.

But Do They Know How to Use the Feedback?

Students often suffer from severe cases of effort–results disconnect. Their task clarity is almost zero. But it isn't for the obvious reason. They *do* get their results. Tests are graded and you know which one is yours, so you are guaranteed either positive or negative feedback, usually pretty quickly. But students don't always know how to *interpret* the feedback in order to improve.

> I studied so hard I deserve a better grade!
>
> —A TYPICAL COLLEGE STUDENT'S LAMENT

The disconnect comes from *a lack of awareness of how they do their work* so that they are unable to process the feedback. In which case, those grades are no more meaningful or motivational than an uncorrected exam would be. In fact, the apparently arbitrary nature of grades reduces the poor student's sense of control over outcomes, which is highly demotivating.

I taught for five years at a large business school, and I would often hear from unhappy students who felt that a poor grade didn't reflect his or her good effort. In fact, undergraduate business majors form long lines outside their professors' offices these days, not to seek knowledge, but simply to debate grades.

When faced with these sorts of complaints, I would patiently explain that the poor grade reflected their poor performance, not the good effort. And I'd suggest that they must have been "working hard, not smart." When I'd probe to find out how they had studied, I would find that they had studied the wrong things, or studied them in the wrong way. For example, memorizing terms and facts won't prepare you for an essay test, no matter how hard you work at it. Nor will reading the wrong chapter. But the students I talked to would make the same study errors on the next test, and the next.

I finally became frustrated enough to do a detailed study of the problem. I asked students on their tests to describe their study methods, expecting to learn which methods were correlated with high grades and then share those winning methods with the entire class. It was a reasonable hypothesis. But it was wrong.

What I found instead was that *any* study methods seemed to produce honors grades. Any methods at all. Didn't matter what they were. If they had a method they could describe, they were getting honors grades.

Students who got below-honors grades, in contrast, were uniformly unable to describe their study methods. They left that question blank. They had simply sat right down and studied without thinking about how to study. They'd done their work without developing *any* sort of strategy or hypothesis about it in advance. As a result of this total lack of inquisitiveness about their own performance, they had no ideas or methods to test, and therefore the feedback could not teach them anything about their performance. (By the way, I'm sure you get the point that this finding applies in spades to most employees, too. After all, my old students are probably your employees by now!)

As a result of this total lack of inquisitiveness about their own performance, they had no ideas or methods to test, and therefore the feedback could not teach them anything about their performance.

So the secret to better grades for any given level of effort is to *think about and try out different ideas* for how to study. It does not really matter which ideas you try. As long as you have *some* idea in advance, the test acts as an experiment and you learn something about how well that method works for you. Then you can modify your hypothesis and try a different approach next time. You *will* improve your performance over time until you, too, get reliably high grades. When I taught this finding to my students, they finally were able to begin improving, and it became possible for them to obtain results proportional to their effort. The same applies to any performance, of course, not just to studying for an exam.

Inquisitiveness Makes Feedback More Useful

Let's apply this surprising insight to your employees. Employees who do their work thoughtlessly, without asking themselves what approach or method to use, *will not have any hypotheses to test.* Whether they get positive or negative feedback, they won't have any mental context for it, and they won't learn anything about how to improve as a result of it.

So any feedback they get from the task will make no sense to them. They won't be able to *understand* the relationship to their performance, even if there obviously *is* a relationship to you, their supervisor. Good feedback won't make them smarter or better, nor will bad feedback. It will just confuse them.

Like the students who do poorly on tests, all your employees know is that they "gave it a good effort," but somehow, "unfairly," it just didn't work out.

So you really need to emphasize inquisitiveness in your employees. Ask them what they *think* about their work. Ask them what *alternative approaches* they see and if they have tried all of them. Encourage them to do a little *experimenting* so they have something to learn from the results. Otherwise, results will be meaningless to them.

You really need to emphasize inquisitiveness in your employees.

The path to wisdom is paved with experiments. Unless employees *think about* their work, no feedback will be of much use.

Respectful Feedback

A hidden but essential component of effective, helpful feedback–positive or negative–is respect. We explored the importance of respect to employee motivation in Chapter 4 and concluded that managers often communicate disrespect for their employees. It is easy to make this mistake without meaning to. And one of the easiest places to run into "respect trouble" is in giving positive and negative feedback.

The importance of respect is really obvious when it comes to negative feedback. If you seem to be attacking the employee instead of his or her behavior, you are communicating a *lack of respect* for

MOTIVATION IDEA 18

"Let's Think About It"

This idea isn't mine. I stole it. And I want you to steal it, too, because it really works.

I worked for a manager many years ago named John whose favorite phrase whenever you asked him a question was, "Let's think about that."

At first, I assumed it was his way of ducking my questions. I figured the guy simply didn't know the answer, so he was putting me off. But then a funny thing would happen. A few days later, he'd bump into me outside my office, and say, "So, did you think about that? Any ideas?"

"Think about what?" was my usual answer at first. I'd long since forgotten my question to him. But then he would patiently remind me of our earlier conversation, and then share any thoughts he'd come up with. And usually they were pretty thoughtful thoughts.

After a few rounds of this, I began to figure out what was expected of me. When I ran into a problem or puzzle worth thinking about, I'd share it with him. And he'd usually say, "Let's think about that." And then we would. We'd think about it on and off, and maybe ask some other people what they thought, too. We wouldn't rush it because John was a patient thinker. But we wouldn't ever forget about it because John hatched every question he ever incubated and you just knew he'd pop up at a quiet moment sometime in the next week or two and say, "So, have you thought about that? What do you think?"

His enthusiasm for thinking was contagious. Everyone in his department did a lot more thinking. And gradually, people from elsewhere in the company (and it was a big company) discovered that we liked thinking about things. They began to use us more and more as internal consultants. People would say, "I've got a problem for you," and describe it, and then ask, "Can you think about that for me?" We were getting good at thinking, and so was everybody else.

Now, what does this have to do with motivation? Well, everything, really. Because we employees got lots of feedback from our work, but much of it was unclear. *Why* did sales drop suddenly in that region? *Why* did that program do so well, but the other one fall flat? *Why* did so-and-so like our last report but not this one? Hmm. I don't know. *Let's think about it.*

Basically, John's "think about it" mentality encouraged us all to think about our feedback far harder than most people ever do. And we were rewarded with a far clearer view of the complex and varied systems that surrounded us. We became better at understanding the subtle links between our behavior and our own and the company's results. And that insight opened up avenues for improvement in our performances and empowered us to improve our own performances in ways that less thoughtful employees could not imagine.

Thanks, John. It's high time someone gave you some positive feedback about that technique. I hope you are still using it!

him or her. This leads to an important respect-based point about negative feedback:

> **You don't want your employees to conclude you think they are the wrong persons for the job or they *will* be!**

So it is important to affirm the worth of the individual at the same time you criticize his or her behavior. This makes it more motivating for your employees, and it also helps overcome the natural aversion we all have toward criticizing others. You instincts are right; you shouldn't criticize others. Just criticize their behavior, not them!

But What If I Don't Respect Them?

Sometimes you are so darn frustrated with poor performance that you just plain feel you have poor performers. No amount of my telling you to focus on the behavior can overcome a strong conviction that the people are the problem. (I'll tell you the story of one manager who reached the point where he decided to adopt an approach to his people he called "management by contempt" in a later chapter.)

When you are feeling truly negative about your employees, it is often because they just aren't responding appropriately to the positive and negative feedback you are giving them. You've reached that point we all remember from our experiences of family life, where a frustrated parent pounds a fist on the table and says, "*How* many times do I have to *tell* you . . .?"

When you are feeling truly negative about your employees, it is often because they just aren't responding appropriately to the positive and negative feedback you are giving them.

Well, you probably have to tell the average child to clean up his or her room an infinite number of times to make much of a dent in that mess. And it's not because you failed to give your children good feedback about their behavior. Heck, you probably have told them when it's dirty a million times. And you may even have praised them when it's clean, if it ever is clean. But they still don't seem to learn. You've reached a motivation wall.

Whenever that happens, whenever you get frustrated with them because you're doing the right sorts of things to motivate them but it just isn't working, *stop*.

Obviously, the motivation or feedback methods you are using don't work. How much negative feedback do *you* need before you figure out you're going about it all wrong?

Obviously, the motivation or feedback methods you are using don't work. How much negative feedback do *you* need before you figure out you're going about it all wrong?

When you hit a motivation wall, please, *please*, change your own behavior. Try a new approach to motivation. And there are other approaches, to be sure. That's why I didn't run out of advice at the end of the first chapter.

By now I'm sure you're getting the idea that the motivation box is virtually bottomless. It's almost like magic the way you can reach in and pull out another concept and another approach. And you know what? It's not a science. *The approach that works is the right one*. So when you get frustrated, change strategies and try out another idea.

In this case, where the manager feels that employees are just not responding to good feedback, whether negative, positive, or both, the natural next step is to *try other forms of feedback*. Wait, did I hear you say . . .

You Didn't Know There *Were* Other Forms of Feedback?

When I advise people to try other forms of feedback, the most common response I get is, "What? I didn't know there *were* other forms of feedback." Precisely! So many people have spent so much time talking about feedback in terms of whether it is negative or positive, that we tend to think of it as either negative or positive. Period.

That's a classic case of what is called bipolar thinking. In the work I do on creativity, one of the easiest ways to help people find new approaches and solutions is to attack their bipolar thinking. Whenever you think there are just two clear, opposite alternatives, you fail to see any others. Bipolar thinking blinds us to other possibilities. Which is okay until the two options we do see no longer serve us well.

Like thinking that the earth has just two poles, north and south. Now, that's a fine model, and it makes sense since the earth's magnetic field orients along the north–south dimension and the Earth spins that way, too. But look at a globe and you will have to agree that the poles are just two dots on it. In theory, you could just as easily pick out two other spots and call them poles as well. In fact, the earth has room for an infinite number of imaginary dots, so there is really no limit to the number of poles we could recognize if it proved useful to do so!

Sure, but why would you need any other poles? Again, watch that bipolar thinking. It keeps you from seeing possibilities. Scientists who think about these things actually recognize more than one set of poles. The magnetic poles are different from the poles defined by the earth's rotation. The theoretical true north at the top of our spinning sphere is in a different place on their maps than is magnetic north. And each has a corresponding opposite on the south side of the planet as well. Two sets of poles when we thought there was only one. Makes you wonder if you could think of a third or fourth type of pole for the earth. Heck, maybe the scientists already have.

My point, which almost got lost over the horizon, is that there are always many other possible ways to think about a topic than the two-category one that is most obvious to us. And in the next chapter, I'll introduce you to several alternative views of feedback that often get you out of a corner when positive–negative feedback ceases to satisfy your needs. But first, let's wrap up this chapter and make sure we have captured all the "keeper" points about positive and negative feedback.

Parting Shots

We've seen that feedback is an essential component of motivation because it tells you where you are and how you are doing. People want to achieve good results, but how can they unless they know what the results *are*? Task clarity comes from clear, obvious links between what you do and what happens as a result.

MOTIVATION IDEA 19

Self-Recognition

People who acknowledge their own good performances are more optimistic and confident when it comes to new challenges. So why not encourage people to recognize good performances in themselves? In a meeting or training session, hand out blank sheets of paper to your employees and ask them to make a list of the five most exceptional things they've done at work in the past year. Help them think of things if they get stuck, and encourage them to put down anything they did that was above expectations or might seem remarkable to others if they knew about it. You can then ask for volunteers to read their lists, but don't force anyone who is embarrassed to do so. (Don't collect the lists; make it clear they will be taking them away with them.)

Benefits. The exercise can be presented as a fun warm-up and will generate some friendly laughter. But it has its serious side as well since it helps build self-confidence and optimism, which are linked with ability to motivate one's self.

One of your most important jobs as a motivator and manager is to provide personal feedback to employees. Especially when they are learning a new task or job, watch them closely and make a point of giving them positive feedback so they will learn what good work looks like and be able to look for it themselves.

Furthermore, your principle task in providing feedback, especially when first teaching a new person or a new task, is to "accentuate the positive" as the old song goes. Remember our discussion in the previous two chapters about emotional motivation? It's an approach in which you build a positive base of optimism and self-confidence upon which internal motivation to succeed naturally develops. Positive feedback maintains this important foundation. But negative feedback provides corrections that are necessary for high levels of success and personal achievement. So a balance is necessary.

Know why people *really* keep pets? Because they provide the positive emotional feedback that's so necessary, but generally so lacking in our human interactions!

Yet, as we saw in the beginning of this chapter, our social traditions do not naturally lead us to a healthy balance between positive and negative feedback. As Chief Justice Earl Warren once observed, even our news overbalances the negative feedback. (I bet you noticed that too, but hang on.) Warren is quoted as saying, "I always turn to the sports pages first, which record people's accomplishments. The front page has nothing but man's failures." (So *that's* why everybody likes to read the sports section first.)

You can think of your feedback task as reporting on performance to your employees–but you won't get it right unless you think like a sports reporter instead of the guy who drafts the front-page headlines.

Once positive feedback is established as a base, you can add negative feedback when necessary. But in all feedback, make sure you praise or criticize the performance, not the performer. In fact, you need to assert the value of the person whenever you criticize his or her behavior in order to show your respect and share your high expectations for him or her. This builds optimism, which your employees may need in order to use the negative feedback constructively. (Think of it as a little emotional nudge to keep them from falling off the motivation path.)

Employees also need an *inquisitive* approach to their own work in order to be able to make productive use of feedback. Unless they are thinking about what they do and how they do it, they won't know why they do well or poorly. They won't be able to use the feedback to improve their own performances. So make sure they are mentally involved in the quest for improvements to their own work methods. Remember, when in doubt, just try that wonderful line, "Let's think about it!" If you say it often enough, your employees just might follow your advice.

"Let's think about it!"

JELLY BEAN MOTIVATION

A. Fill In Jelly Bean Request Form

B. Match Flavor to Employee's Personality Profile

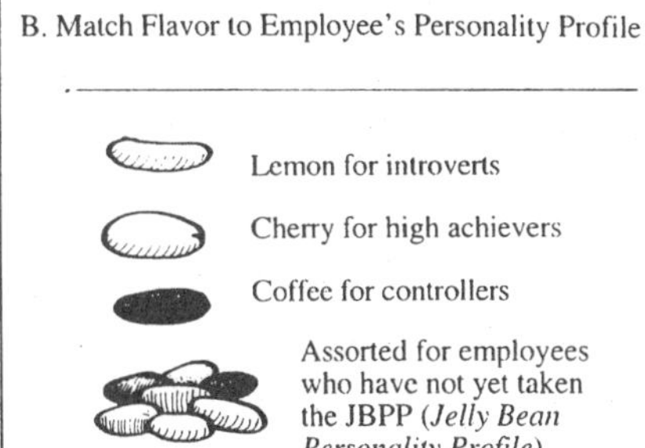

C. Prepare Sweet & Small Reward Form # 6238-B

D. Wait for Approval of Senior V.P., Delayed Feedback and Reorganization

E. Identify Substitute Employees (in case of transfers, layoffs or terminations)

Employee Substitution System
MATCH LEVEL: 86%

F. Sample Reward Materials (for quality control)

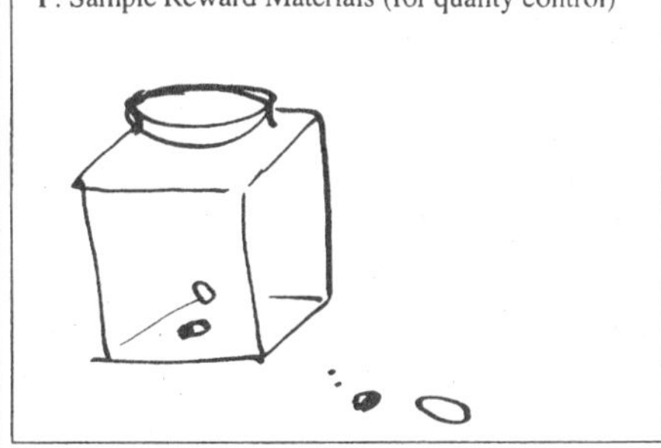

G. Fabricate Rationale for Additional Materials Requisition

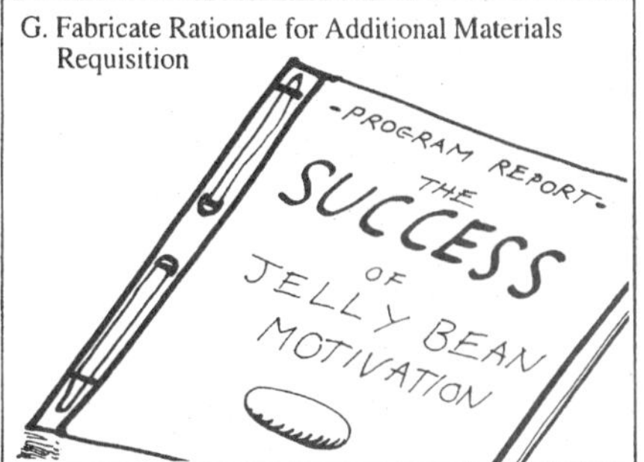

H. Terminate Program for Lack of Funding

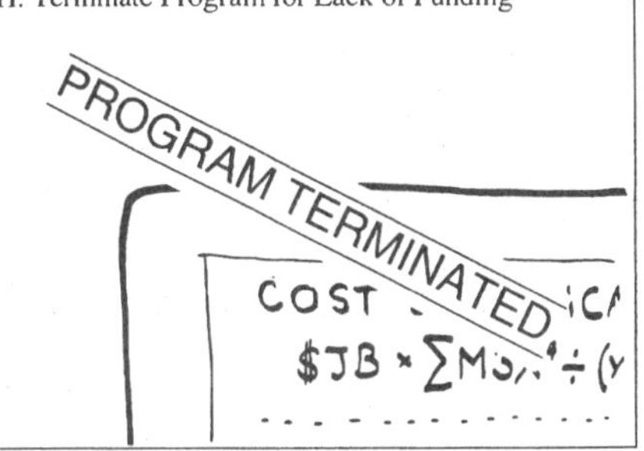

Motivating with Informative Feedback

Chapter 8

The previous chapter explores the two classic descriptions of feedback: negative and positive. It advocates the use of a foundation of positive, behavior-oriented feedback in place of the typical approach, which is negative and attacks the person rather than the specific behavior. And it advocates the use of clear, accurate, timely feedback, delivered in ways that encourage employees to think about their performances and work on improving them.

The shift from an emphasis on negative, personal feedback to positive, impersonal feedback is a healthy one, and does much to build employee motivation. It focuses attention on what to do in order to improve performances, which is precisely where the manager wants the focus to be. And it helps managers "accentuate the positive" so as to build and maintain the emotional foundations of motivation.

The next major issue you need to consider is whether you are using *controlling* or *informative* feedback.

What Next?

But emphasizing positive feedback is just the first key shift you need to consider as you explore your use of feedback and increase its motivational power in your work force. The next major issue you need to consider is whether you are using *controlling* or *informative* feedback. And, just to make sure you have it clear before we go into this subject, I intend to do my level best to convince you that you probably use much too much controlling feedback and need to switch to informative feedback in order to boost employee motivation. Giving people information with which to judge their own performances is far better than telling them what to do, as the farmer who got sick of people ignoring his "No Trespassing" signs realized when he replaced them with a sign that said:

> **"Don't cross this field unless you can do it in 9.9 seconds. The bull can do it in 10."**

Controlling feedback tells people what to do. It can be positive or negative. Informative feedback tells them how they are doing. It also can be positive or negative. But it works much better.

A green light is positive controlling feedback, a red light is negative controlling feedback–to use an example we are well accustomed to.

"Hey, but you said controlling feedback doesn't work well, and most people stop for red lights, so they work, don't they?"

Do red lights work? Depends what your expectations are. Sure, they control people because of the threat of law enforcement and, if conditions are crowded, the possibility of an accident for those who run red lights. But is that the way you want to motivate your employees at work? Usually not. Most managers use controlling feedback in ways that are meant to motivate employees to do better *on their own*. Instead, controlling feedback encourages them to be dependent upon the source of the feedback.

Most people don't really "get" this point 100 percent when I first make it because it's complex and I have a hard time explaining it. So I want you to think about that stoplight example again. Most people are highly motivated to stop when the light is red and go when it is green. They do just what that light tells them 99.999 percent of the time. Great motivation, right? Wrong.

What happens *when the power goes down* in your town and motorists meet at a busy intersection? Has the light trained them to alternate on a twenty-second cycle? Certainly not. It doesn't matter how many thousands of times someone follows the traffic light's cycle. As soon as that light stops working, they do whatever they think they can get away with. Their performance is therefore 100 percent dependent upon the stoplight. And believe me, it's not much fun to be a "stoplight" supervisor at your work. As soon as you turn your back, all hell breaks loose, just like at that busy intersection.

Believe me, it's not much fun to be a "stop-light" supervisor at your work. As soon as you turn your back, all hell breaks loose, just like at that busy intersection.

With *controlling feedback:*

Employees do a better job to please someone who has control over rewards they want.

Or in the case of an anonymous, impersonal control like a stoplight, people do a good job of complying with the control when (and only when) they must to get what they want.

Informative feedback, in contrast, tells people how they are doing instead of telling them what to do. *How* instead of *what.* That's a big difference. Informative feedback is more likely to encourage them to do better on their own because it gives employees control over the feedback. Their control comes from *seeing that they can influence the feedback to make it more positive.* The information the supervisor provides helps the employee see the links between personal behavior and feedback.

When the employee can see what happens based on information about how he or she is doing, this encourages a feeling of control over the results. This feeling of control gives employees an easy pathway to making themselves feel good. They feel good when they do well. It gives them a sense of accomplishment and achievement. And they feel good when they get rewarded for their accomplishments. By performing better, they can make the information about their performance into better, more positive feedback. *The information becomes the reward* the employee pursues.

With *informative feedback:*

A star athlete does not perform to please the coach or the fans.

Employees do a better job to please themselves by making the information about their performance better.

A star athlete (or any highly motivated athlete) does not perform to please the coach or the fans. It's great if they are pleased, of course. But the main motivation is to win. And what does "to win" really mean? It means to improve your score in the game. It's all about an informative feedback system: the scoreboard. To make the next big step up the motivation path, then, you need to start thinking about providing scoreboards on which employees can track their own performance.

Extrinsic Versus Intrinsic Motivation

I've just given you the simplest, clearest explanation of controlling and informative feedback that I can. But I had to skip over a number of interesting points to do so. Now that you have grasped the fundamental concepts, you are ready to tackle it at a higher level.

It gets a little more complicated because to really understand and use informative feedback, you need to distinguish between two kinds of motivation. You have to recognize the difference between

MOTIVATION IDEA 20

Behavior Bingo

Bingo can be used to reinforce desired behavior. It is especially applicable to any target behavior that you don't want employees to do, and that they need to be vigilant about avoiding on a daily basis. In other words, you can use bingo to encourage compliance with regulations, rules, or procedures. Examples: Avoiding accidents in the workplace. Following safety rules. Not violating quality standards or rules. Achieving daily or hourly work quotas. Avoiding customer complaints. Here's how to use it. Put employees who work together on teams. Give each employee a bingo score card at the beginning of a round. (Score cards are 5x5 matrices filled with randomly assigned numbers between 1 and 75.) Individuals win by getting five in a row. A winner typically emerges after you draw twelve to fifteen numbers, and more emerge as you keep drawing. Draw every day and let a round last from a couple weeks to a month. Offer cash prizes, program-related rewards, gifts, whatever you think they'll like.

But here's the hook. Individuals can only play in the round as long as their team has no problems. As soon as someone on your team fails to achieve the goal you've set for the game, then the team drops out. So that encourages team members to help each other out and "police" each other's behavior.

How do you stage a bingo game? You'll need equipment: a container filled with numbered balls from which you can draw at random, a master table or poster with all 75 numbers to record each drawing, and wallet-sized or other bingo cards for each participant. A toy store may stock the basics, or you can contact Safety Concepts, which offers a reasonably-priced bingo cage with 75 balls for under a hundred dollars. (They also have a full-blown program called B-Safe Bingo which includes all the equipment you need to run an occupational safety-oriented bingo game. As of printing, they are located at 417-581-6199, or on the Web at www.bsafe.com.)

Benefits. It's true, this kind of motivation system relies on external rewards, and I certainly favor intrinsic motivation instead. So I'd make sure I combined this game with at least one other initiative aimed more at internal motivation, such as personal goalsetting for individuals based on their own previous performance record, along with some kind of personal record-keeping method that can be turned in for a reward. Maybe a place to record personal performance on the back of those bingo cards, and the option of additional awards from submitting good personal performance records? (In other words, everybody who improves upon poor performance or maintains good performance levels can get a minimum reward. And those who are lucky and on good teams can also get occasional big bingo rewards.)

However, the big benefit of this kind of team bingo game outweighs this possible negative of using an extrinsic motivator. The benefit is that the game gets everyone engaged in helping the supervisors move employees toward the goal. It makes the goal top-of-mind for employees on a daily basis. It provides informative feedback about those goals. And it aligns employees' interests with the supervisors by making it profitable for them to encourage fellow employees to comply. Alignment of interest. That's a powerful thing!

motivation that comes from within, or intrinsic motivation, and motivation that comes from without, or extrinsic motivation.

Intrinsic motivation is motivation that wells up from within. Which means you don't have to supply it. When the employee wants to accomplish and succeed and is eager to tackle the task for his or her own reasons, then you don't have to provide external motivation. The motivation is intrinsic, or within the employee. You simply have to enable the employee to act on this intrinsic motivation.

But when you have to push and prod the employee with external motivations, then you are supplying *extrinsic motivation*. And that means all the motivation originates with you, not the employee. If pleasing you or winning "your" game is attached to important rewards, the employee may amplify the motivation you provide and actually produce a pretty good performance. But only as long as you keep providing the initial motivation and maintaining the external threats and rewards.

Intrinsic motivation is what drives exceptionally motivated star performers, as you want your people to be. It is the motivational style of the motivation path.

Intrinsic motivation is what drives exceptionally motivated star performers, as you want your people to be. It is the motivational style of the motivation path. Extrinsic motivation is the kind that characterizes people who are on the resistance path, as I described in Chapter 5.

A Boy and His Dog

The easiest way for me to visualize the difference between intrinsic and extrinsic rewards is to recall a scene from a playground. Picture this.

A boy and his dog run onto the deserted playground. The boy is carrying a basketball. He positions the dog a few feet from him, says "Stay!" and carefully aims a bounce pass at the dog's head. The dog ducks. The boy says "Bad dog!!!" and the dog cringes. Then the boy pats and encourages the dog and says, "You can do it! Remember your trick?" He demonstrates the trick himself by bouncing the ball with his forehead. Then he repositions the dog and sends the ball toward it again. This time, the dog bumps the ball off its head and back toward the boy. The boy says, "Good dog" and pats the happy pet.

The boy and dog repeat this trick several more times, until the boy is satisfied that the dog is able to return the pass adequately. Then he turns toward a nearby basketball hoop and starts practicing his jump shots. A few minutes later, the dog is sleeping contentedly in the shade of a nearby tree. But the boy is working up a sweat as he continues to practice his arsenal of shots. An hour later, the boy finally quits, whistles for his dog, and the two head off. As they disappear down a path through the park where this incident takes place, the dog finds a stick and keeps presenting it to the boy with the obvious goal of getting the boy to throw the stick. The boy tosses it out a few times, but since he's tired from his workout he gets sick of the stick game and leads the way back home.

If this story is just about the behavior of boys and dogs, then I'm wasting your time with it. And most people would interpret it that way, which is why most people don't bother really watching when boys and dogs take to the nation's playgrounds. But there is much more to learn from this story. The images stay in my mind because they continue to teach me about motivation.

At first, I thought this story demonstrated the difference between people and animals. People pursue higher goals. They prepare for the future. The boy's practicing is all about his ability to anticipate the need for those skills in a future game. The dumb dog "doesn't get it" and so isn't motivated to practice his basketball skills.

But something about the scene doesn't jive with that interpretation. It's the parting view of the pair, where the dog is trying to get the boy to perform a stick-throwing trick and the boy is reluctant to cooperate. I can't see any difference between the dog's desire to make the boy throw a stick and the boy's desire to make the dog return a basketball pass. Each wants the other to play his game. Each has high intrinsic motivation to play his preferred game. And each finds the other's game dull by comparison.

But the boy, having authority by virtue of his "management" position in the relationship, is better able to train the dog than vice versa. However, each of them is depending upon extrinsic motivations ("good dog" and "bad dog" or tail wags and barks) in their efforts to train the other.

At first, I thought this story demonstrated the difference between people and animals.

In contrast, the boy's workout on the basketball court is motivated purely by intrinsic motivation. The dog certainly doesn't tell him what to do. There is no coach either. The boy simply wants to do it. I was taught once in a coaching clinic I attended that "the ball is the best coach." In this story, the ball is the only coach, and it motivates because it provides the informative feedback needed to engage the boy's intrinsic motivation to succeed at basketball. He can readily see what the "score" is by how many of his attempted shots go through the hoop. Trying to improve that score is his main motivation. He feels good when he improves. Give people a game they like and a score they can follow, and they will be highly motivated to improve.

But extrinsic motivation doesn't produce this same urge to improve. That's demonstrated by the dog's behavior. As soon as the boy stops "managing" the dog's practice drill, what does it do? It goes off to sleep under a tree. Ever seen a dog practice its tricks when it is alone? I don't think so!

Ever seen a dog practice its tricks when it is alone?

However, even the dog is fully capable of intrinsic motivation. When it comes to the dog's game, fetching sticks, nobody needs to tell it what to do. In fact, it is so motivated to play that it attempts to motivate the boy to play with it. So the dog, like all animals, is capable of acting from both extrinsic and intrinsic motivation. And if we can say that about somebody's pet, I don't see how anyone could argue that *employees* aren't capable of acting from intrinsic as well as extrinsic motivation!

Intrinsic Motivation and the Motivation Path

The motivation path described in Chapter 5 is the path of intrinsic motivation. The opportunities to develop, grow, accomplish, and succeed are what motivate the employee. That's why much of what I focus on in this book involves getting employees onto the motivation path and awakening their intrinsic motivation.

In contrast, the resistance path depends upon extrinsic motivation to combat employee resistance. And because so many workplaces are on this resistance path, many of our preconceived notions about employee motivation and rewards are based on the extrinsic motivation model. Think about all the ways we are accustomed to motivating employees with external factors:

- Salary is an extrinsic motivator
- Threats of punishment are extrinsic
- Rewards given by managers are often extrinsic
- Promotions for good performance are extrinsic motivations because someone else determines when you deserve the promotion
- Prizes for the best employee suggestions are often extrinsic motivations
- Much of the positive and negative feedback supervisors give is extrinsic

In short, almost all of our traditional incentives and rewards are extrinsic motivations. They take the form of controlling feedback. They poke and pull to move employees. They do not awaken intrinsic motivations. They motivate by controlling, rather than by awakening self-determination and stimulating self-control.

> Our traditional incentives and rewards do not awaken intrinsic motivations. They motivate by controlling, rather than by awakening self-determination and stimulating self-control.

What's wrong with using extrinsic, control-oriented motivations? Well, remember what that resistance path is like. It produces the performance puzzle, in which employees seem to improve, but as soon as the new stimulus becomes routine or the manager lets up the effort, performance falls again. And so the resistance path is a continual chase after new stimuli capable of imposing sufficient control over employees to push their performances up. If the supervisors are absent for a day or a week, what happens to employee motivation? (If the police stopped ticketing people for running red lights, who'd sit and stare at a red light when the road looked clear?)

Let's be honest. A lot less work gets done when "the cat's away." I just spoke with a manager who is on vacation for two weeks, and just got a memo from the office saying that, of the seven employees who are scheduled to cover the main office in her absence, all but one have taken time off for one reason or another.

The work of the office has ground to a halt. The dogs are sleeping under the tree. So much for employee motivation!

The work of the office has ground to a halt. The dogs are sleeping under the tree. So much for employee motivation!

The traditional resistance-path approach uses a lot of incentives and rewards, combined with the implied threat of managerial oversight, to badger employees into mediocre performances. But without the addition of informative feedback, it never moves employees to a state of higher self-sufficiency and self-motivation.

What's Wrong with the Traditional Approach to Motivation?

In business, our traditional approach to employee motivation and rewards is predicated on extrinsic motivation, which uses controlling feedback. *Controlling feedback is any feedback, negative or positive, that imposes management's will on the employee instead of awakening the employee's will.* And in truth, much of the feedback we give employees falls under that definition.

In the previous chapter, I said that the bipolar thinking that leads us to think all feedback is either positive or negative is unhelpful. Now I want to ask you to think about all feedback as either controlling or informative. Informative is the opposite of controlling. The other pole. It speaks to intrinsic motivation and awakens one's own commitment, determination, and will. Which makes informative feedback ideally suited to the motivation path.

Informative feedback is any feedback that tells the employee how he or she is doing. In other words, it *communicates information about performance*. It can be negative or positive, but if too often negative, it will discourage instead of encourage.

Informative feedback *sounds* simple and straightforward. Aren't you already providing informative feedback? Why isn't *all* the positive and negative feedback you give informative rather than controlling? Well, it's a little trickier than that. Much of the feedback we give employees is intended to be informative, but is actually controlling instead. It contains information all right, but the information is more about us than them.

For instance, it is very common to end up giving feedback on how you feel about the employee's performance, which adds you, an external controller, into the equation. Feedback in the form of what you think, how you feel, or what you like makes employees more dependent upon your control, not less.

Informing someone about extrinsic controls is controlling. It's like the driver's education booklets they pass out to new drivers. Full of information, but all of it about controls over how they can drive. Informative feedback is just about them and the task. Period. No you. No reward systems. No bonus programs with their statistics and targets. Just about the employee. (The advertisers' television commercials for automobiles speak to one's intrinsic motivation to drive. Compare them with that driver's ed manual. Which is more compelling? Which needs a vast system of law enforcement behind it, and which doesn't?)

How Do You Break the Control Habit?

In commitment-based leadership trainings, trainers teach employees how to break the "control habit." It *is* a habit, which is why we don't even recognize that we are using controlling feedback most of the time. For example, trainers teach employees to recognize the hidden controls in the following statement: "If you keep making such quick progress toward that goal, you will be in line for an excellent performance evaluation at the end of the month."

What are the extrinsic controls in this statement? Did you notice them? Right. First, the supervisor expresses an opinion about the employee's progress rather than just making objective information available to the employee. When possible, give information, not opinions. Second, the supervisor emphasizes his or her control over the employee's performance evaluation. That's a powerful external threat. Better to explain how the good work helps the company or benefits an internal customer or fits into the department's quality goals. Those are informative messages.

> It is important to expect, support, challenge, and inform, but if you want to encourage internally motivated, self-directed achievement, do not overly control.
>
> —DAVID MYERS

This employee is receiving very positive feedback, so the supervisor no doubt thinks it is highly motivational and supportive. But it isn't. Not in the least. The controlling nature of this feedback makes the employee's performance increasingly dependent upon the supervisor's presence and persistence. Bad move if you don't want to have to carry your employees up the hill whenever you need peak performance from them.

Okay, if that's the wrong approach, then what the heck *can* you say to employees? I thought you'd never ask! Here are two examples of how C-Lead trainers teach employees to translate the statement from its current control form to an informative version instead:

> "You are making excellent progress toward the goal—faster than most people do."(That informs them of their progress relative to coworkers.)
>
> "Did you see that your progress scores are way above average for someone with your level of experience?" (That teaches them to inform themselves about their progress relative to coworkers.)

Such statements focus attention on the performance, keeping the supervisor in the background. You are simply making sure the employee is aware of the information and keeping it in mind. You are being purely informative. Your approach encourages the employee to focus on the performance, not you. And when the employee stays focused on informative feedback about performance, then progress in performing the task becomes a motivating pursuit for the employee.

When the employee stays focused on informative feedback about performance, then progress in performing the task becomes a motivating pursuit for the employee.

The difference between the two statements, by the way, is that the first one keeps the supervisor in the feedback loop. It is the supervisor who knows whether the performance is better than average. So the supervisor must provide this information for it to have motivational power. The second statement takes advantage of an information system in which there is objective information that the employee has access to, as well as the supervisor. So the supervisor can step even farther back. The supervisor needs only to make sure the employee is watching the scoreboard. He or she doesn't need to shout out the score.

Is all that crystal clear? I didn't think so. In truth, informative feedback is *the most confusing topic in the whole subject of motivation.* Which is why nobody but me even tries to teach you about the power of informative feedback. (It just so happens that I enjoy confusion!) But on the other hand, when you become skilled at giving informative feedback, it becomes one of your most powerful motivation tools. So it is well worth while to master this tricky art.

So if you are at all uncertain of your ability to supply informative feedback to your people, let's go one more round with it and make sure it really is clear enough to act on.

Why They Invented Scoreboards

Another simple story helps illustrate the concept of informative versus controlling feedback. Imagine you are coaching a very strange basketball team. It plays in a league where there are no scoreboards, and nobody is allowed to tell players what the score is. Instead, the officials keep a private tally and announce the winner at the end.

> Imagine you are coaching a very strange basketball team. It plays in a league where there are no scoreboards, and nobody is allowed to tell players what the score is.

If that were the case, how would the players know whether they were doing well or poorly? They'd have to check with their coach. That's you. And, of course, you would try to keep a mental tally of the score so you'd know how the game was going, but since you couldn't tell them the score, you'd have to tell them what to do based on your knowledge of the score. So players would look at you to see what your mood was and get cues from you about how hard to play. And you'd often have to shout at them to tell them what to do.

If you had to leave the bench for a few minutes to visit the bathroom, how do you think your team would do? Not very well. They'd be a mess until you got back and told them they were down and needed to pick up the pace. Or what if *you* lost track of the score?

It's a stupid example because nobody would be willing to play under those conditions. Because how could any team really play without a clear score posted all the time? They'd be almost helpless, always depending upon their coach to tell them when to be motivated. It would simply be stupid. Nobody would do it. Yet when you use controlling feedback, that's exactly what you do in the workplace. And work is an even more complex game than basketball, with a far more complex set of scores to keep track of. So unless you use "scoreboard feedback" extensively, most employees really have no idea how their team is doing, or even what game the company is playing!

Players would soon come to question their coach, and wonder whether they could trust his or her feedback.

When I tell people about my idea of a secret-score basketball game, they sometimes point out another reason why it just wouldn't work. Players would soon come to question their coach, and wonder whether they could trust his or her feedback. And they'd start interpreting it in complex ways that would get in the way of their understanding of the game.

Why? Because the coach would certainly prefer to tell them they had to work harder than to tell them they could glide. So even if they were ahead, would the coach tell them to relax? No way. He'd *always* be telling them to give it their all. He'd just be shouting that message louder some times than others. So why should they give it 100 percent each time the coach shouts to give it 100 percent? They'd probably give it 85 percent, and that way they wouldn't be too worn out in case the coach never gives them that chance to regroup. Controlling feedback tends to produce a *lower level of performance* on average for this very reason. The resistance path never climbs as high as the motivation path. And controlling managers (or coaches) never get as sustained an effort as informative ones.

So playing basketball, we agree, is a stupid idea unless the scores are known to all. If one team's coach posted the scores in a code that only his or her team could read, and the other coach just shouted at the players when they were down, which team would win the most matches? It's a cinch. Yet most employees play the great game of work without any clear scoreboards in sight. They have to keep glancing toward the bench to see how their coach is doing and try to interpret his or her cues. It makes for a dumb game, one that certainly is not played well enough to attract a crowd and sell out a stadium! As I pointed out in the first chapter, there is much to be learned from cases in which people operate at truly high motivation levels, and the basketball court routinely produces peak performances just as the workplace routinely fails to. Are we really digressing then when we spend time thinking about basketball instead of work?

Mastering Informative Feedback

If you want to make your people less dependent upon your motivating them and more self-motivated, then you need to practice recognizing and using informative feedback. You will need to change your own behavior and also to make sure that information systems are available to do some of the informing. Why should you have to hold the scoreboard in the air or flip the numbers on it when the employees could do it or some computer could do it for them? So in the short term, you can simply communicate the information you possess. But in the long term, you should always be seeking ways to make the information accessible directly to employees so you can step even farther back and "let them play."

In the long term, you should always be seeking ways to make the information accessible directly to employees so you can step even farther back and "let them play."

Tapping into Intrinsic Motivation with "It" Statements

Much of the feedback untrained managers give employees is about them. They use statements with the word *you* in them or at least obviously implied. "You messed up." I've talked repeatedly about the importance of depersonalizing your feedback so that it's about the behavior, not the employee (see Chapter 7, for instance). And in the next chapter, I'll review a classic interpersonal tool to help you do this, the "I" statement. In the "I" statement, you tell the employee how you feel about his or her behavior and why. That makes the behavior informative rather than controlling. "You" statements are controlling by nature.

I want to encourage you to take this strategy to an even higher level now by practicing the use of *it statements*. It, in this case, is *the task performance* itself. So *it statements* talk about how the task is going, not about how the person is doing or what you feel about how the person is doing.

It statements are preferably based on objective data about the task, and they bring that data to the attention of the person performing the task. So they answer the question, "How is it going?" in place of the question, "How am I doing?" For example:

> "This control chart shows an out-of-spec situation today." (The attention is squarely on the undesirable result, so it is easy for employee and manager alike to get to work finding the cause of the problem rather than dealing with anyone's defensive reactions about it.)
>
> "Did you hear that our department exceeded this month's quota by 10 percent?" (This positive feedback is purely informative and focuses on the accomplishment, not on you or the employees. In that respect, it is just like a posted score in a game.)
>
> "The client told me your report was very good. I'd say they liked it more than most of the reports we've done for them."
>
> "Did you see that the customer satisfaction index went up three points last month?"
>
> "I noticed in the latest report that our division submitted 20 percent fewer employee suggestions than the others."

Slight, subtle variations in your wording can make all the difference!

In all these statements, the manager has carefully avoided telling the employees about her view of the situation or how she feels. She is instead bringing specific performance-related feedback to their attention. She lets it stand on its own to make sure they get the message that she wants them to notice the score. Even though she might later discuss how to improve upon the score, or praise someone for his or her effort, she does not let those topics "contaminate" her informative feedback. The *it statement* is *only* about the score. It is informative.

Asking the Player the Score

It statements can also take the form of questions. The manager does not always want to have to tell employees the score. The best employees know the rules of the game and track their scores themselves. Once employees get used to watching their own scores, the manager can ask them the score instead of telling them, using statements like:

> "How is it [the job] going?"
>
> "What kinds of results did your team get yesterday?"
>
> "How do those control charts look today?"
>
> "Any trouble with customer satisfaction this morning?"
>
> "How many of those have you been able to complete per hour?"

In each of these questions, the manager asks the employee what the score is. The questions stimulate the employee to collect his or her own informative feedback. That's a great habit for employees to develop.

The questions stimulate the employee to collect his or her own informative feedback. That's a great habit for employees to develop.

What if there isn't a "scoreboard" for the information? There is always some information that you as a supervisor are in a better position to obtain or interpret, so you can't always use scoreboard motivation. Until you can develop a way to get that information posted routinely for employees to track, you will have to provide it with informative feedback. Even though you make the employee dependent upon you for the information, this sure beats making the employee dependent upon you for the motivation!

Psychologist David Myers illustrates informative feedback with cases in which the information is the subject of the *it statement* in the following quote (from *Psychology*, Worth, 1995, p. 423):

> **Note that we can use extrinsic rewards in two ways: to control ("If you clean up your room, you can have some ice cream") or to inform someone of successes ("That was outstanding–we congratulate you"). . . . Rewards that inform people they are doing well can boost their feelings of competence and intrinsic motivation. In one experiment, Thane Pittman and his colleagues asked college students to work on puzzles. Those given informative**

complements ("Compared with most of my subjects, you're doing really well") usually continued playing with the puzzles when left alone. Those given either no praise or a controlling form of praise ("If you keep it up, I'll be able to use your data") were less likely to continue. So, depending on whether we use rewards to control or inform, they can either raise or lower intrinsic motivation.

Understanding Rewards and Incentives

This book's title addresses both motivation and rewards, but you've probably noticed that I emphasize the motivation topic over the rewards topic. The real challenge is after all to motivate employees, not to reward them. Most managers find it far easier to solve the problem of finding a suitable reward for great performance than to solve the problem of not having any exceptional performances worthy of rewards.

But right now I want to shift gears and talk about rewards because you can think of them as tools in your feedback toolbox. Rewards are used to give feedback and can be either highly effective forms of feedback or ineffective or even have a negative effect. And now that you have a more detailed understanding of feedback than most managers do, you are in a great position to gain some real insight into how to use rewards more effectively.

You can think of rewards as tools in your feedback toolbox.

To explain the use of rewards as feedback, I want to first convince you that all true rewards *are* feedback. They are simply one form of feedback, not different in their basics from personal one-on-one comments, a note of thanks, or a statistical process control chart. To convince you of this, I have got to ask you only one thing. Can you name any reward that is not a form of feedback?

Take something like a prize or trophy. It obviously is a symbol, a symbol that conveys some power because it represents honor and recognition. But recognition and honor for what? For doing whatever it recognizes. Winning the game. Submitting the suggestion that saved the company the most money. Being the most valuable employee of the month. Whatever the reward recognizes, it is a performance. And so the reward is a form of performance feedback. It's positive performance feedback. Nothing more or less.

So that means that:

The rules of feedback govern rewards.

Which also means you know a great deal about rewards without even having to study the subject since you have only to apply your growing understanding of feedback.

For instance, you know the following essential principles of good reward programs:

1. Rewards should provide positive feedback to everyone.
2. Rewards should provide feedback about performances, not people.
3. Rewards should provide attainable, timely, and accurate feedback.
4. Rewards should provide informative feedback.

I'm going to end this chapter with a quick look at how to implement these four principles when you design any employee rewards.

The rules of feedback govern rewards.

Positive Feedback for All

Let's take point one first even though you might be thinking it is so obvious it doesn't need explanation. Of course, rewards are positive. That's their nature. You don't give out "Worst Employee" awards, you give out "Best Employee" awards. So it's a lot easier to follow the "good news" rule of feedback when giving rewards than when giving other forms of feedback. But notice that I said rewards should provide positive feedback to *everyone*. That's the wrinkle I want you to keep in mind.

The problem is that sometimes a reward gives positive feedback to one person and negative feedback to others. For example, take an employee suggestion system in which one suggestion is selected by a committee of managers to receive the Best Suggestion of the Year award. The employee whose suggestion is selected receives a trophy

> Success or failure in business is caused more by mental attitude even than by mental capacities.
>
> —WALTER DILL SCOTT

and prize money at a recognition ceremony in front of all the other employees. This employee has certainly just received very positive feedback about his or her suggestion. I guarantee the employee will submit more suggestions next year.

But what about the employees in the audience? None of them won the prize. Some of them didn't submit ideas, so they understand perfectly well that they weren't in the running. They might be more motivated to submit ideas next year by seeing the winner receive the recognition and awards. They can experience the positive feedback vicariously, if you will. But others might have submitted perfectly good ideas. In fact, I guarantee there are plenty of employees in that audience who "know" their idea was better, and who believe the committee should have chosen them instead. To them, the perceived loss of this positive feedback is negative. One person's win may be another person's loss. And I can't help wondering whether they will take this competitive situation well or poorly.

A loss either can stimulate people to try harder next time or can discourage them from trying as hard. Too often, competitive reward programs have the latter effect.

The problem is that individuals differ significantly in the extent to which competition motivates them, which means that in any group of employees, *there are plenty who don't like competition*. And in your business, since cooperation is probably vital, you may not want to turn off the majority who are averse to a highly competitive, make-others-lose attitude toward work.

So far, I've focused in this book on competence-oriented motivations. That is to say, I've guided you toward motivational approaches that encourage your people to seek higher levels of competence and the intrinsic rewards that come from applying that competence to achieve success and recognition. But competition can also be rewarding in and of itself. Many people just love to win and hate to lose. They are motivated to play games of luck by this urge to win, so their urge to compete can obviously be separated from competency-based motivations to succeed. These are the people who will participate disproportionately in any competitive reward system, such as a trip to Hawaii for the highest-selling salesperson or a trophy and cash prize for the best suggestion. However, other people may not be good at coping with the stresses of competition and may avoid participating when they anticipate the possibility of a loss.

In addition, there is the very real possibility that many employees will feel the competition was unfair. They will think they should have won, as I mentioned. So big prizes tend to raise that fairness issue and risk damaging motivation as a result.

What I recommend is that you (1) check out any competitive rewards or awards your organization uses to make sure they are fair, and (2) consider whether they are really the best approach. Sometimes they are. Sometimes you need to recognize real leadership and if you don't that feels like negative feedback to the employees. But other times, the competitive reward is just an artificial level of competition that distracts from what you really want employees to focus on: competing with themselves to attain increasingly high levels of competence and performance excellence.

And when you focus on employees' development paths, you begin to favor more personal and less competitive rewards. The coaches who get the best developmental results are the ones who track individual needs and set individual goals, then provide constant feedback about how their players are achieving their individual goals. They create lots of little scoreboards, each one unique to a player's needs. That is the bedrock of feedback. If you win a league trophy, great. But if you lose, the players are still better at the end of the season because they've been winning little rewards through their own development all along.

> It's not enough to succeed. Others must fail.
>
> —GORE VIDAL

Apply this same thinking to your role as a supervisor since your team is with you for the long haul and you can't recruit a whole new one for the next season. Develop them as best you can with individual rewards and recognition. If you want to spice up your personal approach to feedback with the occasional contest-oriented reward, great. But make sure it is fairly judged in your employees' minds, and make sure they all get enough positive feedback as individuals that they don't mind losing when someone else wins that big reward.

I just took a little break from my writing to tune into ESPN in the "conference room" of my offices (it far more often is my "break room," but don't tell anyone, please!). The reason I tuned in was to see how the Cardinals versus Cubs baseball game is going. And by

> The achievement of high athletic performance should never take precedence over psychological and personal growth and development of an athlete. Although athletic achievement and personal growth are not incompatible, they often become so when athletes are pushed or forced by others or by themselves beyond their level of physical or personal maturity.
>
> —DORCAS SUSAN BUTT, SPORTS PSYCHOLOGIST

good luck, Mark McGwire had just stepped up to bat when I turned the TV on. Within seconds, he'd punched a line drive into left field, bounced it off the windows of a restaurant high in the stands, and tied the record for most home runs in a season. As he circled the bases, the stadium erupted in a joyous standing ovation. Many people had brought signs reading "61," and now they waved them wildly. All his teammates jumped up and rushed over to congratulate him, and the other team applauded, too. Nobody felt as though his victory was their loss. Everybody felt good about what he'd done.

Tying that homerun record (and, as it turned out, breaking it before the season ended) is a reward that is obviously highly competitive, but is nonetheless highly motivating to everyone. It makes other players feel proud of their sport and probably encourages them to spend a little more time in batting practice in the hope of improving their records.

Notice how a home run record is tied or broken. *One hit at a time.* Everyone gets his turn at bat, and some people hit more homers than others. Nothing could be fairer. Performance is tracked each step of the way. The best man wins, but everybody competes with a will. Because along the way there are many smaller victories (60 so far for McGwire), each bringing the prize a little closer. That's a great model for any competitive awards or prizes you do decide to offer your people. Make sure there are steps along the way, and that your employees get the positive feedback of achievement each time they take another step. If they get only one turn at bat, it isn't going to do much for their motivation or anyone else's.

Reward Performances, Not People

Of course, you have to give the reward to a person, not a performance, but please make sure the reward is obviously linked to and in recognition of that person's performance or the performance of a group or team the person represents.

This seems obvious, yet many reward programs fall prey to the error to some degree. I've seen lots of cases in which an annual reward dinner looks suspiciously like a popularity contest. "MVP" type rewards in which a supervisor or management committee "anoints" someone as the most valuable employee are supposed to reflect overall performance, but sometimes seem to be about the person instead. Just listen to the speeches if you doubt me. "Joe's a truly great guy." "We've all enjoyed working with Jane; she's a real inspiration."

So what? What did they *do* to earn the reward, aside from just being themselves? Unless the speaker can list some very specific and exceptional things the winner actually did to win the reward, the reward shouldn't be given. *Prizes and awards have to be for something, not someone.* Make sure you subject yours to this acid test before you announce any winners, and please keep the speech focused on the performance, not the person. Thank you!

Prizes and awards have to be for something, not someone.

Make the Reason for the Reward Crystal Clear

In Chapter 7, I reviewed the case of the mysterious salespeople. Remember? They were the ones who outperformed the others in spite of lacking the "right" personality profile and lacking the option of big commissions. What they had that lower performers lacked was clear links between their behavior and results. They could see the links between what they did and what happened more clearly, which encouraged them to improve their own performances and made it more personally rewarding when they succeeded.

Rewards should obey the task clarity formula if you want them to have any impact on motivation and performance. But they seldom do. Because formal rewards are, well, formal, they tend to be separated from the behaviors they reward. It is often hard for employees to see exactly how they did or didn't get the reward.

For example, let's have a look at the following program described in Bob Nelson's *1001 Ways to Reward Employees*:

> **Tina Berres Filipski, editor and director of publications for Meeting Planners International in Dallas, took her staff of eight to the Texas State Fair one Friday afternoon, paying for their admission. The field trip was not only fun, but served as a good chance to help the group get to know each other better.**

Now, I enjoy a state fair myself, but I'm at a loss to explain exactly what this was a reward *for*. In fact, I run into this problem with lots of rewards. When you have to resort to explanations like "it helps them get to know each other" (as if they don't spend more than forty hours a week with each other already), you are probably on shaky ground. If they indeed don't know each other very well, that's a problem. Rewarding them for it won't send the right message. Face it, Filipski took her people to the fair because she wanted to go, and she was feeling generous toward her people and wanted to bring a little fun and pleasure into what had probably been a rough week.

In which case, that trip to the fair was not a reward. How could it be a reward unless it was a reward for something? It wasn't performance feedback either, unless you call giving someone a reward for not getting to know their fellow workers a form of feedback. I doubt that's what was going on in any of their minds.

When you see something like this trip to the state fair presented as a reward, remind yourself that it isn't. That's not to say you shouldn't ever do anything nice or fun for your people. But if you do something like this, you need to recognize that you are giving a *gift*, not an award or reward. If it's something nice you think they'll like, but it isn't related to performance, it's not a reward. It's not feedback. It's a gift.

You need to recognize that you are giving a *gift*, not an award or reward.

Which is okay. Sometimes you feel like giving people gifts. Sometimes a gift helps set the right emotional mood for motivation even though it doesn't motivate in and of itself. Sometimes the situation demands gifts, like when someone is retiring. Gifts symbolize your warm feelings toward someone. They speak to that person's worth as a human being–not to anything specific they've done (it's a no-brainer to have a birthday or make it to retirement). So gifts are mostly about *who*, and not really about *what*. That makes them the opposite of feedback. Which means they have none of feedback's power to motivate people to develop and achieve through their personal performances. You can't tell me that I'm going to do better next year if I get more birthday presents, or worse if I don't.

Should you give your employees gifts? Sure, why not? Sometimes you want to express your warm feelings toward them. A gift tells them you like them, admire them, or want them to feel good about themselves. I think we should give far more gifts in our society than we do. So if Filipski wants to take her staff to the fair, more power to her. (It was a nice thing to do and it helped with their emotional state, which is why Nelson included it in his book.) But there are some pitfalls to look out for when you give employees gifts.

First, if they are valuable gifts, like cash bonuses or merchandise, then they may seem like a part of the overall compensation picture to the employees. In which case, you've reduced the links between compensation and performance by bringing some of that compensation into the realm of gift giving and out of the realms of base pay and performance-related feedback. You might run into the fairness problem if you don't give everyone equivalent gifts. It gets messy in many possible ways if the gifts are economically valuable instead of symbolically valuable (is it taxable income?), so I'd just stay away from expensive gifts entirely if I were you.

Should you give your employees gifts? Sure, why not? But there are some pitfalls to look out for when you give employees gifts.

Second, gift giving is reciprocal in most societies. Adults exchange gifts. The only people who aren't expected to reciprocate are young children. Yet employees aren't expected or even permitted to give gifts to their managers in most companies, so is one-way gift giving to employees an accidental way of treating them like children? Does it show a fundamental lack of respect for them? Is it overly controlling? Wow, these are deep waters. I'm not sure that gift giving always raises these respect and control issues, but sometimes it does, so you want to just think about that, too.

Third, I want to make sure you don't blur the line between gifts and rewards. If you sometimes hand out restaurant gift certificates to employees who have just done something extra special, then that's a good example of performance-related reward and recognition. But what if you also hand out gift certificates to employees as gifts? For instance, maybe you give them out on birthdays. Or on days when you've just landed a big new account and are feeling really up. Now you've accidentally blurred the line between gifts and rewards, and the problem with blurring the line is that it makes it harder for employees to recognize the links between their performance and the awarding of gift certificates. Sometimes certificates are awarded because of performance. Sometimes they are given regardless of performance. So if you want to give out gifts, make sure they are obviously gifts. Don't use the same things you use for rewards. And present them according to the conventions of gift giving (use wrapping paper, and so on). Don't present them the same way you do rewards for good performance.

If you want to give out gifts, make sure they are obviously gifts. Don't use the same things you use for rewards.

Wow, there sure are a lot of ways to run into trouble when you try to reward employees! No wonder most workplaces aren't exactly bursting with motivation.

Oh, and one other problem. Rewards that are given infrequently, like at an annual employee dinner, are pretty far removed from the performance events they recognize. Big, infrequent rewards have less power than the same amount of effort and money invested in little, frequent rewards or just plain old one-to-one feedback. The big rewards are less powerful at awakening intrinsic motivation because they are further removed from the performances they inform us about. They break the timeliness requirement of feedback and therefore reduce the clarity of the feedback.

So if you are wondering whether to introduce or continue using some big, infrequent reward, my advice is to think hard about alternatives that are more timely instead. In fact, I'm willing to bet that you easily get your money's worth by replacing an annual trip to Hawaii that costs your company $3,000 with, say, a program of weekly recognition and rewards that includes the use of restaurant gift certificates, allows all employees to win them at least a few times, and costs you two times as much. Or you can cut the cost of rewards to a fifth of the old cost, say, $600 worth of small gifts, and it may still be more effective than the old program. Because the small, frequent rewards should easily be ten times as effective at boosting motivation and improving employee performances.

I'm not ruling out trips to Hawaii, mind you. I'm just asking you to work on routine, tight links between rewards and performance first. If you've got a program in which there is a lot of positive, informative feedback on a daily, hourly, or even minute-by-minute basis, that's a great start. Add rewards and public recognition on a weekly basis, and you're adding more steps along the motivation path. Once you've taken care of all that, you can consider a big reward as a climax. Kind of like McGwire breaking the home run record. The event is exciting, but wouldn't happen without lots of home runs along the way. And it serves to remind us of all those home runs and focus us on the importance of hitting homers in baseball. The same should be true of that trip to Hawaii.

Reward programs too often violate the principle of task clarity. When you make the links between performances and rewards tighter, you get much more bang for your motivational buck.

Reward programs too often violate the principle of task clarity.

Make the Rewards Informative!

Some rewards are controlling. Some are informative. Just like any feedback, rewards can convey useful information about performance. Or they can just tell you what the supervisor wants you to do. Think of it this way. Would giving drivers a special reward when they've waited at their millionth red light be a good idea? I don't think so, at least not if your goal is to make them any less dependent upon traffic lights. You'd never phase out traffic cops and big fines and get people to adopt some sort of honor system just by rewarding them for not running red lights. Why? Because the red light is a controlling form of feedback, not an informative one. Dogs don't practice rolling over when their masters aren't there to give them a treat or a pat. Drivers don't wait for red lights just because they want to. Employees don't try harder and get better because it says they should in the employee manual. Adding rewards, recognition, and prizes won't make controlling feedback more powerful. You've got nothing until you have an information loop that you can base the reward upon. It's got to be based on how they do. Not on what you tell them to do. So let's state a general principle that many managers seem not to know about:

> **Rewarding compliance doesn't generate motivation. At best it maintains the compliance.**

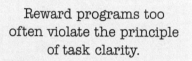

How about rewards for the fewest sick days? They are quite common in businesses. What do they reward? They reward compliance with the policy that says you shouldn't call in sick unless you really are (a policy most employees violate occasionally). And they reward compliance with the expectation that you will have good health.

Is there any useful informative feedback involved in either of these rewards? No. Employees probably know when they are sick. Let's assume that. If not, they'd be coming to work sick instead of staying away. So we don't really need to provide them with feedback informing them of their health status. Their bodies take pretty good care of that. And employees also know if they are calling in sick dishonestly in order to "take their sick days" as people always put it. In fact, you as supervisor know less about this behavior than they do, so there's no point in your trying to put yourself or your administrative systems into their feedback system.

The other side of this example of a reward for least sick days taken is that it will seem to many employees to be providing feedback about something they have little or no control over. Telling someone they've got the flu does nothing to prevent them getting it again. Rewarding someone for staying healthy does little to ensure they will stay healthy next year, or that others will become more healthy to "be like them." It's basically a stupid thing to reward people for health since it isn't very informative and they don't have a great deal of control over the portion of those sick days in which they are actually sick.

Telling someone they've got the flu does nothing to prevent them getting it again.

But sometimes these programs do actually increase the attendance of employees and reduce the number of sick days taken. How come they work at all if I think they are so stupid? Well, it's because they are pushing employees along that resistance path. They are controlling employee behavior. In exchange for approval and whatever tangible rewards you offer, employees are dragging themselves in some days when they have a cold and are taking fewer unjustified sick days, too. So you are getting some compliance. But you have not "fixed" the motivation problem in the least; you've just temporarily tipped the balance by imposing some pressure on them. Stop giving out those rewards, and sick days will climb up to the old level or higher within weeks. I guarantee it.

Now, perhaps it's more economical to spend a little cash bribing your people into complying with your sick-day policies than to have them away from their posts and unproductive. There is a tradeoff here that many managers are willing to make. But, remember, if you decide to use a controlling reward like this, then you are simply buying a little compliance. I'd rather see that sort of purchase put right into the job description and made part of the base salary so that we can get it out of the way early on and focus on building real motivation on a daily basis.

And if you use controlling feedback, you'll divide your company into those two groups Cyrus Curtis describes in the quote in the margin.

There is a very large hidden cost to investments in compliance. The cost is that you can't get people onto the motivation path nearly as easily if you are pushing them onto the resistance path at the same time. We don't partition our responses to management initiatives to such a degree that we can be compliance oriented about sick days but development oriented about the quality of our work, for example. So that reward for least sick days sets a compliance-oriented tone to the entire employer-employee relationship. For you to swim against that current as a supervisor is a difficult task. You'll have to develop special ground rules that apply just within your group and make sure you never violate them. Better by far to cancel that silly program and replace it with rewards for important aspects of personal performance. If you do, performing well will become more motivating, and people will want to show up so they can perform. Then you won't have to work on motivating them just to show up any more!

There are two kinds of people who never amount to much: those who cannot do what they are told and those who can do nothing else.

—CYRUS H. K. CURTIS

Rewarding Length of Service

Take the classic reward, the one given out more than any other in businesses across America and Europe. It's the reward for length of service. Many companies and other institutions award their people with gold pens or whatnot in elaborate ceremonies for serving ten, twenty, or thirty years. Is it informative feedback?

It isn't informative unless it conveys useful information about some important aspect of performance. Does reward for length of service convey any useful information about performance? No. None at all.

Do you want to give your employees a fish, or teach them how to fish?

First of all, the employee knows perfectly well how long he or she has been there. It doesn't take any additional informative feedback for an employee to keep that score. So if it is important to stay a long time, everybody already has enough information in their pocket calendar and long-term memory to track their own performance with high accuracy.

And second, it probably makes little or no difference how long an employee stays. Does someone who's been there five years automatically perform 24 percent better than someone who's been there four years? If they were sure to be even 2 percent better, I'd say, let's reward them big time for each year of service. But nobody's made that claim at your company, I bet. There aren't many jobs where lengthy tenure is the key performance goal. So why bother recognizing and rewarding it as if it were? The same companies that hand out length-of-service awards at deadly employee suppers are now switching their hiring priorities to select people who have a track record of shorter tenure in past jobs. They find these people are more self-motivated and well rounded than people who stay in one place for many years. But they are still rewarding that kind of immobility within their company.

By the way, you are probably assuming I'm against ceremonies and awards recognizing those who've been with the organization for a long time. Not necessarily, I just don't want you to think you'll buy any motivation or performance with them. If you simply like these occasions to bring people together, and if they create a positive feeling in your people, go for it. But remember, you're giving them gifts because of who they are, not because they've done anything special that has an impact on the bottom line. Gift giving is not a bad way to make people feel good about themselves, which is a great way to build those emotional foundations of motivation. It just isn't any substitute for motivation itself, which arises from informative feedback, not gifts.

So if you are thinking about what to spend your time and money on in the area of feedback and rewards, don't bother about retirement dinners, tenure-based awards, and other forms of employee gifts. Stick with real performance-related feedback. Invest in developing more scoreboards. On the other hand, if you want to

MOTIVATION IDEA 21

Monopoly Money at the Bank

This idea is inspired by a bank that holds an annual auction put on by managers. They auction away their own services, for example, "Doing your job for a day," as well as an assortment of merchandise. Just like any community auction event. The unusual thing about their auction is that you can use only play money to pay for things, and each employee is given the same amount of play money before the auction. That makes the event entertaining and fun. For a further development of the idea, consider giving everyone the ability to earn additional play money as recognition for their accomplishments.

Benefit. This event creates a sense of community and adds an element of fun to the workplace if managed well. To manage it well, keep your sense of humor, but also a strong sense of respect for employees. Make sure you offer lots of funny prizes along with the serious ones, and make sure the joke is never "on them." Also make sure there is a way for everyone to take away something they will enjoy in the future so the fairness issue doesn't derail your event. Think of this event's main benefit as the change of pace it offers. People will be taking a break from their desks to do something fun together. So schedule it after any period in which you've had to call on them to work extra hard as a way to say thank you. And tell them clearly that you know they worked extra hard, and that's why you scheduled this event so that they will get the point that this is positive feedback for performance.

invest in a nice party or event to help people feel good about themselves and their work, well, then go ahead. But think hard about what the best way to make people feel good is before you order another chicken dinner. Make sure you give them a fun time, not a dull time. I bet you can imagine a bunch of fun alternatives if you try. Or you could simply ask *them* to design the next fun event. That gives employees more control (which is motivating), and it gives them a chance to do something well (which stimulates their urge to succeed in other areas, too, so is also motivating). There is always a better way. And now that you know so much about what motivates people, you can think of lots of better ways!

Encouraging Employees to Act Like Owners with ESOPs

"I wish my employees would act like they owned the place. They just don't seem to care." This classic complaint reflects the differing interests of a company's owner and its employees. The owner is in it for the long haul. The employees often are not.

And there is a very simple way to overcome this clash of interests. Give the employees a significant share of ownership in the company. That's what Employee Stock Ownership Plans do, and they are currently in use in approximately 10,000 companies, with about 10 million employee participants, which works out to about 10% of the U.S. workforce according to the ESOP Association. So about one tenth of U.S. workers own at least a small fraction of the companies they work for. Are they more motivated? Yes, on average, according to a variety of studies. Their employers tend to perform a little better than the average company, and to register higher productivity increases, too. And their employees tend to stay longer and be more committed. Which is why some people say ESOPs are essential if you are serious about employee motivation.

Analysis. But the impact of ESOPs is often subtle. They aren't a silver bullet. For instance, the ESOP Association found that 54 percent of its member companies had an increase in productivity as a result of their ESOPS. The others didn't, but they presumably still incurred the full costs. So is an ESOP right for your company, or will it just be a costly mistake? I think the main issue is whether you are really willing to make the ownership interest of each employee significant enough to put them on your side of the fence. If they get an insignificant share, then it will have an insignificant impact on attitude and performance. You don't really feel and act like an owner unless you see your ownership as a major asset, one that you stand to benefit from substantially if all goes well.

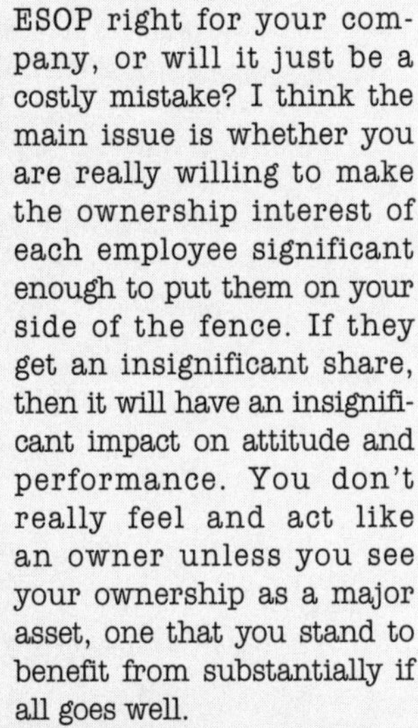

So are you really willing to make employees your partners, then stick with them through the (probably rough) transition from clock-punching to a real sense of ownership? If so, then an ESOP, cooperative, collective or other joint ownership structure is definitely for you. If not, then don't bother. Lip service won't change anyone's heart.

Parting Shots

In this chapter, I've argued that you need to make the switch from controlling to informative feedback and rewards, just as you need to switch from an emphasis on negative feedback to a foundation of positive feedback.

There are lots of basic, commonsense points in both these chapters on feedback. I rarely meet anyone who argues these points. You probably have agreed with me, too. But what I do see all the time is practice that violates these sensible principles of feedback and rewards. I see lots of programs that are compliance oriented. I listen to lots of managers giving negative feedback far more than positive. And I rarely see managers who put their creative energy into giving employees as many and as accurate scoreboards as possible.

If you want people to perform better, throw yourself into the quest for better ways to track and reward their performance. Study their jobs with them to gain insights into what makes for better or worse performances. Think of ways to track or measure components of performance. Provide feedback and rewards based on your growing knowledge of performance variables. And seek ways of empowering them to track their own performances so that you can gradually take yourself out of the feedback loops to the greatest extent possible.

I rarely see managers who put their creative energy into giving employees as many and as accurate scoreboards as possible.

That means a lot of commonly praised employee reward programs are not nearly as good as they seem on the surface. Take the company that maintains an apartment in New York City for its managers to use for personal trips on weekends. Nice idea. But why reward someone for being a manager? It doesn't give the manager information about his or her performance. It's about who they are, not what they did. So this is just a part of their compensation package, a perk that might be necessary to maintain parity with compensation offered by competing companies. But that's its only possible justification. It certainly isn't a useful form of performance feedback. It won't make them do any better when they come back from that weekend in New York.

Or what about an "outstanding management achievement" reward with the prize of a trip around the world? This is offered by one of the big hotel chains, which selects a hotel manager as the recipient. But the relationship between personal performance and winning the reward is fuzzy. If you manage an older hotel in a dog of a location, you aren't going to win. If you luck into a great location in a booming area, that may help you win. And even if you did do something to turn around performance at the hotel and you get the prize, what exactly did you do that was so good, and will you or your fellow managers know what it is and be able to replicate it next year? Maybe not because task clarity is pretty low with this reward. I'd say it's 75 percent gift, 25 percent true performance reward at best.

I could go on, but then again, you've been with me for eight chapters, so you already know that. Instead, I'm going to ask you to be a skeptic when it comes to employee feedback and rewards. You don't need me to rant and rave about ineffective techniques or programs because you know enough to sniff them out yourself. Make sure you use informative feedback and rewards, and you will do far better than the typical manager when it comes to building real motivation in your people.

Be a skeptic when it comes to employee feedback and rewards.

Uh-oh! Looks like it's time for performance appraisals again.

Using Your Interpersonal Intelligence

Chapter 9

"Ninety percent of management is interpersonal skills. I don't know why everybody ignores them." That's what Bob Carkhuff, the president of Human Resource Development Press, says. In fact, he usually says it at least once each time I visit his office (Bob publishes my training and assessment products, so I seem him pretty regularly). But what does he mean?

The brain is a wonderful organ; it starts working the moment you get up in the morning and doesn't stop until you get into the office.
—ROBERT FROST

The conventional view of management is that it involves "analysis, planning, and control." That serious-sounding trio appears in the opening chapter of most textbooks on management. Analyze those numbers. Write thick, impressive plans. Control those feeble-minded people to make sure they don't mess up the plans too badly. And to do these three things well, managers need to be analytical, rational, and authoritative. Are you?

When pressed, no doubt, you can perform all those tasks. You can analyze, plan, and control. But I've gotten enough calls from panicky managers over the years asking how to write a business plan, strategic plan, or marketing plan that I know for a fact many managers are not naturally analytical planners and controllers. And those requirements are a burden for many managers, one they feel bad they cannot carry with greater ease. In spite of what the textbooks say, the vast majority of managers will never be brilliant technocrats.

But that's okay. If the classic trio of analysis, planning, and control doesn't feel quite natural to you, your instincts are correct once again. Because that view of management probably represents about 10 percent of what it takes to be a successful supervisor, manager, or executive. The other 90 percent comes down to *how you relate to your people.* Bob Carkhuff's comment that it all comes down to interpersonal skills is right on the money. (And he should know; he spends his days developing and publishing materials to help people manage better.)

Bob's right about interpersonal skills for the simple and obvious reason that managers don't do the work themselves; they do it through others. This creates what those management textbooks call "the management challenge," usually defined as *the responsibility to achieve results through other people's work.*

In other words, management comes down to motivating other people to do what needs to be done. And that's all about how you relate to and interact with those people. About generating relevant commitment and competence in others. Not about analysis, planning, and control.

As a result, study after study shows that people with high interpersonal skills are the most effective managers. They are able to get their people motivated, help them develop the needed competencies, and keep them on track for continuous high-level performances.

The Concept of Interpersonal Intelligence

A best-selling book called *Emotional Intelligence* popularized the idea that there might be more to intelligence than one's ability to perform mental gymnastics with a calculator and piece of graph paper. But this idea goes back to the work of psychologist Howard Gardner and his theory of multiple intelligences. He argues that these multiple intelligences include things like logical-mathematical intelligence, linguistic intelligence, spatial intelligences, and what he terms personal intelligences, which are similar to the emotional intelligences of Goleman's interesting work.

According to Gardner, "These intelligences typically work in harmony, and so their autonomy may be invisible. But when the appropriate observational lenses are donned, the peculiar nature of each intelligence emerges with sufficient (and often surprising) clarity" (from his book, *Frames of Mind,* Basic Books, 1983, p. 9).

Yet when most people think about intelligence, they think of it more narrowly since traditional IQ tests emphasize abilities in the area of logical-mathematical intelligence. That logical-mathematical intelligence of the traditional IQ test may be a good asset when doing analysis and planning, but it isn't at all relevant to the interpersonal side of management. As long as you aren't a total, blithering idiot in the realm of logic, you have enough IQ to work with people. But do you have the *interpersonal competencies* needed to succeed in one-on-one and group interactions with people?

We all have a considerable amount of interpersonal intelligence to start with.

We all have a considerable amount of interpersonal intelligence to start with since humans are a very social species and we grow up interacting with other people in a great many contexts. But since interpersonal skills are generally acquired by watching others perform them, we tend to learn the interpersonal skills and styles of those around us.

In other words, our interpersonal intelligence is limited by tradition, by the models we have at hand. People tend to interact with their children using the interpersonal styles they learned from their parents. And people tend to manage using the interpersonal styles of the managers they learned from, including their own past and present supervisors, and the teachers and parents who managed them in childhood.

People tend to manage using the interpersonal styles of the managers they learned from.

Oh, and yes, interpersonal intelligence is learned and learnable to a far larger degree than traditional IQ-oriented intelligence. That's the good news. You can work on increasing your sensitivity to what others think and feel—that's termed empathy. You can work on better understanding and expressing what you think and feel—that's termed genuineness. Although some people are naturally better in these areas than others, all can improve dramatically with effort. You can also develop specific interpersonal skills by studying and practicing specific techniques and methods, such as the many in this book. Heck, there's nothing to stop you from acquiring a new interpersonal skill every day of the week. So interpersonal intelligence is both absolutely critical to management success, and highly learnable. You can become an interpersonal genius if you so desire. And believe me, interpersonal genius is an awfully good qualification for motivating employees!

Why *You* Need an Exceptional Level of Interpersonal Intelligence

So we all inherit a range of interpersonal skills and habits, and thus have a decent level of interpersonal intelligence to start with. The question is, are these interpersonal skills and strategies sufficient to produce the motivation levels and performance highs you aspire to for your work force? In general, they are not. In general, *people have to raise their own interpersonal intelligence quotient in order to get more and better efforts out of their employees.*

Why? Because it simply takes more than average interpersonal intelligence on your part to create higher than average motivation and performance in others. You don't get above average results from average effort. And if you aren't willing to be exceptional in *your* approach to managing, how can you ask your people to be exceptional in *their* approach to their jobs?

In addition, your investment in increased interpersonal intelligence is a natural consequence of your realization that the best way to improve employee performances is to make changes in your own behavior rather than theirs. You probably agree that saying "do that" or "do that better" or "do that harder" is not a promising approach to motivation. And you probably agree with the thesis we've pursued in earlier chapters, that you can generally get your people to do what you want more easily with an indirect approach, in which you change some aspect of your behavior in order to move them along their own motivation paths and create a situation in which it is the natural thing for them to do what you want.

In order to find and use those personal levers that connect your behavior with theirs, you need a high level of interpersonal intelligence.

And if you think about it, much of what I've given you as methods and solutions so far falls into the general category of interpersonal skills. So what you have been doing all along in this book is working on appropriate interpersonal skills. You've been raising your interpersonal intelligence. We've discussed listening skills and ways of giving good one-to-one feedback, for example. We've talked about increasing your sensitivity to how your employees are feeling and about using your interpersonal skills to boost their morale. We've talked about the difference between behaving in a controlling and an informative manner. We've talked about understanding how employees evaluate their jobs in order to diagnose and eliminate any basic biases or problems that might interfere with motivation and performance. All these approaches are powerful motivational tools, and all depend heavily upon interpersonal skills to execute them.

What you have been doing all along in this book is working on appropriate interpersonal skills. You've been raising your interpersonal intelligence.

So you have actually been building your own interpersonal skills as you read other chapters in this book. Good work! But I want to use this chapter to highlight a few areas of interpersonal skill

MOTIVATION IDEA 22

Give 'em the Old Two-One

Most reasonably sensitive people realize they need to show some support and offer some praise when they provide negative feedback. So they typically think of something positive to say to go along with and "soften" their criticism. That's a good instinct. But the trouble is, we almost always make a mistake in how we deliver that mix of good and bad news.

Almost all managers lead with the good news. They say or write something like, "You've done a great job, Alex, and I really appreciate your effort." They may even offer some specific examples and praise. Then, once they get up the courage, they launch into the negative feedback. They say something like, "But there is just one little thing that I want to talk to you about. I really don't think it works to do _________. I guess it's my fault for not telling you sooner, but the way you did this project isn't a very good approach. I mean, you did a good job considering, but because you failed to _________ before you ________, things just didn't work out as well as I expected." And so forth.

I call this the old one-two because it knocks 'em down every time. When you start with praise, then switch gears and end with negative feedback, you leave them feeling very down. The praise at the beginning actually makes the criticism feel tougher, not softer. They feel, somewhere deep inside, that they just can't please you, no matter *what* they do. They feel like throwing up their hands and saying, "F**k it." In fact, they usually do, but not until you are out of earshot. The old one-two always upsets employees' emotional balance and can easily knock them off the motivation path and onto the resistance path. Depending upon how resilient and independent they are, it may take anywhere from a day to a month for them to recover their equilibrium and regain their former level of motivation.

Managers using the old one-two don't mean to destroy motivation. They think (and are often right) that the feedback is necessary if the employee is to improve in the future. Necessary, yes, but not sufficient unless the foundation of a positive attitude is present. That's why I recommend you reverse that traditional order and hold back your praise until you've given them all the necessary negative feedback. Criticize first. End on an up note with as much praise and reaffirmation as it takes to overcome their discouragement and get them pumped up again. Give them the old two-one! By reversing the order, you stand a good chance of reversing the effect on morale as well.

development that I haven't had the chance to delve into in depth in other places and that are especially relevant to the manager who wishes to motivate employees to peak performance levels.

Are You Attacking Them or Motivating Them?

When you want to motivate employees to perform better, or when you just want to let them know you feel they aren't giving it their all, what do you say?

Typically, we say things like, "The new productivity goals are posted above your workstations, and I hope you will all try to meet them. You'll get a notice later today explaining the new goals and the rewards you can earn if you achieve them quickly."

Or maybe we say, "I've noticed you have been coming in to work late repeatedly, Bill, and I want to talk to you about how to improve your record."

Or perhaps, "Whenever I ask you to get me a report, you keep me waiting for several days. You know I really need this information when I ask for it, not the next week."

Or even, if you are feeling especially happy about how things are going, "You guys did a better job this week than you have for many months. Good work."

Statements such as these appear perfectly fine. They are the kinds of statements good managers are supposed to make. You wouldn't for a moment think you'd just made a big mistake if you said something in this vein to your employees.

But if your goal is high self-motivation, then you cannot allow yourself the luxury of such statements. You can't talk to your employees like that. To you, that sort of approach should appear to be obviously and deeply flawed. A mistake. A boo-boo. A no-no of the first order.

You can't talk to your employees like that.

Well, I bet I have your attention now if only because you think I just went off the deep end. But give me a minute to explain.

The common problem running through all those statements is that they are "you messages." They have to be reframed as "I messages" before they are going to work as motivational statements for your employees. If you go around talking like that, your employees may not see exactly what's wrong. But they will feel it, and it will tend to push them off the motivation path.

Here's what those two terms mean:

- *I messages* explain how you react to the employee's behavior and why you are concerned about it.
- *You messages* communicate your judgment of the employee's behavior or your requirements for how it must change.

To put it most simply, *I messages* explain, *you messages* tell. And whether you tell them they are doing poorly, adequately, or well, it's you telling them. And that is a style of communication that fits on the resistance path but not the motivation path.

The *you message* style of speaking is commonly used when we speak to small children, pets, or employees.

Replacing "You" with "I"

How does the *you message* sound from the receiver's side? From the employees' perspective, you aren't sharing the decision with them in any way. You aren't treating them like adults. It's disrespectful. And it automatically raises defensiveness. When someone starts talking about you, you are naturally put off by it. It's just not polite.

Yet the *you message* style of speaking is commonly used when we speak to small children, pets, or employees.

By the way, someone once pointed out to me that the best methods for producing motivated employees are those used by animal trainers. His argument was, "Hey, look at my dog. I've trained her to roll over whenever I tell her to. She's 100 percent reliable. And I don't even have to give her a treat each time, just every now and then to keep her enthusiastic. Now that's motivation. I'd like to see the employee who does what he's supposed to 100 percent of the time."

What's wrong with this argument? I stewed over it for a few days before the fatal flaw struck me. Then, the next time I saw the guy, I said, "I just want to ask you one question about that highly motivated dog of yours. Does she *ever* roll over when you aren't around to tell her to?"

Again, the results are striking. A full 100 percent of the time, dogs do *not* do their tricks when nobody is there to tell them to. Never.

Ever see a dog out in the backyard practicing its tricks for the next time it has a chance to perform them?

The reason you don't is that the owner trains them using the doggy equivalent of the *you message*. He just tells that dog what to do. The dog learns quickly that, by complying, she can get the owner to give her a treat or a pat, at least some of the time. Perhaps it looks, from the dog's perspective, as if the *owner* is being trained!

Since the dog has a strong intrinsic motivation to stimulate humans to feed and pat it, the opportunity to do a few tricks and get some rewards is not one to be passed by. But the experience fails to create even the slightest motivation to do those tricks. They are the last thing on the dog's mind. It's entirely about the rewards. And if you persist in using *you messages*, work will be the farthest thing from employees' minds. They will do work only out of their preexisting motivation to earn their compensation and avoid getting in trouble with you. Which is enough for the resistance path and mediocre performances (as long as you are watching), but it will never, ever get you to the high end of the motivation curve. And it certainly won't satisfy their urge to develop and grow since it reduces their work to the simple performance of routine tricks in exchange for rewards.

The *I message*, on the other hand, looks a lot more like what employees want to see. It incorporates respect, invites commitment, provides open communication and fuller information. By explaining decisions or policies, it often makes them seem much fairer, too. So the *I message* is fully consistent with the motivation path, and you need to begin using the *I message* formula in order to build any significant levels of internal motivation in your people.

Here is the formula to follow in developing *I messages*, according to Kimberly Stott, the training director at Devereux, a large nonprofit that provides services to people with mental health and developmental disabilities:

The *I message* looks a lot more like what employees want to see. It incorporates respect, invites commitment, provides open communication and fuller information.

Description of Behavior + Feelings + Effects on Me

It's easy to transform *you messages* into *I messages* using this formula. For example, take one of the *you messages* I quoted earlier:

"I've noticed you have been coming in to work late repeatedly, Bill, and I want to talk to you about how to improve your record."

The supervisor might transform this into an *I message* by:

- Making sure he or she uses a clear, accurate, and fair description of the behavior (eliminating any anger or exaggerations). Something like:

  "Arriving ten to fifteen minutes late several times this week."

- Identifying and describing his or her feelings about this behavior accurately. Something like:

  "Surprised you haven't apologized or explained, feeling my authority is questioned, worried everyone will start doing it if you don't stop."

- Identifying and describing the negative effects on him or her. Something like:

  "It makes it difficult for me to maintain my authority and I'm afraid others will start coming late, which will get me in trouble because we'll miss our productivity goals."

- Creating a new version of the message that uses these components, such as:

"I feel my authority is at risk when you come in late several times in a week, as you did this week. I'm worried that if others think they can get away with showing up late, I'll get in trouble with my boss for missing our productivity goals."

This is a classic *I message* version of the original *you message* statement, which I'll reproduce here for comparison:

"I've noticed you have been coming in to work late repeatedly, Bill, and I want to talk to you about how to improve your record."

The new *I message* is so much more engaging and positive than the old *you message* that it is far more likely to generate a positive result. It invites the employee to see your perspective and to take on some of the responsibility for the effects of the behavior. Responsibility is opportunity–in this case, an opportunity to help you achieve the productivity goals.

And when you open up and share your observations, feelings, and concerns (the *I message* formula), you invite the employee to open up to you also. The use of *I messages* stimulates more open communication in both directions. Soon employees start using *I messages* when they talk to you, so you get more informative feedback about their feelings and concerns.

The use of *I messages* stimulates more open communication in both directions.

For instance, the employee might respond to the *I message* about his coming in late with an *I message* explaining the behavior. Perhaps something like:

"I feel bad that my tardiness upsets you and I didn't mean to make you look bad, but my wife is sick this week and I've had to drop my son off at nursery school on the way in to work. So I felt like I didn't have any choice, since they open at the same time my shift is supposed to start."

An answer such as this is helpful, and I'm sure you could work something out easily with this employee if you got a response like that. You'd probably say something like:

> **"Well, now that you explain it, I certainly understand and I'm sympathetic to your problem. I'd be willing to make an exception in a case like that. But [here comes another I message] I feel confused and hurt that you didn't trust me enough to talk to me and ask me if it was okay in advance. When you don't talk to me about problems like that, it makes me feel like you are trying to see how much I'll let you get away with."**

A discussion like this that is based on *I messages* generally leads to a cooperative problem-solving approach. For instance, in this case, the supervisor and employee might decide on a plan for similar situations in the future, such as the employee calling and leaving a message on the supervisor's voice mail. And the cooperative problem-solving approach stimulated by the *I message*'s sharing of feelings and effects (the problem) leads the employee to feel responsible for being part of the solution. That's a step toward self-motivated performance, a step up the motivation path.

In contrast, most resolutions of problems that are based on the use of *you messages* are imposed by the supervisor and are seen as controlling and frustrating by the employee. They lead down the resistance path.

Encourage the employee to see the bigger picture and to consider how his or her behavior affects the organization.

"I" and "We" Messages

When you deal with employees, you are representing the organization, not just yourself. Often the things that upset you about employee behaviors are bad because of their impact on the organization, not their personal impact on you. So whenever you can, you should take yourself out of the effects component of the *I message* formula and replace yourself with the organization. That way, you encourage the employee to see the bigger picture and to consider how his or her behavior affects the organization. This reduces employee dependence upon you. It increases the likelihood that they will feel motivated to "practice the trick" when you aren't around. I call *I messages* with broader reference to the organizational effects of the behavior "we messages."

A *we message* is one that describes employee behavior from the organization's perspective, not just your own. It incorporates information about the effect their behavior has on all of you, not on you personally. And it relates how you feel about their hurting the organization, not just how you feel about it personally.

Everything is more complicated than it seems.
—MURPHY'S LAW

The *we message* is especially useful when you are representing the company's perspective. There is probably a good reason why coming late to work is bad for the company, for example. What is it? Can you turn it into a *we message* so as to communicate this perspective in the form of useful feedback? If so, your comments will be viewed as respectful and as sharing an adult, concerned perspective with the employee, instead of just telling him or her what to do as if he or she were an irresponsible child.

Here is a transformation of the earlier *I message* into a *we message*:

> **"I feel my authority is at risk when you come in late several times in a week, as you did this week. I'm worried that if others think they can get away with showing up late, we will miss our productivity goals. And it's important for us to achieve our productivity goals because the organization is facing tough competition and we need to increase profits to avoid budget cuts and possible layoffs."**

Now the employee gets information on many levels with which to analyze his own behavior. He sees why it bothers the supervisor by putting her at risk of not being able to make productivity goals. And he sees why the supervisor feels the productivity goals are important for the health of the company–something both employee and supervisor want to maintain in order to protect their jobs.

Note that you will have trouble delivering *we messages* if you don't know why a specific behavior is bad or good for the organization. If you can't think of any compelling reason why flexible work hours are bad, for example, then you really can't criticize flex-time using the *we message* format. The only way to insist everyone gets in and goes home on the same schedule is to use an arbitrary-sounding, authoritative *you message*. And that will hurt employee motivation and push people down the resistance path.

So you really cannot get away with rules and rulings that are not obviously justified in terms of their benefit to the organization. It's either-or. Either stick with fair, justifiable decisions or give up on the motivation path and accept that motivation levels will be low and resistance high. Which do you want? Most managers, once aware of this tradeoff, decide they would rather stick with justifiable decisions and pursue the motivation path. If a moderate use of flex time doesn't hurt the organization in any way, then the manager who values employee motivation will allow employees to use flex time. If it begins to threaten results, for example, by keeping employees from being able to collaborate on joint projects, then the motivation-oriented manager has a good case for a *we message* and is willing to take the case to employees and engage them in a cooperative search for a solution.

Are You an Abusive Boss?

So far in this book, I've addressed you as a fellow seeker wishing for nothing more than to help your people perform better. My approach assumes we are both "on their side" as our basic starting perspective. It assumes we are inherently nice and helpful people who are just looking for better ways to help our people succeed.

They hurt people on a routine basis.

But are we? Heck, let's be realistic here. Nobody's nice *all* the time, and on top of that, I happen to know that a significant percentage of supervisors and managers out there in business are guilty of a routinely negative and unfriendly approach.

They may not mean to, but they end up being abusive, mean, spiteful, and downright nasty. They hurt people on a routine basis. My informal estimate based on years of visiting and working with all types of organizations on multiple continents is that *about a quarter of managers are actively toxic* and seem to go out of their way to do more harm than good.

So I can't help thinking that perhaps a quarter of my readers fall into this little-acknowledged but large category as well. If you aren't one of these people whose behavior leads others to view you as toxic, then you no doubt have an associate or (horrors!) a supervisor of your own who is toxic in his or her behavior.

So we really need to talk about this taboo subject. And you really need to think about it. You need to examine your own behavior at work to see if you are sometimes a monster to your employees. And you need to think about other managers' behavior and honestly identify any who fall into this category. Until we acknowledge the problem, we can't do anything about it. And it is a very serious barrier to the motivation path because it prevents any positive emotional foundations from being raised and crumbles any that may already exist. Abusive behavior also dashes employees' expectations of reasonably fair and respectful treatment, which is another strike against motivation.

> A slip of the foot you may soon recover, but a slip of the tongue you may never get over.
>
> —Benjamin Franklin

Have I scared you off yet? I don't think so, but I do think you are sitting back in your chair and trying to get a little distance from me. So far I've been pretty warm and fuzzy. But now I seem to be accusing you of some absurd crime you never heard of. I bet (based on the "live" discussions I've had on this subject with other managers) that you don't really think there is a major, widespread "toxic manager" problem. You think I've finally gone off the deep end.

Well, let me give you a little more information to help you see it for yourself.

One of the most striking pieces of evidence I've ever encountered is sitting next to me here on my desk. It's a thoughtful book on verbal abuse in personal relationships by Patricia Evans, one of the leading people in the field of counseling and recovery for battered women. She has worked with thousands of abused people, a majority of them women who are verbally and sometimes physically abused by their male partners. And she gets hundreds of letters from them each week as a result of her lectures and books, so she has her ear well tuned to this group's experiences and needs.

But what does that have to do with your behavior as a manager?

Well, here is why I find this book beside me so powerful. On the back cover, it has a simple paragraph that sums up Evans's diagnosis of abusive relationships so the potential reader can find out if it applies to her. It reads like this:

> **If your partner: seems irritated or angry at you several times a week; denies being angry when he clearly is; does not work with you to resolve important issues; rarely or never seems to share thoughts or plans with you; or tells you that he has no idea what you're talking about when you try to discuss important problems . . . then you are the victim of verbal abuse.**

Although there are far more nasty examples of abuse within the book itself, the behaviors described on the jacket are indeed intolerable. You shouldn't put up with them from anyone you are in a personal relationship with. *Such practices constitute abuse* in the eyes of the world and certainly among the professionals who handle abuse cases.

But now let's read Evans's quote a second time, with one minor change. Let's substitute the word *supervisor* for the word *partner*. And let's imagine that we are asking these questions of *your employees*.

For instance, let's imagine I asked your employees this question: "Does your supervisor seem irritated or angry at you several times a week?"

Or how about this question: "Does your supervisor not work with you to resolve important issues?"

Or, how about, "Does your supervisor rarely or never seem to share thoughts and plans with you?"

And so on.

I think you get the point. Most employees answer those questions in the affirmative for most supervisors. We ignore such behavior in the workplace, but it does go on routinely. And, *if most supervisors behaved at home the way they behave at work, they would be wide open to charges of abuse.*

If most supervisors behaved at home the way they behave at work, they would be wide open to charges of abuse.

MOTIVATION IDEA 23

Managing Critical Incidents

People often assume motivation is built up incrementally, day after day, task after task, interaction after interaction. But a critical incident can overwhelm these routine experiences, turning an employee off for good, creating alienation, and stimulating anger and resentment. By tracking critical events in the emotional lives of employees at work, you can prevent demotivating traumas, or, if not preventable, turn them into opportunities for motivation recovery—which often build greater commitment than before!

For example, take the case of a manager who uses frequent positive feedback and tries to create a friendly, supportive work environment. But every now and then, say once or twice a quarter, this supervisor becomes upset about a missed deadline or a messed-up project and loses his temper. He chews out the nearest employees and stomps off to slam his door and not come out again for hours.

The employees who are in the line of fire for one of these outbursts are liable to be traumatized. They probably feel that the supervisor is overreacting, and is blaming them unjustly for a problem that is far bigger than them. These rare outbursts are actually critical events in the emotional life of the office, and they undo all the good work the supervisor has done in the weeks preceding them. Yet this supervisor, like many, does not recognize that one traumatic event can outweigh dozens and dozens of routine ones and poison the motivation climate.

So make sure you focus on the critical events. Don't underestimate the importance of an inappropriate criticism, a lost promotion opportunity, a problem that requires employees to stay late, and other events that loom large in employees' minds. These set the tone for daily motivation. You need to help employees recover from negative events, and you need to try to balance them with positive events. If you've just lost your temper at your employees, you owe them one. Acknowledge that this was an important event and counter it with an apology and perhaps a positive event as well. Employees remember critical incidents. So manage them!

I find it fascinating that we hold managers to a far lower standard of conduct than we do the people whom we spend the other half of our time with. We rarely call managers on the rug for verbal abuse. As long as their abuse doesn't cross the lines into assault, discrimination, or sexual abuse, it can be as emotionally abusive as they want. And many managers have no idea how abusive they are. Do you?

Common forms of verbal abuse: criticism, blaming, withholding, ordering, and diminishing.

Recognizing and Working on Your Problem Behaviors

Now I'd like to open Patricia Evans's book, *Verbal Abuse: Survivors Speak Out on Relationship and Recovery,* and use some of her insights from abusive personal relationships to make sure you aren't accidentally falling into the abusive supervisor syndrome.

Let's start by learning a little more about verbal abuse in general. A great way to do that is to take a peak at a page from a journal of one of her patients. Evans recounts the story of Ann, who "has just recognized that she is in a verbally abusive relationship, and as she thinks about the previous day's events, she writes in her journal." Her approach, a powerful one for victims who are seeking to understand abusive behavior and heal its wounds, is to (A) list the specific abusive behaviors she remembers, and (B) identify the type of abuse involved since diagnosing it helps her recognize and cope with it. Here is an entry in Ann's journal, and it refers to an abusive man with whom she is in a personal relationship:

This is what happened yesterday morning:

A	B
He turns away.	Withholding
Come out and say it.	Criticism/ordering
His tone of contempt.	Undermining
You interrupt etc.	Accusing and blaming
Never mind.	Blocking and diverting

We're leaving.	Ordering and demanding
You rehash everything.	Accusing and blaming
Said angrily.	Abusive anger
The discussion is ended.	Withholding/ordering

The journal documented nine incidents of verbal abuse on that particular morning (and according to Evans, there were twelve incidents that day when the evening log was added in). Now, each one of these incidents might not be too debilitating, as best we can infer from the cryptic entries in Ann's journal. You can forgive anyone the occasional grumpy behavior. But when ten or more are dished up each day, that's thousands a year. They add up to a crushing load of emotional abuse. They signal scorn and disrespect. They are obviously bad for one's frame of mind and destructive of motivation and performance. And people subjected to that level of verbal abuse at home are chronically depressed and unable to accomplish anything significant and satisfying in their lives because they develop seriously low self-esteem.

I'm fascinated by this and other peeks into Evans's patients' experiences because I just keep flashing on management behavior I've witnessed over and over in the daily routines of supervision. If your employees worked with Evans or another expert to learn how to identify abusive techniques like withholding, ordering, and demanding, they would probably recognize quite a few incidents in your relationships with them. Maybe even a dozen a day. I know I've sometimes acted like this toward my employees and children in the past. Wonder what their logs would have looked like if they'd kept careful journals! Scary thought. Anyway, it's my strong feeling that the average manager is doing a lot of this sort of verbal abuse, and so I can't help wondering if it could apply to you.

It's my strong feeling that the average manager is doing a lot of this sort of verbal abuse.

Checking for Common Forms of Verbal Abuse

But let's not base this inquiry on my judgment alone. It's *your quest* for motivation, and they are *your employees*, not mine. You're the only one who can decide how much of this might apply to you and

Is "Good try" an example of positive feedback? Sometimes.

your people. So I want you to read the following definitions of common forms of verbal abuse and see if you use them in your interpersonal interactions with those you supervise.

Diminishing

This is when you use words and body language to make someone feel small. It's the opposite of encouraging. Sometimes it's done in the guise of encouraging, as when a manager says, "Good try, Jimmy." Is "Good try" an example of positive feedback? Sometimes. But not if it's delivered in a tone or style that implies Jimmy couldn't be expected to do any better. Try saying it in a genuinely encouraging tone of voice. Now try saying it in a dismissive or undermining tone of voice. It can cut either way, can't it?

Other diminishing behavior is more obvious. "I didn't expect you to be able to handle that." "You really made a mess out of this one." "Oh boy, you've done it again!" And so on. Note that negative feedback taking the form of *you messages*, as defined earlier in this chapter, is always diminishing.

And how about passive forms of diminishing, like when the manager looks right past an employee when soliciting input, as if to say, "We won't bother asking you because you obviously don't have any idea what's going on." I've heard the lament, "Why didn't he ask me?" so many times that I know this form of diminishing exists in many variants and is widely practiced.

Note that diminishing focuses on people's weaknesses, not their strengths, which, as we saw in Chapter 5, sets the stage for the resistance path instead of the motivation path. If you ever engage in diminishing behavior (and I think a large majority of managers do), you are unintentionally thwarting all of your efforts to motivate your people.

Withholding

Withholding involves being unwilling to share information or feelings. In abusive personal relationships, it often takes the form of refusal to discuss the relationship. When the abused person feels that things are going poorly and wants to improve them, withholding by the other party makes it impossible to do so. Withholding one's self is only one form of withholding, however. People also withhold things, from access to money to use of the car in order to flex their power in the relationship. The boyfriend who refuses to go to movies or restaurants his girlfriend likes is withholding these pleasures from her.

When it comes to withholding behaviors, I am again floored by the many examples I've seen in business. In fact, withholding is one of the absolutely most common behaviors of managers everywhere. Managers routinely:

- Refuse to discuss their relationships with their employees, preferring to set the ground rules entirely themselves.
- Withhold information that is important to employees, even when there is no justifiable security issue involved (and there rarely is).
- Use their control over budgets, supplies, parking spaces, lunch breaks, and anything else in order to flex their power and demonstrate their higher status.
- Withhold themselves, refusing to open up and be genuine or personal with employees.
- Refuse to communicate openly about subjects of mutual concern and interest.

Refusing to communicate freely is a form of withholding. It's abusive and damages the employer–employee relationship in ways that seriously damage performance potential.

This last form of withholding–withholding communication–is employees' number-one complaint about their managers, if you'll recall our discussion of it in Chapter 3. Refusing to communicate freely is a form of withholding. It's abusive and damages the employer–employee relationship in ways that seriously damage performance potential. As Patricia Evans observes, "You can't have a relationship with a noncommunicator." Most managers desperately want to have a meaningful relationship with their employees, for that is what is required if they are to motivate and manage them. Yet most managers are "noncommunicators" from their employees' perspective.

There may be certain occasions in which a supervisor or manager can make a good argument for withholding information or resources from employees. Control is one of the manager's func-

Judging and criticizing someone is definitely a form of abuse. It makes them small and you big.

tions, after all. But those occasions are relatively rare. Most of the time, we withhold without thinking or even recognizing the behavior in ourselves.

Judging and Criticizing

When you give feedback to employees, are you judging them? And is judging really a form of abuse? Let me tackle the last question first. Yes, judging and criticizing someone is definitely a form of abuse. It makes them small and you big. And for your employees to succeed on the motivation path, you need to make them bigger, not smaller. So if you judge them and criticize them, you are working against your goal of achieving high motivation and star performances.

Now to the first question. Are you judging employees when you give them feedback? Probably, but you don't have to. I went on at some length about the importance of giving feedback about the behavior, not the person, when I talked about how to use negative and positive feedback in Chapter 7. I also addressed this vital issue earlier in this chapter when I talked about replacing *you messages* with *I messages*. If you avoid forms of feedback that judge the individual, positively or negatively, then you will avoid this form of abuse. But it is easy to forget and find yourself telling employees what you think of them instead of what you think of their performance. In fact, judging and criticizing are very common forms of verbal abuse in business settings.

Trivializing

When you send signals that say, "You're not as important as me," that trivializes the other person. It is another way to make them smaller and you bigger. Forgetting an appointment with them is a variation on trivializing, too. So is undermining, as when you undermine someone's statement or position in a meeting.

And guess what? Trivializing is also an amazingly common form of management behavior. I'm sure you've worked for bosses who trivialized you in many subtle ways. You might not have recognized it as abusive behavior at the time, lacking a formal term for it, but in retrospect, you know it was.

I remember one boss years ago when I worked for a multibillion-dollar company that was long on titles and hierarchy. This boss was a master of trivializing employees. When I told him my wife had just given birth to a baby boy, he nodded vaguely, as if hardly hearing me, then asked me when I'd have a report ready for him. My life obviously was trivial in his eyes. And he routinely cut into your answers to his questions, saying something like, "That's enough," and then turning to ask someone else a question. As a result, people at his staff meetings got pretty nervous whenever he'd ask them something, and would try to say the minimum possible. He rarely heard much of what was going on in the department because of this, but he acted as if it didn't matter to him.

Managers who employees describe as "on a power trip" are often exhibiting this kind of behavior. Employees sense there is something wrong, but don't know quite what. They often think there is something wrong with them, rather than with their boss. But bosses who trivialize employees instead of showing them respect can hardly expect to motivate their employees to peak performances.

When the Rabbi Gamaliel told his servants, "Bring me something good," they brought a tongue. The Rabbi said, "Now go to the market, and bring me something bad." Again the servants brought a tongue, saying, "A tongue, my master, may be the source of either good or evil. If it is good, there is nothing better. If it is bad, there is nothing worse.

—The Talmud

Abusive Anger and Accusing and Blaming

These are the two most common categories of verbal abuse in personal relationships, but I'm covering them last here because I believe they are far less common in supervisor-employee relationships. Most supervisors don't rant and rave at work because they feel inhibited by the more public setting. Few let their anger really hang out, few scream or curse at employees. And few shout accusations and blame in an angry tone of voice even though that's a very common pattern in abusive households. The public nature of the workplace and the possibility for many supervisors that *their* supervisor may be watching inhibits the majority of tempers and channels verbal abuse into the more subtle and low-key forms described earlier.

But abusive anger does occur on occasion, and accusing and blaming occurs with higher frequency. And if you ever engage in these behaviors toward your employees, I think you'd know it without my having to go into a song and dance about what they are. Do you ever blow up at someone or at a group of people? Do you ever go off about how they messed up? Do you lose your temper at your employees? If so, well, I guess you know by now that it's a major problem.

A really major problem. If you can't control your temper, your interpersonal intelligence is probably best expressed as a negative number. And I don't think you should even bother reading about how to motivate employees until you learn how to stop losing your temper at them. So I strongly recommend you put this book down and schedule a visit with a therapist or psychologist who has a track record of success with helping people control their tempers. You can call this person a counselor if you feel there is a stigma associated with seeing a therapist or "shrink"–my sister Claire is a therapist and she tells me lots of people don't like those terms. But call them what you will, you should go anyway...or I'm going to get *really mad* at you!

When you have spoken the word, it reigns over you. When it is unspoken, you rein over it.

—ARABIC PROVERB

How to Defuse Your Own Anger at Employees

I want to share with you some useful findings from the field of psychology about how to cope with one's anger because it is entirely possible that you may be able to improve in this area on your own, especially if you don't have a major problem with anger but are instead an occasional abuser, as many of us are.

Extensive studies of how people cope with anger and what works and doesn't work to cool them down reveal that most of us fall prey to some widespread myths about how to handle our anger. (I'm roughly following the conclusions of Carol Tarvis in her book *Anger: The Misunderstood Emotion.*)

First, many people believe that *acting out aggression* helps cool us down by providing an appropriate catharsis. Pounding fists, kicking walls, throwing things, even striking someone in anger, are all common attempts to resolve one's anger. *They don't work.* Aggressive actions just keep the pot boiling. They often boomerang on you when the other person gets mad at you and things escalate. Even if the other person doesn't rise to the bait, your aggression rehearses your anger, increasing its intensity or duration. So forget about it, those behaviors won't help. That's why people who are in the habit of acting out anger never seem to get it out of their systems for long. They cool down, sure, but you know they might be "touched off" by another incident at any time.

Second, most people believe that *talking out your anger* helps get rid of it. In fact, people generally divide into two camps–those who act out anger and those who talk it out. Unfortunately, plenty of studies indicate that "ventilating" one's anger does nothing to diminish it. Talking to an associate or another employee about your employee's "stupidity" or "chronic mistakes" or "bad attitude" won't do anything to make you feel less angry about the problem. It will probably just strengthen your feelings of anger and rehearse them, and may lead you to find even more aspects of this person to be angry about.

Third, *suppressing the anger* isn't very effective either. Lots of people advise you to "count to ten" or "take a walk." But the reality is those solutions don't generally occur when we are seeing red. We forget about suppressing the anger most of the time. If we do remember, and succeed in imposing our will over our feelings, those feelings of anger will just percolate beneath the surface and erupt later on when that irritating employee "does it again." It's very, very difficult to stifle feelings of genuine anger. It's like trying to keep the tide from rising.

Well, that pretty much covers the waterfront in terms of the popular wisdom on how to control your anger. Three popular theories, often attempted, but none of them have been proved to be successful.

What the research shows instead is that *there is one and only one powerful way to defuse anger*. It's to understand why the person you're angry at behaved as he or she did. *Understanding* is the best antidote to anger as far as I've been able to learn. Seeking the cause of the anger and working on understanding or eliminating it is the only sure way to eliminate that anger.

For example, if I explain to you why an employee you are angry at acted the way he did–what pressures he is under, how he saw the situation, and so forth–then your anger will probably give way to empathy. "Oh, yes, I guess that makes sense," you may say to yourself.

Understanding gives you the ability to fix the cause of your anger. You can work on the employee's problem when you know there is a problem. Control over your environment is empowering.

> If a couple doesn't deal with what is *causing* their anger, it will remain, or worsen.
>
> —MURRAY STRAUS, A SOCIOLOGIST STUDYING FAMILY VIOLENCE

So the best way to work on not getting mad at your employees is to try to understand the roots of their irritating behaviors.

Lack of control leads to frustration and anger. And understanding makes the difference between helplessness and control.

Empathy with an employee's problem, by the way, does not necessarily lead to sympathy. You might not like the employee's behavior any more as a result of understanding it, in which case you won't sympathize with the employee. You might feel the employee reacted inappropriately or even irresponsibly. But you'll empathize because you know what the employee reacted *to*. When you understand the causes of his behavior, you understand how he was feeling and what led him to act the way he did. That's empathy, not sympathy, and it provides insight into his behavior without requiring acceptance of the behavior.

So the best way to work on not getting mad at your employees is to try to understand the roots of their irritating behaviors. Next time you feel frustrated by someone's behavior, immediately stop and ask yourself why he or she behaved that way. Refuse to allow yourself to think about anything but why. *Go off and puzzle it out.* Postpone reacting to the behavior until you are able to find out why it occurred.

The choice when an employee does something that irritates you is therefore:

Anger or understanding. Which will it be?

You do have a choice! And it's interesting to note that, if you've read this book from the first chapter onward, you have actually been enriching your ability to understand your employees' behavior to a considerable extent. Each chapter has given you new insights into the root causes of employee behavior. For instance, when I talked about and diagrammed the performance puzzle in Chapter 5, I explained the roots of one of the most common sources of management frustration–initial progress toward a performance goal, followed by degeneration of performance as employees slide down the back side of that wave. You learned to look at the underlying emotional state, and to recognize that a lack of optimism and self-confidence in your employees produced that performance puzzle by pushing them down the resistance path instead of up the motivation path. That knowledge is a powerful thing when you face frustrating performance deterioration after working hard to get a new

Listening Better at Pillsbury

If feedback is the breakfast of champions, why don't supervisors need it even more than employees? They do, and not only from above. In fact, feedback from your employees is the most important indicator of how well you are managing them. But ask your employees how you are doing and they are unlikely to speak their minds freely. They worry (quite rightly) that negative feedback to the boss will lead to negative consequences for them.

So bosses are starved for feedback from their employees. They regularly go without breakfast. What to do? At Pillsbury, the solution is to offer a 100 percent safe and secure third-party service for submitting your feedback. Here's how it works. The employee calls a number and provides input. The number rings in a remote office with no direct contact to Pillsbury. An employee there, who doesn't know anyone from Adam, simply types up the feedback and adds it to the pile. Periodically it is distributed to the relevant managers, minus any indication of which employees submitted it. Just an anonymous report about how employees feel and what they see.

Analysis. The head of personnel at Pillsbury explains that this system's main objective is "to have employees get in our face." The way managers routinely get in employees' faces. Which not only gives managers more and better performance feedback, but also gives employees a greater sense of control. They know they can be heard at all levels of the company if they have something important to say. By helping to make communications more open, this program does a great deal to maintain a healthy motivational climate.

procedure or program up and running. Instead of losing your temper, you now know to check the emotional foundations of motivation.

Similarly, you can apply your knowledge of employees' evaluative criteria, as described in Chapters 3 and 4, to find out if there are some basic problems with the workplace that are getting in the way of motivation and performance. These, too, may be at the root of irritating employee behaviors that might well lead a less knowledgeable manager than you to lose his or her temper.

I just have to add one caveat to my advice to defuse anger by seeking understanding of the employee's irritating behavior. I want you to promise you won't implement this advice by demanding that the *employee* tell you why he or she "behaved that way" or "did it." *You can't delegate the task of understanding the root causes of your anger.* That's an abusive thing to do, too. And it won't help employees or defuse your anger if you start shouting at them to "tell you why." They probably don't know, and if they do, they'd be crazy to tell *you* when you are in their face like that. So leave them alone while you sort it out. Thanks!

I'm great at telling people what's wrong with their interpersonal behavior. But I guarantee I'm not a perfect model.

Parting Shots

Look, I have to make a confession. It is far easier to write about this sort of thing than to implement it. I'm great at telling people what's wrong with their interpersonal behavior. But I guarantee I'm not a perfect model. (Thank God, my wife and children don't get to add their two cents worth to this chapter!) The fact is, it is very, very hard to change yourself. Therapists working with abused women tell them not to even bother thinking they can "reform" their abusive husbands or lovers. A common piece of advice given to abused or battered women is, "People don't change."

Damn it, I don't accept that. I know it is the best advice when you are trying to empower someone to face up to the facts and get out of a dangerous relationship. But when it comes to reforming ourselves, we have to believe we have the potential to change. In fact, the most powerful thing about the field of motivation is it shows us that people do change for the better given the right circumstances and attitudes. Let's apply that to ourselves as managers. Let's plan to change by making sure we recognize any inappropriate or abusive interpersonal behaviors we may engage in and begin the long process of retraining ourselves.

A great way to do this is to record your own behavior. A journal like the one I showed you from a therapist's patient is helpful, except you need to keep it on *yourself* since you can't reasonably ask any of your employees to do so.

But maybe you sit down and stare at a blank page in a notebook after a morning of interactions with your employees and can't think of any behaviors worth noting. Did you do something abusive you need to remind yourself to avoid next time? Can't remember, or aren't sure. Did you make good use of I statements in giving helpful, informative feedback? Hope so, but can't remember exactly what you said. It's awfully hard to be your own supervisor.

> Who is strong? He that can conquer his bad habits.
> —BENJAMIN FRANKLIN

For instance, it's hard to remember exactly what you said or guess whether it sounded abusive or not. If you lost your temper and shouted at someone, you'll remember that. But did you diminish someone in a subtle way? Did you forget to give informative feedback, using a controlling approach instead? Some of this stuff is pretty subtle, after all. So I want to make another recommendation. I recommend that you get one of those small-format tape recorders and stick it in your pocket to record yourself as you talk to your people.

Take it to meetings. Run it when you walk around to see how people are doing. Slip your finger in your pocket or desk drawer and punch the record button when an employee approaches you with a question. It won't be hard to get good recordings in spite of the lack of power of the microphone in a cheap recorder because you need only to hear your own voice clearly. You are going to use it to study yourself, not your employees.

After you've collected at least a few hours of tapes of yourself speaking to employees, listen to some of them. Start with the last and work backwards in time because you will have been on good behavior for the first hour or two. But after a while, the recording gets to be a habit and you will stop thinking much about it as you interact. Then you will capture your real self as employees hear you on tape. And you will be able, simply by playing those recordings back, to get a good idea of how you sound to your employees. It

You will truly know yourself as others see you.

won't be nearly as hard to "diagnose" your own verbal behavior. Make a point of noting and studying any good or bad examples of interpersonal behavior. This is great feedback, and it will permit you to increase your interpersonal intelligence at a rapid rate.

I think many of my readers will resist this little experiment, but of those who are brave enough to try it, I'm pretty darn sure that 90 percent of them will find that they do engage in one or more of the abusive verbal behaviors described earlier, at least once a day and probably much more often. If you have the fortitude to find this out about yourself, you are well on your way to achieving an unusually high level of interpersonal intelligence. You will truly know yourself as others see you, and will find this knowledge is the most powerful tool of all in your efforts to help your people achieve higher levels of motivation and performance.

Oh, by the way, I recommend keeping this self-study project to yourself. Reuse or chuck those tapes after a few weeks. Don't label or file them anywhere official. Buy the equipment with your own money and store it at home when you aren't using it. And if you keep notes to analyze the tapes (you should), don't put your name or any employees' names on them, store them at home, and discard them after a month or two. Why all the concern with security? Because your sincere efforts to understand and improve your own behavior might be turned to other purposes by an unfriendly associate, boss, or employee.

You may be creating a positive emotional environment for your people, but in all likelihood not everybody in your organization is reading this book. So it's better to keep documentation of your "faults" private and work on them in your own way. Also, every now and then you may be involved directly or indirectly in one of those cases in which an employee claims he or she was harassed. In which case, you'd hate for your tapes and notes to appear in court as evidence that you were abusive!

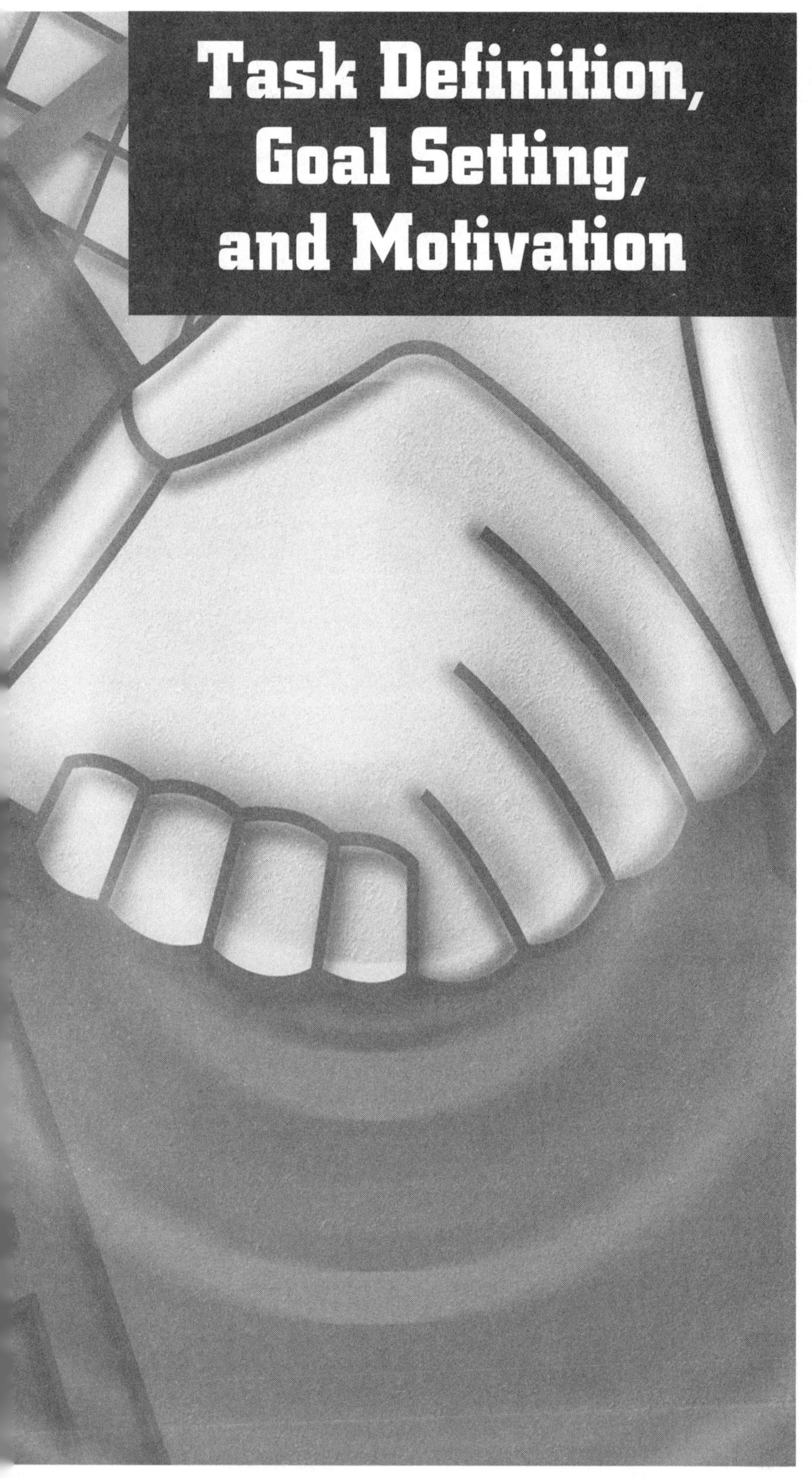

Task Definition, Goal Setting, and Motivation

Chapter 10

What do you do in tough cases like this, where nothing seems to work?

I sometimes talk to managers who are doing all the right things, and are trying their best to be understanding, supportive, and positive, but are absolutely at their wit's end and ready to shoot their employees because "they just don't get it!"

Here's a good example. A friend of mine manages a group of Wall Street traders. These people are doing a challenging, responsible job requiring a lot of care and intelligence. They are highly compensated, carefully selected, and are as bright, well-educated employees as you could ever hope to find. But they keep messing up on obvious details. Time after time, year after year, they forget about something obvious and important. Or fail to do something right even though they know perfectly well how to do it. My friend said he was sick and tired of all the theories about management, and was convinced that there was simply something wrong with them.

His new philosophy? He calls it "management by contempt." He simply can't help feeling, and expressing, his contempt for people who act so irresponsibly and take so little interest in learning about and improving their own work.

What do you do in tough cases like this, where nothing seems to work? Do you go on trying to motivate them by giving them challenging opportunities? Not if you just know they will mess those opportunities up. Do you take a very deep breath, count to ten, and try to smile and think positive thoughts so as to reset the emotional frame? Not if you think they are already contented and happy–happy to get grossly overpaid for making mistakes they ought to know enough to avoid. Do you fight down your feelings of contempt and try to give them respectful positive and negative feedback about their behavior? Not if you think they won't pay any attention to that feedback or learn a thing from it because they haven't before.

The answers I've given you so far *will not always work*. In my friend's case, where he felt he'd tried everything and was simply at his wit's end, these answers obviously haven't worked as well as he wants them to.

What most managers do when they run out of positive, people-oriented strategies is to fall back on the old command-and-control approach. In this classic method, management is the controller, forcing compliance from witless employees.

When individuals fail to perform an assigned task in command-and-control management, you reprimand them and tell them to try again. If they keep failing, you conclude they aren't ready or able to take charge of that task on their own, and you supervise them more closely. Specifically, you *direct* their performance by watching over them and correcting them whenever they mess it up. In other words, you have to provide the brains part of the work, and they just provide the sweat. (And if they won't sweat enough, you fire their asses.)

But what happens when you tighten the reins by being highly directive with those experienced, intelligent, well-paid, highly educated employees who still seem to mess it up? They don't like it one bit. Their self-image is the same as your image of them after all, with only one exception. They see themselves as experienced, intelligent, well-paid, highly educated employees, too. They just don't see the messing-up part. So their self-image is inconsistent with being treated like little kids or ignorant laborers. They do not want to give up their control and autonomy and the status it represents. They will strenuously resist any efforts to infantilize them through heavy-handed supervision and control.

If you try to direct their work more closely, they will lose any motivation they currently have and will make life miserable for you in every way they can. And believe me, an experienced, intelligent, well-paid, highly educated employee can be amazingly resourceful when it comes to making managers miserable!

An experienced, intelligent, well-paid, highly educated employee can be amazingly resourceful when it comes to making managers miserable!

Resolving the Performance Dilemma

So you face a dilemma that the traditional approach to management cannot resolve. On the one hand, you have people who are capable of responsible, self-supervised performances and know it. On the other hand, you have performances that seem to call for step-by-step direction and control. The interpersonal style you need to keep them from messing up is not going to work because it clashes with their emotional requirements. Task requirements pull one way, people requirements another. Damned if you do, damned if you don't. (Exactly *why* did you want to be a manager?)

The reason this dilemma is so frustrating is that it cannot be resolved. There is no solution. My poor friend will never get those traders to perform up to his expectations. They simply are not ready and able to perform their jobs as well as he requires, at least not the majority of them. Either he's got to change his expectations of them or change their jobs. But most managers don't seriously consider doing either one. They just keep trying to motivate or direct their employees to better performances.

I like it when I think I've upset my readers. I know I have their full attention. And telling someone midway into a book on employee motivation that *there are cases in which it is impossible to motivate employees* is probably a great way to upset my readers. Right? I mean, I'm sure you expected this book to be full of solutions, not problems, when you picked it up.

Motivating people to do a job that isn't right for them simply will not work.

Well, okay, I guess I'll show you how to solve this problem, too. There *is* a solution, but it is an out-of-the-box one because I spoke the truth when I said those people could not be motivated to do much better than they already do. The fact is, sometimes you run into limitations and reach the point where you have to admit motivation alone will not produce better performances, *given the current task structures*. The problem isn't the people, it's their jobs. And the reality is:

> **Motivating people to do a job that isn't right for them simply will not work.**

Are You Making the Fundamental Attribution Error?

All too often, managers are frustrated about employee performance and believe they have a motivation or attitude problem when it's not the people at all. It's their jobs, or some other aspect of the situation. There turns out to be good reasons why performance isn't everything you want it to be, and when you eliminate those reasons, the people will take care of themselves and what looked for all the world like an attitude problem will disappear as if by magic.

MOTIVATION IDEA 24

Project Identification

It's old hat (no pun intended) to put your organization's logo onto clothes, hats, pens, mugs, and so forth. And I don't knock that. It can help encourage identification with the organization. But let's be real. In today's business climate, most people aren't working primarily out of a sense of shared identity and destiny with their employer. Working for your company isn't the same as being part of a family or something. It's a temporary arrangement, sustained as long as it is of mutual convenience. So the company logo and identity are really more for the sake of the customer than the employee.

But employees are often highly motivated by and attached to specific, challenging projects. An important project assignment gives them a chance to really engage themselves. It lines up those vital intrinsic motivations: the opportunity for achievement and personal development and the chance to be recognized for significant accomplishments. That's what really turns employees on. So when you put together a project or plan and assign people to it, why not give that project it's own special identity? Name it. Design a simple logo for it. And then have some mugs made up with the project identity on them. Or better yet, have some nice binders or dress shirts or other daily-use items made up to remind them of their identification with this special opportunity to excel. If you were trying to sell a new product to your customers, you'd do all this as a matter of course. Why not when you are trying to sell a new project to your employees?

The reason we misdiagnose other problems as motivation problems so often is that we humans have a basic bias to attribute performance problems to aspects of the *people* rather than the *situation*.

Psychology researchers call this the fundamental attribution error, and they worry that it contaminates their own studies of interpersonal behavior too often. It is easy to focus on aspects of the people involved when you study human behavior and to forget about the circumstances surrounding that behavior. Once psychologists realized they were often barking up the wrong tree, they began to track aspects of the situation more carefully. And they began to document our attribution errors, too. For example, take the experiment in which seminary students are on the way to give a lecture on the parable of the Good Samaritan when they encounter someone who needs help. Which of them will stop and be Good Samaritans themselves, and which won't? Some of these students are more religious than others, so most people assume that the most religious ones would be most likely to stop. In other words, they assume something about the individuals themselves will predict their behavior. Not so. The best predictor is whether the students are late or not. Those who are running late don't want to stop, whether they are religious and profess a firm belief in helping others or not.

So the truth is, we all tend to look at aspects of our employees and to attribute performance shortfalls to their motivation, skills, or other aspects of them. Not to the external situation, the context in which they perform. But when you simply can't seem to make good motivation theories work with your people, it probably isn't them. It isn't even you. It's not behavioral. It's more likely something about the circumstances in which they must perform. Heck, increasing the lighting might be more effective than providing more feedback. It could be anything.

We all tend to look at aspects of our employees and to attribute performance shortfalls to their motivation, skill or other aspects of them. Not to the external situation, the context in which they perform

The Culprit May Be Job or Task Structure

But when something external to the individual is messing up their performance, it is usually *the way their work is structured.* And fortunately, you as their supervisor have considerable control over that situational variable. You can fix it with ease once you know how. I'm going to teach you the basics of getting people's assignments right so that they have work that is inherently challenging and motivational for them. These are the three steps you must take:

1. Make sure you understand what each individual's competence level is so you know what he or she can and can't handle.
2. Figure out what tasks they should be responsible for based on that, which may mean modifying their job to suit them.
3. Define the feedback mechanisms and goals to make it easy for them to perform and improve.

To clarify how to perform each of these steps, I'm going to go into them in order. Let's start with assessing the individual to see what he or she can handle.

Assessing the Employee

Each employee is unique. We know that. Yet the habit in most organizations is to overlook much of what makes employees unique. If you want them to follow the motivation path instead of the resistance path, you need to take a developmental approach. And that requires attention to their individual capabilities and requirements. You simply have to accept that you will need to manage one on one to a considerable extent. That's how you get the most out of individuals–by treating them as individuals!

But how? Does this mean catering to their every need? No. You aren't running a luxury hotel, you're running a business. So your focus should be on three things: competence level, commitment level, and maturity.

Competence level is specific to the task you want them to do. Ask yourself how skilled and experienced they are, and how much knowledge they have of relevance to the task. Are they already experts? Or perhaps intermediates? Or are some of them actually beginners? Some of the beginners may be experienced employees who've been with the organization for years. It doesn't matter that they are expert at other things. The issue is are they beginners at the task in question? When experienced employees have to learn a new task, like how to operate a new piece of equipment, you have to treat them like beginners. It's not reasonable to assume they will be expert at the new task, too. You will need to inform them about the new task, direct their initial efforts, and develop their competency. You will have to be a directive manager to start with, then a developmental manager, and only when they have established a high level of competency at the new task will you be able to delegate to them, as you are accustomed to doing.

Often, employees who seem to be unmotivated and put in poor performances were never properly prepared for their work in the first place!

Building a solid foundation of competence is an important step for any manager. Often, employees who seem to be unmotivated and put in poor performances were never properly prepared for their work in the first place! It is discouraging to fail and not know why. It's the same feeling my old college students used to get when they'd study all night, then bomb an exam. They felt cheated because their grades didn't reflect their effort. Same with employees who haven't

MOTIVATION IDEA 25

Opinion Candy

How good or bad is customer service today? Most methods for getting feedback require a relatively high level of customer involvement, and so fail to capture the opinions of most customers. An easy way to get lots of immediate feedback is to offer free candy, mints or gumballs, to all customers. The only constraints are that they can take just one at a time and that they must decide whether to take one from the Good Work or the Bad Work machine. How does it work? You put two identical gumball-type machines side by side and keep both full of the same candy. Put a basket of tokens for the machines on your service counter or have each employee pass out tokens whenever they interact with a customer or upon request from a customer. Then let the customer cast his or her vote by putting the token in the Good Work or Bad Work machine. At the end of each shift or day, count the tokens, and calculate or plot the ratio to inform employees of how their customers viewed their work.

Benefits. Provides timely, relatively accurate information about how customers perceive the quality of service. Attracts employee attention since they need to participate in maintaining the system and educating customers in its use. Ought to lead to employee motivation to improve on the "gumball measure." Just make sure customers can cast their votes out of sight of employees!

been properly taught and coached. It sets them up for failure. You need to give them enough knowledge of their tasks to ensure that they can use feedback constructively.

To make sure you think this competence issue through, I recommend you use an activity from the Commitment-Based Leadership training materials I developed for HRD Press's line of training products: the Task Analysis Worksheet. It includes a form called the Task Planner, and I want you to look at the first section of this planning tool right now because it shows you what information you need to assemble in order to begin the process of assessing an individual's competency to perform a specific task.

TASK PLANNER

WHAT: (Define/describe the task)

____

____

____

____

____

WHY: (Relate the task to an important goal)

____

____

____

____

____

HOW: (Key skills/issues for performing task well)

____

____

____

____

____

When you answer the What, Why, and How questions for a specific task, you are preparing to manage for a peak task performance. These questions force you to clarify in your own mind what the task is, why it needs to be done, and how it should be done. Unless you think these questions through for at least a few minutes, you won't be ready to explain the task to someone or motivate him or her to do it.

It's amazing to me how often managers complain that employees don't seem to be highly motivated to do a task, but then admit upon being questioned that they can't explain why the task is important enough to justify high motivation. Make sure you know what, why, and how before you try to motivate someone to do it!

How competent are your employees on each of the specific skills or abilities the task requires?

Now that you've analyzed the task in question, you are ready to evaluate the individual employee's competence to perform this task. How competent are your employees on each of the specific skills or abilities the task requires? For example, take a very simple task, like answering phone calls from customers or clients. This task seems so simple that most managers don't bother analyzing it. They just say, "Will you answer the phones, please?" Then they get mad when incorrect messages are taken or customers aren't treated with proper respect or the employee is unable to answer simple questions like "What business are you in?" or "Do you know when Joe will be available to talk to me about this problem we've got with the last order you guys shipped us?"

In truth, handling customer calls requires a lot of competencies, such as:

- Sufficient knowledge of the business to answer questions appropriately and professionally.
- An ability to write down names and numbers 100 percent accurately.
- Excellent phone manners.
- Knowledge of who the important customers and prospects are and how to treat them.
- Knowledge of how routine calls should be handled.
- Knowledge of how problems should be handled.

- Knowledge of how your staff likes to have their phone calls handled (for example, do some not want to be disturbed ever, and others insist that they be interrupted whenever a client calls?).
- Technical knowledge of the phone systems (it's easy to vaporize a message or send a call into a dead end in modern phone systems if you aren't well trained!).
- An understanding of customers' expectations for how their calls will be handled, including an appreciation of the "norms" in the industry so as to know what will and won't frustrate them.

Like all tasks in business, answering the phone is more complex than it seems at first glance. Unless you analyze the competencies involved, you won't know whether an employee has sufficient competencies to succeed in this task.

Here is another form we use in the C-Lead trainings that is helpful in analyzing the competency requirements of any task and rating an employee on each of these competencies.

Unless you analyze the competencies involved, you won't know whether an employee has sufficient competencies to succeed in this task.

COMPETENCE DEVELOPMENT PLAN

THE TASK REQUIRES THE FOLLOWING SKILLS AND ABILITIES	DOES FOLLOWER NEED TO WORK ON THIS SKILL/ ABILITY?	
1. ______	Yes____	No____
2. ______	Yes____	No____
3. ______	Yes____	No____
4. ______	Yes____	No____
5. ______	Yes____	No____
6. ______	Yes____	No____
7. ______	Yes____	No____
8. ______	Yes____	No____
9. ______	Yes____	No____
10. ______	Yes____	No____

> Good leaders don't ask more than their constituents can give, but they often ask—and get—more than their constituents intended to give or thought was possible to give.
> —JOHN W. GARDNER

From this form, you can decide which things you need to teach the employee in order for him or her to succeed at the task. You can also decide whether the employee has enough competencies to be likely to succeed. If you've checked lots of No answers, then you can predict a pretty bad performance regardless of the employee's motivation level or any incentives you create. You can't succeed if you don't know how, no matter how motivated you are. If that's the problem, then you are able to diagnose it and you know that what you have is a task problem, not a person problem. It's not the person's motivation, its the job that's the problem. Maybe you should redefine the job.

For example, take that task I analyzed earlier–answering the telephone. If an employee lacks most of the competencies I listed, he or she is going to handle important customer calls poorly. Period. The employee needs to learn a lot before you entrust these most important calls to him or her. So why define the task so broadly? Break out this critical part from the rest of the calls that come in. Perhaps you'd do better to ask this employee to forward all calls from important clients to someone else with more experience, at least for the first few weeks until the employee gets a better foundation of knowledge about how the phone system works and what appropriate phone manners are.

I'm anticipating the second step, which is to modify the job to suit the employee. Let's go on to that step now.

Adjusting the Task

Once you have the detailed information about the task requirements and the employees' competencies, it will feel perfectly natural to adjust their work to make sure it is appropriate. You will be able to see how to structure tasks and goals appropriately so that they have a sufficient level of challenge to make their work highly rewarding and engaging for them.

Your role as a supervisor is *to design tasks, not assign tasks.* By customizing the task to the individual, you are able to make sure everyone is working at an appropriate level of challenge. Not too much nor too little. The idea is to make sure people aren't out of their depth. That sets them up for failure and attacks the emotional foundations of motivation. But nor should the tasks lack challenge, or they will be boring, which attacks the emotional foundations of motivation too by making the work seem meaningless and dull.

You need to make a judgment call as to how much of a new challenge will be motivational for the individual employee. Perhaps on average a "stretch goal" that asks about 10 percent more of them than they are currently giving is a good one. It should appear attainable, but challenging, to them. If the task demands 50 or 100 percent more of the employee, then you know the task must be broken down into smaller components and the employee given only one of these to start with. If the task is too easy in terms of the employee's level of competency–say it uses only 80 percent of their ability–then you know you need to enlarge the task to make it more personally challenging.

To get good at adjusting the tasks you assign your people to do, you can use the *chunking* and *grouping* techniques.

Chunking is breaking out pieces of a larger task to make smaller chunks of it. I gave an example earlier, in which I recommended chunking out the task of handling important client calls from the other phone duties of an office. This is an example of chunking by function. Those specific calls serve a specific function. Handling them is a whole unit of work, and so is handling the other calls that come in. Chunking by function is a good way to break out jobs into smaller tasks that you and the employee can focus harder on in the pursuit of excellence. Another example is to chunk out the job of retail sales clerk by assigning individual clerks to specific departments of a store, as many stores do.

You can also chunk by process instead of function. That's when you divide the work up into steps and give an employee a step instead of asking him or her to complete the whole task. This is commonly done on a production line, for example. In fact, most production lines chunk too much so that each employee is doing such a small, dull, repetitive chunk of the overall process that it is impossible for him or her to sustain high motivation. You could chunk the work of a retail sales clerk by assigning some clerks to handle only the register and others to handle stocking the floor and helping customers find what they want.

When preparing for each new competitive event, the athlete might be directed to strive for a personal goal that is 10 percent greater than before.

—ROBERT N. SINGER,
SPORTS PSYCHOLOGIST

The opposite of chunking is grouping. Grouping means combining two or more functional or process chunks into one task or job assignment. Grouping is a good idea when an employee is underchallenged by his or her tasks.

Another way to make tasks more challenging is to set higher performance goals for them. Quality, productivity, or other performance goals can be raised, which adds challenge for the employee. You can do this without changing the nature of the task if you think the task is adequately defined. In the next step, I'll show you some techniques for setting stretch goals with employees.

"Do better" is not a performance goal

Defining Feedback and Setting Goals

"Do better" is not a performance goal. Nor is "Do much better." Nor is "Be the best." Yet managers often state so-called goals like this. The reason these aren't goals is that they are not specific enough to be clearly relevant to performance. They set the employee up for a fall because they are low in task clarity. What does a manager expect when he or she says to do a good job? What's the manager's definition of good? What does he or she care about? Employees wrestle with these dilemmas every day, and they are generally pretty bad for motivation levels because you can never seem to guess quite right.

When the manager surprises the employee later by saying, "I told you to do a good job and look at the mess you've made of it," the employee is usually puzzled and hurt by the feedback. Why is it a bad job? The employee didn't *mean* to do a bad job. People don't go to work to do a bad job, as we observed in the first chapter. When they do, it's an unhappy accident for them and their supervisors. But saying, "Do a better job" is a controlling approach. It makes the employee dependent upon your judgment of what is good and bad, rather than making it clear enough that they trust their own judgment and know why you like some work better than other work.

So you need to define exactly what your performance goals are for the employee. Break it down. Be specific. Communicate in detail what your concerns and objectives are. For instance, what are the possible mistakes you want the employee to avoid when answering calls from important clients? What are the consequences of these mistakes? How will the employee know if he or she makes one of these mistakes? You can't take this kind of knowledge for granted when you assign tasks.

One great way to make sure the employee has appropriate performance goals is to set goals in a meeting with the employee so that you can discuss each one and make sure they make sense to both of you. Here is a methodology for participative goal setting that is also part of the C-Lead program.

PARTICIPATIVE GOAL SETTING

Consider negotiating the performance targets or goals with the employee. Here is a four-step process you can use:

1. Meet one on one to share your draft Task Plan with the employee, and ask the employee to evaluate it and let you know if there are parts that he or she finds unclear or inaccurate. Fix anything necessary, then ask the employee what performance targets or goals he or she can commit to. Listen to the employee's opinions and collaboratively negotiate a final set of performance goals. Make sure the employee agrees that the performance goals are reasonable.
2. Modify the worksheet or fill out a new copy to reflect the agreed-upon goals. If you like, both you and the employee can initial it to signify your agreement. Make a copy for your files and give the original to the employee.
3. Follow up by asking the employee to report progress toward each goal at regular intervals. Also make notes in your calendar to check with the employee if you haven't received a progress report. (Set the intervals based on the time frame of the project. Make sure you have at least four intervals for employees with low-to-moderate competence and/or commitment. Fewer reporting intervals are acceptable for high-commitment, high-competence employees.)

> Goals begin behaviors. Consequences maintain behaviors.
> —THE ONE MINUTE MANAGER

> To do some idiotic job very well is certainly not real achievement. What is not worth doing is not worth doing well.
>
> —ABRAHAM MASLOW

4. After the task is complete, meet again to see how well the plan worked out. Ask the employee for suggestions about how to improve the planning and goal-setting process next time, then remember to use any valuable suggestions in future task planning.

This four-step process is based on the Task Planner worksheet, which I excerpted earlier. I include a clean copy of the entire form as Figure 10-1 so that you can use it with your employees for goal setting.

Figure 10-1

TASK PLANNER

This worksheet will help you define a task well so that it is easy to explain and teach it, and so that the task itself is motivating. Use it to "rough out" a task description before assigning someone to the task. And also consider using it again for participative goal setting and follow-up.

WHAT: (Define/describe the task)

____

____

____

____

WHY: (Relate the task to an important goal)

____

____

____

____

HOW: (Key skills/issues for performing task well)

____

____

____

____

INDICATORS

Measure *Target or Goal/Date*

A. FEEDBACK PROVIDED BY LEADER

______________________________ ______/______

______________________________ ______/______

B. FEEDBACK PROVIDED BY TASK

______________________________ ______/______

______________________________ ______/______

______________________________ ______/______

C. FEEDBACK PROVIDED BY PERFORMER

______________________________ ______/______

______________________________ ______/______

Completion Date? ________

Note that the form includes room at the bottom to define different types of feedback and then set goals based on the feedback. For example, if you track customer satisfaction with some sort of periodic survey, you might make higher customer satisfaction scores a goal for an employee who interacts regularly with customers. (Just make sure there is task clarity, that the employee can see how his or her work affects the score.) Or you can use a productivity or quality indicator as a source of feedback and set a performance goal for it.

One of the best and simplest sources of feedback is *completion*. Setting a date for completing a project or a step of it makes your performance goal clear and measurable.

If you are worried an aggressive completion date will lead to poorly done work, then switch from completion to acceptance. Create some quality criteria (write a checklist you'll use later), and give these criteria to the employee up front. Tell the employee the project has to be acceptable by the required date according to the criteria in the checklist. Now you've incorporated quality concerns into the deadline, so it has to be not only done, but done well.

You may be puzzled by the three types of feedback the form in Figure 10-1 calls for. Feedback provided by the leader is what you tell them about the work. It's usually the simplest type to define and get started on. The example I gave earlier, in which you tell them when the work is good enough to be acceptable, is obviously a form of feedback provided by you. Also any ongoing verbal or written one-on-one feedback falls into this category. You can negotiate with them how often they want you to check in and give your opinion of how their work is going. Or you can just tell them you plan to give them some feedback each day or week, and that they should come and solicit that feedback if you haven't gotten around to it on schedule.

Tasks provide their own feedback to some extent. If you hit a nail with a hammer, you can see quite easily whether you gave it a good hit or whether you just dented the wood beside the nail. What are the types of feedback that are inherent to the task you are assigning?

Tasks provide their own feedback to some extent. If you hit a nail with a hammer, you can see quite easily whether you gave it a good hit or whether you just dented the wood beside the nail. What are the types of feedback that are inherent to the task you are assigning? If you are expert at the task, you know what to look for. You can get lots of useful feedback about how you are doing just by being sensitive to the feedback the task provides. For example, when speaking with a customer on the phone, you probably can tell if he or she is growing impatient or frustrated by his or her tone of voice. But will the inexperienced employee pick up on this important cue? Often not, unless you identify "tone of voice" and list it under the Feedback Provided by Task category on the Task Planner. But once you make it clear that they should pay attention to the caller's emotional state, you can teach employees to track it and try to achieve a record of 100 percent of all customer calls ending with customers sounding happy, not frustrated.

Feedback provided by the performer is often overlooked, too. But often it's the best type. The idea is to create systems and techniques whereby *the employee is able to evaluate his or her own performance*. Then when the employee wants to ask that all-important question, "How am I doing?" he or she doesn't have to depend upon you to answer it. The employee can just check for himself of herself.

The total quality movement can be thanked for putting this type of feedback on the management agenda. When you train employees to measure a sample of the parts they are producing at a workstation and plot them on a control chart, they are providing their own feedback. If they see that the machine is getting out of adjustment, they can adjust it. They are collecting and reacting to their own informative feedback. If it's positive, they keep going. If it's negative, they take corrective action.

Often, all you need to give employees are some simple yes–no questions.

Now, lots of people assume that this simple concept from the field of statistical process control is hard to apply to nonproduction jobs. Without complex machines and engineering specifications, what use is a complex control chart system? None. But that actually means it's far easier to apply the concept, not harder. Often, all you need to give employees are some simple yes–no questions. A checklist they can look at as they work. No need for calculating moving averages or standard deviations. Just a simple check against some clear criteria to see if they are doing it well or poorly. A simple scoreboard they can post their own scores on as they play. So don't overlook the possibility of developing systems for the employee to provide some of his or her own feedback.

Aerial Combat at Ford Motor Credit

Imagine winning a sales contest and being sent to aerial-combat flying school. That's what employees from eight Ford dealerships did. They attended Fighter Pilots USA, a combat-flying school in Chicago that uses simulators to create a compelling combat experience. The program, called Top Gun Incentive Awards, briefs the group the night before, then puts people into cockpits with trained F-16 fighter pilots. Disney and other companies have used the program, too, and participants find it a highly memorable experence.

Analysis. The thing I like about this case is that the participants experienced a new and difficult challenge, and were able to rise to it (no pun intended). Most people rightly view flying an F-16 in combat as a difficult and challenging task, even a scary one. By proving to themselves that they can do it, they get a real emotional boost that carries over to other challenges in work and life. (In psychological terms, it builds self-efficacy.) Personally, I'm not that keen on shooting down airplanes, so I might prefer another challenge. Maybe rock climbing, a ropes course, or an Outward Bound adventure. Any difficult personal challenge will do, as long as it seems a little intimidating and a lot exciting, so that you get a real sense of pride and accomplishment when you succeed. And I might consider opening the opportunity to others, not just the top performers, since the benefits should be noticeable in anyone's job performance. Some companies use such experiences almost like rites of passage, as part of new employee orientation or team-building efforts. The real reward in all these adventures is the sense of accomplishment in the face of severe challenge. And that's a reward you want to hook your people on early and often, so that they will seek the same reward in their daily work.

Quantifying Performance Goals (Please Do!)

I've walked you through a careful three-step process for defining tasks and selecting appropriate types of feedback and goals. The feedback should be measurable in some way, shape, or form so that you can easily define performance goals. Even if the feedback is just your opinion–negative or positive feedback in the form of a quick note, for example–you can still make it into a quantifiable measure.

For example, you can say:

> **"I'll give you my opinion on how this work is going each day, and I want you to track the number of positive and negative responses I give you. At the end of twenty days, I think it's a reasonable goal for you to have no more than five negative responses since that will indicate that I'm pleased with the results of your work 75 percent of the time. Do you think you can achieve that goal?"**

There is always a way to quantify the performance goal and track it on a chart.

Then you could suggest 90 percent positive versus 10 percent negative feedback for the next twenty-day period, and so on. Or you could just have the employee accumulate feedback notes from you and work out the ratio each time he or she receives ten or twenty.

There is always a way to quantify the performance goal and track it on a chart. In the example I just gave, you are quantifying the most difficult type of feedback to keep track of: personal, informal feedback based on supervisor judgment. If that can be quantified and tracked and used to create performance goals, then anything can!

The Difference Between Motivation and Manipulation

Here is one of the most common pitfalls in all of management. You think you are motivating your people. But they think you are manipulating them.

Take the case of an employee I interviewed to evaluate some new incentives a manager had introduced to her department. The incentives were straightforward rewards and recognition of the type used in thousands of companies. So I was shocked to discover that this employee had a strong, negative emotional reaction to the new system.

She couldn't explain exactly why, but she knew the rewards were "insulting." She felt that the manager "treats us like children" and "doesn't respect our intelligence." Her feelings were echoed by other employees, too. Obviously, the manager's well-meaning efforts to motivate employees had backfired badly and were threatening to poison the motivation well for a long time to come.

I haven't described the reward system in detail because it wasn't the problem. Changing it didn't help. The problem was that the manager was manipulating instead of motivating. And this problem had its roots in *how managers set performance goals* for employees. It is all about the task and how it is presented, not about the rewards and incentives.

Here's what I discovered in this case. The employees did not really understand what the manager was looking for. They received a lot of confusing and contradictory messages about what he expected of them. The goals were unclear, the rules of the game unpredictable. So when he told them he would reward them for certain things, they felt it was manipulative and dishonest, not motivational.

The goals were unclear, the rules of the game unpredictable. So when he told them he would reward them for certain things, they felt it was manipulative and dishonest, not motivational.

For example, this manager was eager to get more ideas and suggestions from employees. He had learned (probably by reading books on motivation!) to tell employees he valued their ideas. And he had instituted some rewards to give out to recognize good ideas from employees. Sounds okay, except...

Employees said that he "didn't really mean it" when he asked for their input. They cited many cases in which their input had been ignored by him, and other cases in which he had failed to pass their good ideas along to his superiors. So sometimes he liked their ideas–they thought it was only when they were his ideas, too–and other times he ignored them. When the recognition arrived, then, employees were cynical about it. They felt he was trying to manipulate the situation and create the illusion of a participatory workplace. They figured it was just supposed to make him look good to his superiors.

To prevent your efforts at motivation from becoming manipulation, make sure you think all the likely outcomes through in advance so *you* won't be surprised by what happens.

They were being manipulated to help him accomplish his personal goals, and they resented that deeply. People love to be motivated, but they hate being manipulated!

How can you avoid this trap? How can you make sure your feedback and incentives don't feel like manipulation to others? I'm raising the issue here in the chapter on tasks and goals because they hold the key. *You need to define tasks and set goals clearly, in advance.* They are the ground rules of the performance, and they have to be clear and fair to avoid the manipulation trap.

If you think about it, manipulation simply means making people do something they didn't know about or didn't agree to up front. If employees ever say, or even feel like saying, "But you didn't tell us that . . ." or "Hey, how could we know that . . .?" then you have manipulated them in their eyes. You are no better than a con man tricking them into something they didn't understand up front. And con men motivate people to do something only once. The mark will never do it again after discovering the trick. So you can see why it is essential to avoid the appearance of manipulation.

To prevent your efforts at motivation from becoming manipulation, make sure you think all the likely outcomes through in advance so *you* won't be surprised by what happens. You can't make it clear to them until it's clear to you!

That manager who turned off his employees with his requests for ideas and input made this mistake. He didn't think through the options. He got some feedback he was prepared to use, but a lot of other feedback he didn't expect and didn't know what to do with. For instance, employee suggestions that were relevant to another manager's turf were hard for him to deal with because he hadn't negotiated a way to pass them on before he started his program. As a result of his failure to think it through, he overpromised to his employees. He was unable to act on many of their suggestions, and it ended up looking to them as though he didn't value their ideas and was just doing it for show. He should have defined the areas in which he was prepared to act and asked for ideas only in those areas.

Please make as much use of the goal-setting and task design methods in this chapter as you can. If you think about it, an appropriately designed task and clear, agreed-upon performance goals and measures take much of the uncertainty out of what you are asking them to do and rewarding them for doing:

- *Clear goals* ensure that people are aware of what you expect them to do.
- One-to-one *goal-setting sessions* ensure that people have agreed to the goals and measures of their performance.

If you use these two techniques, then your efforts to get them to do what you want will seem motivational, not manipulative.

Setting Realistic Expectations for Change

One reason managers have difficulty building motivation for their goals is that they simply have *too many goals*. They are trying to accomplish so many things at once that it is not realistic to expect employees to buy into them. No one could be highly motivated to do that many things at once.

One reason managers have difficulty building motivation for their goals is that they simply have *too many goals*.

The motivation path requires focus and is fueled by employee absorption in challenging, engaging tasks. If you get somebody going on an interesting challenge, then interrupt the employee to ask him or her to tackle another one, then interrupt again, well, you've pretty much spoiled any motivation those tasks might have engendered. But that is just what many companies are doing to their employees these days.

Businesses experiment with new management methods in a bolder and more constant manner than ever before. Total quality management (TQM) arguably started this trend, as Japanese companies showed auto and electronics giants from the United States and Europe that new management methods could more than substitute for experience and economies of scale. But in a survey I performed to track U.S. management methods, I was startled to find that most respondents said their firms were engaged in not just TQM or engineering or just-in-time management or teaming, but *all* these, and usually another handful or two as well.

This was not true eight or ten years ago, when the majority of midsized and large companies reported that they had TQM processes

Hiring Motivated People at Intel

Intel's incentive programs are focused on "rewarding individual excellence" according to the company's policies. And this emphasis is especially helpful in recruiting motivated individuals who want to excel and are looking for a company that will reward them for excellent performance. Intel's approach to hiring, according to its Jobs at Intel Web site, is to "hire people that we believe will help make Intel successful." And, the site goes on to explain, "We share that success with our employees." Specifically, Intel's recruiting materials make the following points about their employee reward programs (I've summarized these statements and left out the legal qualifications):

Bonus programs. Intel has two bonus programs based on company and business unit performance that reward their employees for their contributions. (They include a profit-sharing plan called the Employee Cash Bonus Program that is based on financial performance of the company and the employee's business group.)

Stock programs. The Stock Option Program gives employees shares based on their past performance levels and anticipated future performance levels. There is also a Stock Participation Plan in which employees can buy additional shares at a discount.

Awards. According to recruiting information, "Outstanding performance by individuals and organizations is recognized and encouraged through Intel's awards programs. Awards range from formal recognition at the corporate level to spontaneous employee-to-employee awards presented at the department level."

The point of telling potential Intel employees about the reward programs is to make it clear that performance-based rewards "may add significantly to your compensation package" as the recruiting materials put it. And that means applicants will tend to self-select. Those who feel confident in their abilities and willing to take responsibility for earning rewards will see Intel as a place where they can succeed. Those who are looking for a comfortable berth will get the message that Intel is not for them and may not even bother to apply. As a result, applicants will tend to have high internal motivation. And if you hire people who are driven to succeed, you won't have to work nearly as hard to motivate them. The challenge then is simply to avoid spoiling their motivation and drive. Get out of their way and watch them perform!

Analysis. The theory behind Intel's recruiting approach is a sound one, but there is one major pitfall to beware of: the control over results issue. Will the best candidates feel that you are offering them enough *personal control over their rewards*, or will they worry that poor performance of the company as a whole might counter their own good performance and reduce their rewards? An emphasis on rewards tied to companywide performance suggests individuals won't have sufficient control over their own bonuses to make them truly motivating. Intel's programs are generous, but they emphasize stock performance, and in a company that big most employees won't have much control over the performance of the stock, no matter how good they are or how hard they try. On the other hand, some relationship between individual rewards and company performance makes sense since it aligns employee and employer interests.

So a balance is needed, in which some parts of the bonus package are tied to individual performances that the company believes are key to overall performance. Other aspects of the bonus package can be more general. In fact, a hierarchical structure in which, say, a third of the bonus is directly based on the individual's performance, a third on the business unit's performance, and a third on the company's overall performance might make the most sense. Then the high performer shopping for a new job will see your company as a place where he or she is assured of at least some of that generous bonus plan, and can hope to earn all of it in good years as well. ▣

in place but not much else. Now senior managers seem to feel they must try everything, all at once and constantly, in the hope of hitting a great many home runs simultaneously.

According to a *Training Magazine* survey of more than a thousand U.S. firms, the following initiatives are commonplace in U.S. firms:

MANAGEMENT INITIATIVE	PERCENT OF RESPONDENTS
Total quality management	58
Development of an organizational vision	51
Transition to teams-based structure	44
"Partnering" with suppliers or customers	34
Downsizing	31
Reengineering	31
Increasing use of temporary workers	20
Increasing use of outsourcing	14

They get a similar result to mine although they asked about different types of initiatives. Mergers and acquisitions, new production technologies, new information systems, relocations of facilities to take advantage of cheaper labor, and other changes also occur periodically. There are obviously a lot of new things in the wind in most every company. My best estimate is that the average company is working on six or seven major companywide initiatives at any one time.

With an average of six major new initiatives in companies at any single moment, we're talking about some very busy managers and a great many concurrent changes for employees.

What the trend toward concurrent change programs means is a kind of self-imposed constant turmoil. But if there is any benefit from even one of those simultaneous change initiatives, then companies have to join the fray to avoid being left in the dust. Rather like an arms race, the management innovation race cannot be easily called off once it is under way. So I can't in good conscience advise you to drop any major initiatives in order to solve the problem of building motivation to other initiatives. Somehow, you must now motivate employees not only to do their job better, but to accept and contribute to change after change, initiative after initiative. The motivation problem is getting bigger as we struggle to adopt new strategies and practices in business. The faster pace of change within companies demands a constant redirection of employees.

Though I probably can't get you to bring your company's mad embrace of each new fad under control, I can certainly convince you to introduce as much focus as you can *within your own span of control.* Supervisors have to play the role of buffers for their people sometimes. You know what the company wants from you and your employees in the long run is simply good results, and you know you need to have a focused, motivated, happy work force to produce them. So pick your winners and try to duck as many distractions and disruptions as you can. Keep your ear tuned to the pacing of work and change in your group. Don't let outsiders disrupt a productive, healthy rhythm once you get one going. You know better than anyone else how much change your people can handle at any one time. Try to balance the external demands with the realities of human performance. It's a tough job, but someone's got to do it!

You know better than anyone else how much change your people can handle at any one time.

Parting Shots

In this chapter, I've asked you to check that what looks like a motivation problem isn't really a job problem instead. If all those darn employees keep messing up, maybe it's not them, but their jobs. You don't want to overlook the way you define and assign tasks or how you set goals for performance. These are factors that are outside your employees' heads and well within your control. So control them. It's a simple way to get more out of your people by making sure their tasks and goals are well designed and well assigned.

There is a strong link between feedback and goal setting. Or should be. If you are setting goals for employees in a vague, abstract manner, then you are setting the employees up for failure because they won't have accurate feedback to track their performances against those goals.

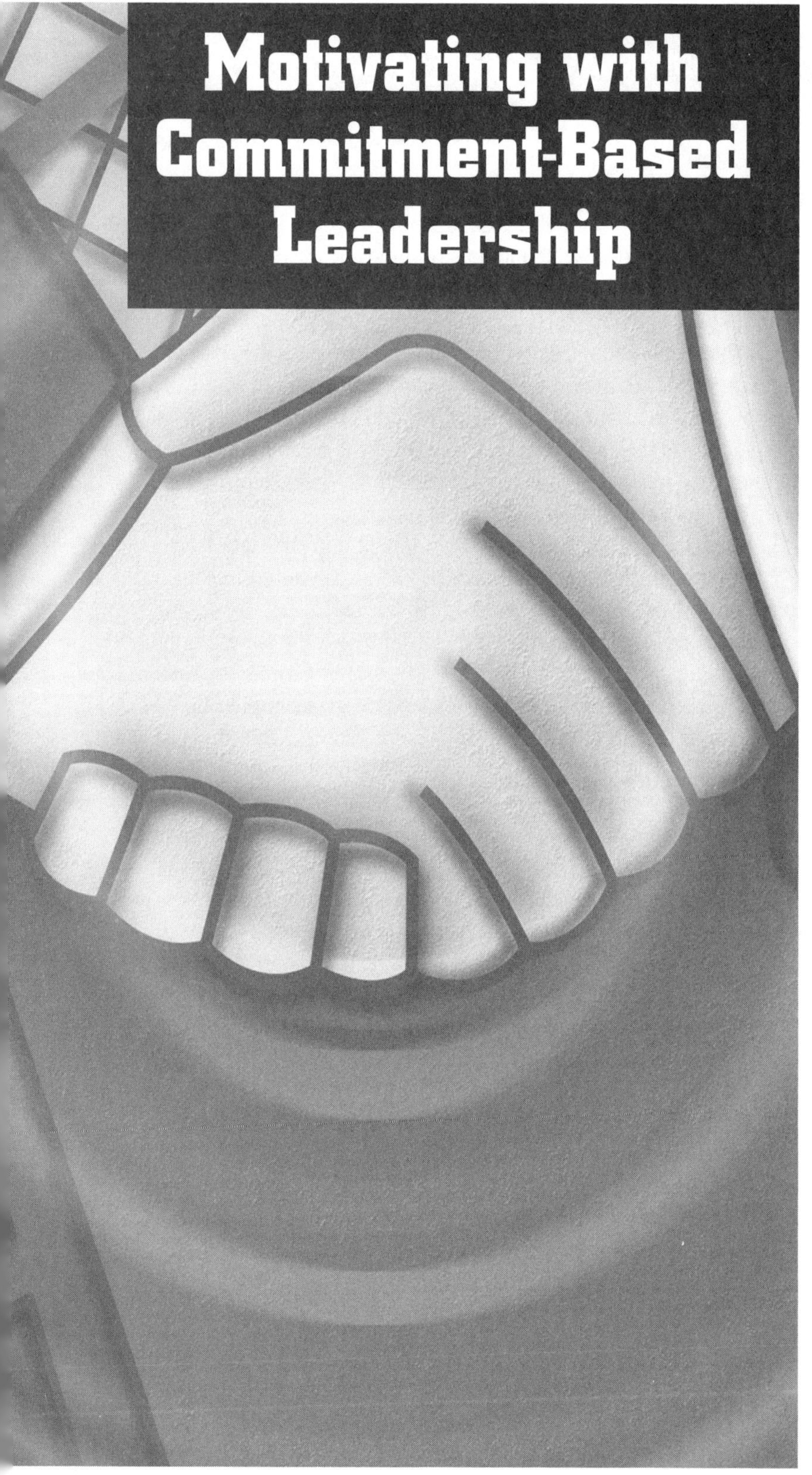

Motivating with Commitment-Based Leadership

Chapter 11

When you decide to pursue the motivation path instead of the resistance path, you begin a rewarding journey with your employees. You focus on motivating your employees by encouraging them to develop and grow in their work, by offering them opportunities in which they can pursue stretch goals and do more meaningful and challenging tasks. You make sure their feedback is accurate, frequent, informative, and not weighted toward bad news. If necessary, you simplify their tasks to make sure they have more successes than failures. That way they will get more positive than negative feedback, and this will encourage them to feel good about their work and strive for greater successes.

When you provide the right environment and the right feedback, employees then use this feedback like a scoreboard to challenge themselves to "play better" and try harder in their work.

This concept of motivation is consistent with the views of highly motivated people we captured in the first chapter, people who are deeply engaged in personal challenges, and experiencing the flow of absorption in meaningful work. It is also consistent with our visual image of what true motivation looks like–that photograph by Ken Kipen of the boy racing down the dock. It is easier to comprehend why people most often have these highly motivated and memorable experiences outside work now that we have looked at so many aspects of management behavior and job design. In truth, the typical approach to management is *not* consistent with high motivation. It shouldn't work, based on everything we've reviewed about motivation in this book. And it doesn't.

Instead of being highly motivated, employees are struggling to persist against emotional resistance. It's an uphill struggle for them to do the work, and an uphill struggle for us to make them do it.

Instead of being highly motivated, employees are struggling to persist against emotional resistance. It's an uphill struggle for them to do the work, and an uphill struggle for us to make them do it.

When we add rewards, awards, bonuses, recognition, and other incentives to perform, we can tip the balance for a while and boost motivation and performance. But to the extent that these levers over performance have as their fulcrum an external source of motivation, we are simply pushing harder against a natural resistance to peak performance. As a result, managers struggle and their people struggle. Managers go out and buy books like this one in the hope that there is a better way. Employees fantasize about a whole new career that is more meaningful and rewarding.

If you are willing to embrace the motivation path and turn your back to the resistance path, you can find a new and better alternative for yourself and your people. It's a far more rewarding and productive pathway for supervisor and supervised alike. It is an approach to leading your people that builds and profits from their commitment rather than your authority. Your success is the result of your investment in their commitment. What you are doing when you walk the motivation path is providing commitment-based leadership to your people.

Commitment-Based Leadership

The commitment-based leadership method is based on a model of how people reach peak performance levels. It portrays peak performances as resting on a foundation of high commitment, combined with a solid superstructure of competence. Commitment and competence, but commitment first, or high competence will never be pursued and acquired. The commitment-based leadership method is therefore a practical how-to approach to motivating and managing employees on the motivation path.

I developed the commitment-based leadership model and training methodology over a lengthy period of study and practice. I've produced a variety of teaching tools based on it, including an electronic course for the Internet (published by UOL Inc.) and the Commitment-Based Leadership line of assessment and training products (published by HRD Press). I've also tested the method and training tools with a wide variety of people at small and large businesses, schools, and nonprofits. This experience has been a wonderful one for me since it's allowed me to meet many enthusiastic managers and observe their efforts to achieve high levels of employee commitment firsthand. I have great admiration for those who manage in this inspirational style and also a firm conviction that it is a practical and rewarding alternative to traditional styles for those who wish to pursue it.

I have great admiration for those who manage in this inspirational style.

You need to recognize three levels of employee commitment and how they develop so that you can nurture them.

The C-Lead approach incorporates much of what I've already covered in this book. The approach to feedback and rewards I've described is completely consistent with C-Lead's methodology. And C-Lead relies on the kinds of interpersonal skills and understanding of employee needs and motives that this book addresses. So in a sense you as a reader are better prepared for using the C-Lead approach than anyone else! It should not be difficult for you to become a commitment-based leader.

To do so, you simply need to learn a little more about the nature of motivation. You need to recognize three levels of employee commitment and how they develop so that you can nurture them. And you need to review the eight C-Lead styles. Leadership styles are specific ways of interacting with your employees. It's obvious to any intelligent manager that you can't treat your people the same way all the time. And you can't treat different people identically even at the same moment in time. Different people have different needs. The C-Lead styles give you a simple way to define their needs and address them in a professional leadership role. And these styles are designed to develop motivation and commitment to the highest level possible in a workplace setting, so by using them you will have little difficulty in staying on the motivation path.

To "bring you up to speed" on how to be a C-Lead manager, I'm going to divide the rest of this chapter into two sections. First, I'll review the development levels of the C-Lead model. This involves one new wrinkle for you: the recognition of several different forms of employee commitment and the need to develop and nurture each in turn in order to achieve highly motivated performances. The second part of the chapter will address the specific styles you may use in order to accomplish this goal.

But first I want to clarify the distinction between the words *motivation* and *commitment* to the extent that there is one. Many people use the terms interchangeably, as in "my people just don't seem motivated" and "my people just don't seem committed." When someone doesn't perform well and seems indifferent to making significant improvements, it's safe to say he or she is neither motivated nor committed. Whereas when someone is performing at peak levels, his or her motivation and commitment must be high. So the two terms are interchangeable in those instances.

But it is also possible to have motivation without commitment or to have commitment without motivation. Take the case of someone who, in the heat of first love, made strong vows of loyalty to a lover. The vows represent a firm commitment that, when it was initially coupled with motivation, felt very comfortable to the inspired lover. But what happens if the love fades and the lover no longer feels that same strong motivation? The commitment lingers but now, lacking motivation to support it, is difficult to sustain.

Employees make a commitment to work hard for the betterment of their employers. That's implied if not stated from the day they begin their jobs. And, often, the employees are eager to get to work and excited about their new jobs, so they have plenty of motivation to back up that commitment. But the motivation often fades in the light of inappropriate management behavior, poorly defined tasks, and other problems such as we have reviewed in this book. Then the employee is left with a hollow commitment, one that is difficult to pursue with much vigor. The employee–employer relationship is on the rocks, and may stay that way for many years. These employees who have hollow commitment without real motivation are on the resistance path, not the motivation path.

In contrast, commitment-based leadership seeks to build genuine commitment based on a strong motivation to perform. My dictionary gives two distinct meanings for the word *commitment*. They are, first, an agreement or pledge to do something in the future, and second, the state of being emotionally compelled. It is this second meaning of commitment that is most compelling and durable in the workplace. When employees feel compelled by their own emotional and intellectual commitment, then you see high and lasting levels of commitment to the work at hand. That's the objective of commitment-based leadership, and it should be the objective of every manager. You don't get someone to give a task his or her all by tricking the person into making a verbal or written commitment to do so. You stimulate that level of motivation only by generating real, durable emotional commitment to the work.

When employees feel compelled by their own emotional and intellectual commitment, then you see high and lasting levels of commitment to the work at hand.

Now let's look at the nature of commitment to work and how you can build it up in your employees. (My treatment follows the *Leader's Handbook & Guide for Commitment-Based Leadership* published by HRD Press.)

What Is Commitment?

Commitment is defined in C-Lead as a strong motive or desire to do something. Commitment can come from outside us or within, but is stronger and more sustainable when it comes from within. C-Lead methods are designed to build the kind of commitment that comes from within so that employees will feel a strong urge to accomplish, perform, and learn.

The workplace or other leadership setting must be one in which the employee feels good about performing.

Most leadership methods treat commitment simplistically—someone is either committed or not. But in real life, commitment is made up of several layers, each of which has to be present to ensure the motivation of the employee. Let's look at each one.

The First Layer: Participation Commitment

First, the employee must feel good about participating in "the game," the situation itself. The workplace or other leadership setting must be one in which the employee feels good about performing. Otherwise, the employee won't want to "play the game" in the first place.

Imagine a playing field dotted with dangerous, hard-to-see holes. Would you play soccer or baseball on it? Not unless you didn't mind the risk of a sprained ankle!

Or, how about a playing field that is so small anyone can easily hit a home run or score a goal? Here, too, you might not be enthusiastic about performing, but this time because it's too easy and boring, not because it's too risky.

The playing field in these examples represents the context in which leadership and "follower-ship" are supposed to take place. Some workplaces seem like dangerous playing fields to employees. Others are like toy playing fields where it's so easy to win that there isn't any point to play. Either way, the leader needs to fix the playing field before he or she can recruit a team and teach the team members their positions. Until you have the right sort of playing field, there is no point in saying, "Let's play ball!" Nobody will want to come out on the field with you.

To put this concept in psychological terms, the leader needs to make sure that employees feel *the right level of challenge*. Not too much, and not too little. We all perform best when there is a reasonable chance of success, but also enough chance of failure in our eyes to make the game worthwhile. A normal playing field creates a context for the game in which players who play hard have a reasonable chance of scoring. So should the normal workplace.

To put this concept in psychological terms, the leader needs to make sure that employees feel *the right level of challenge*.

Figure 11-1 shows how participation commitment works. When employees feel too low a level of challenge, they are bored and complacent. They will never be fully committed to the game. When employees feel too much challenge, they are fearful and preoccupied with survival. Only when the level of challenge feels right for them will they be ready to commit.

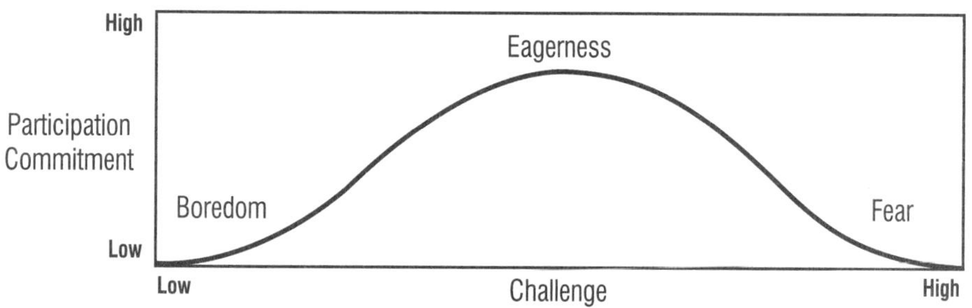

Figure 11-1

In commitment-based leadership, leaders check the level of challenge their employees feel and, if necessary, adjust that level to an optimal point. They challenge employees who are bored, and they reassure employees who are fearful. When employees are eager to participate, then the leader moves on to the next layer of commitment.

When the employee's heart and mind are fully engaged, then high commitment is possible.

The Second Layer: Cause Commitment

Next, the player must feel committed to *winning* the game. Is it a game they like? One they want to win? Did anyone even tell them what game they were playing?

The second layer of commitment is called cause commitment. It concerns the employee's desire to accomplish the leader's goal or pursue the leader's cause. When employees believe the destination is a good one, they are much more willing to commit to the journey.

Figure 11-2 shows the key components of cause commitment. Full commitment requires the "whole-brain" support of the employee. When the employee's heart and mind are fully engaged, then high commitment is possible. And so leaders need to give employees the rational arguments and information behind the plan, and to help them feel good about the goal, too.

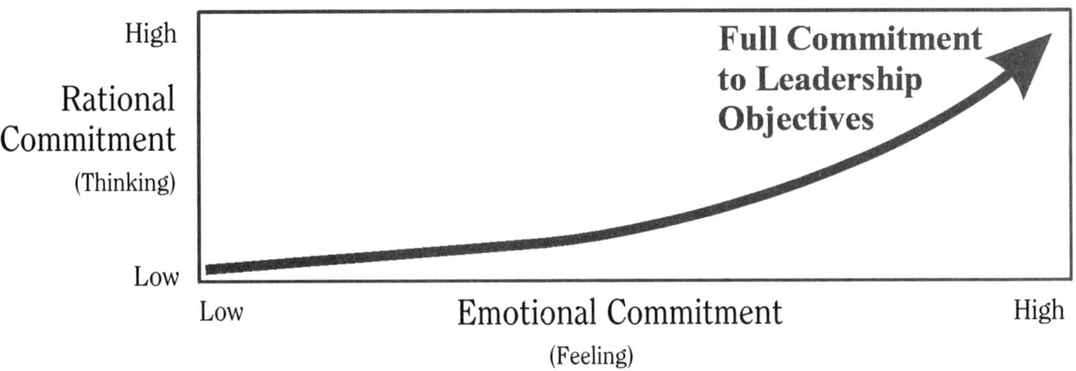

Figure 11-2

In commitment-based leadership, leaders inform employees who are not rationally supportive of the plan or goal. And they empathize with employees who are not emotionally supportive in order to better understand the employees' feelings and relate those feelings to the goals. By so doing, leaders build cause commitment in a natural, easy way over time.

The Third Layer: Task Commitment

Imagine a soccer player who has high participation commitment–she wants to get out there and learn the game. And she has high cause commitment–she "gets" the point of the game and is eager to help her team score goals. So far, so good. She is a committed beginner.

But what happens when her coach says, "go out there and follow that fast player from the other team. That's all I want you to do. Just stay near that player all the time. Don't try to chase the ball or score, just stick to her like glue."

If she is like most novice and intermediate soccer players, she will do a poor job of it. She won't stay near the person she was asked to mark, at least not all the time. She'll get tired and lag behind, or she'll get distracted and run after the ball. The reason is that she won't understand why her job is important to winning the game. She will lack commitment to the specific task she was given. And without task commitment, her high participation and cause commitment will not translate into a good performance.

Task commitment is a strong motivation to do your part, your specific task. It arises only when you are able to understand your task clearly.

To return to our earlier example, the coach needs to tell the soccer player that she must shadow the other team's "play maker" so that this player won't be open for passes, and therefore won't be able to set up scoring opportunities for the other team. Once the reason is made clear, the player will be able to see why the apparently dull task of shadowing someone is vitally important to the goal of winning the game. Her task will come to life in her mind and become highly motivating. She will gain task commitment.

In C-Lead, we use the term *line of sight* to describe the employee's view of his or her task. There needs to be a clear line of sight to the cause and also to the task itself. When both are in clear

Task commitment is a strong motivation to do your part, your specific task. It arises only when you are able to understand your task clearly.

view, then the participation and cause commitment can translate to task commitment.

View to cause is the employee's view from his or her task to the overarching purpose–the cause or goal. Employees who already are committed to a goal are willing to commit to tasks that have a clear view to the goal. The leader simply needs to clear that line of sight by helping the employee see why the task is important.

There is one other aspect of task commitment, as Figure 11-3 illustrates. It is called *view to task*, and it is defined as the employee's ability to see how well he or she is *performing* an important task. It is the line of sight in the other direction, from the employee to the task instead of from the task up to the goal. When employees get plenty of clear, useful, timely feedback about their task performance, then they have the view to task needed for high task commitment. (This is the task clarity I described in Chapter 7.)

Unfortunately, leaders must often hand out task assignments that do not explain themselves.

The apparently thankless task of shadowing a star player from the other team is an easy one to "see" from a view-to-task perspective. Either you do or you don't manage to stick close to that player and prevent her from receiving passes. If you drift too far away, she will get into the play and you will know right away that you goofed. Thus (to return to our soccer example again), the coach need not worry too much about view to task when she assigns a player the job of shadowing another player. The task *explains itself* quite clearly.

Unfortunately, leaders must often hand out task assignments that do not explain themselves. As a result, leaders may need to provide direct feedback or (better yet) give the employee the tools and skills needed to generate accurate feedback about their own performance. (To make it easier for the soccer player in my example to track her performance, the coach could just tell her to keep count of the number of times that star she's shadowing touches the ball. The lower the better. That's an example of empowering the individual to track her own performance using a feedback measure she can do on her own.) Creating a clear view to task is an important leadership role.

In commitment-based leadership, leaders check that employees understand their tasks by checking the line of sight. They make sure the view to cause and view to task are clear. If not, they explain the purpose of the task, and they make sure there is plenty of good performance feedback, too. The result is high commitment to task.

A simple way to think about the leader's role in raising task commitment is to remember that the leader needs to explain the *whats, whys,* and *hows* of the task. And don't forget that "How am I doing?" is the most important how of all!

Figure 11-3

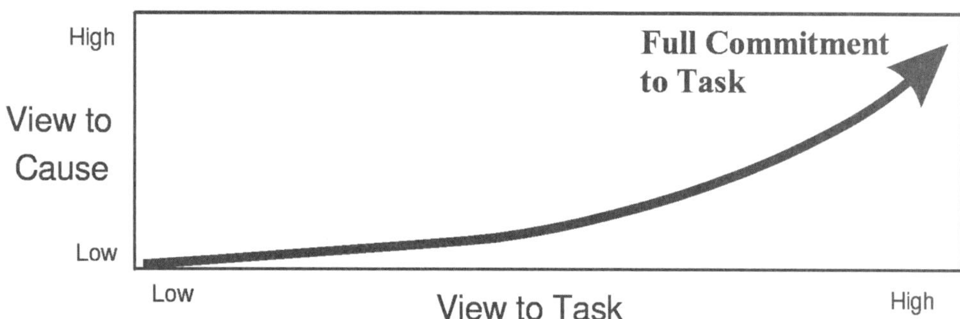

Full Performance Commitment

Employees have full commitment when (and only when) they are eager to participate, they are motivated to accomplish the goal, they understand why their task is important, and they are able to see how well they perform that task. Such employees are ready and eager to perform. In fact, it is hard to keep them *off* the playing field.

But will they win the game? Not necessarily, because winning takes more than a desire to win. It also takes some skill. So competence is the next concern of the commitment-based leader who has made sure that all three levels of commitment are in place.

People learn best and perform best when they are given the right experience and the right information.

Competence is ability to perform a task well. Which sounds simple, and in a sense it is. But when you look closely at ability, you find that it is a combination of the right experience and the right information. People learn best and perform best when they are given the right experience and the right information. In commitment-based leadership, competence is defined as *ability to perform at a high level as a result of the right experience and information.* In Chapter 10, I gave you some methods from the C-Lead training materials for assessing employee competence. These tools help you define the necessary skills and information, and decide whether you need to give employees more information and training before they have sufficient competence to perform a task. And in Chapter 3, we explored the issue of how to provide open communication to your employees. This approach helps ensure that they receive enough information to achieve high competence levels.

Once you have a solid foundation of commitment, you can work on building up competence

Over time, employees with high commitment will develop their own competencies, continually seeking insights into how to do their job better. If they lack the foundation of high commitment on all three levels, then they will not take strong interest in self-development. You will be frustrated with their lack of passion for competency development. So commitment is really the key to high levels of competence in your work force.

Once you have a solid foundation of commitment, you can work on building up competence from low to medium and eventually to high levels. During this development process, you can often set your motivational hat aside and focus more on the acquisition and development of skills. You can play the role of a guide, helping the employee on his or her journey up the motivation path to high levels of skill and superb performances.

Now that you understand the general framework of the commitment-based leadership model, you will be able to appreciate the specific styles in which C-Lead leaders are trained. They are the subject of the final section of this chapter, and each corresponds to one of the components of commitment-based leadership: participation commitment, cause commitment, task commitment, and task competence (see Figure 11-4).

How Do You Use the C-Lead Styles?

Each of the C-Lead styles is a natural approach to leadership, and so you are probably already familiar with all of them. In fact, you've probably behaved toward your employees in ways that are consistent with each of these styles although you might not have recognized at the time that you were using a specific leadership style. Read the

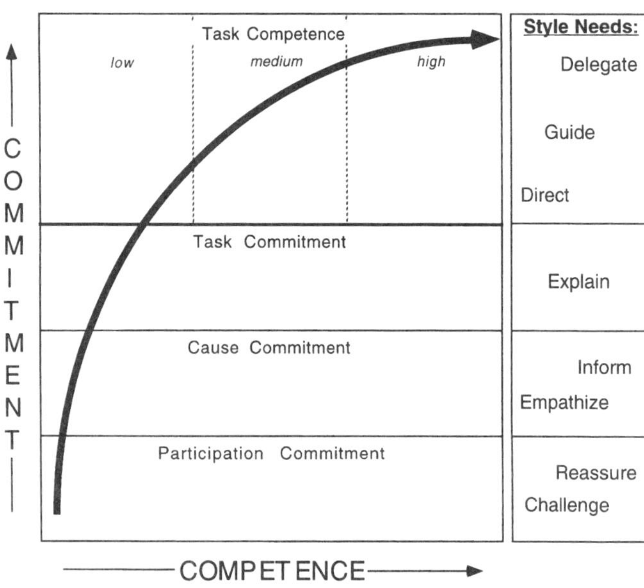

Figure 11-4

short descriptions of each style to get a quick feel for what the style is. Then check out the style's orientation to get a feel for the underlying principles that drive the style.

Each style has a basic orientation toward building commitment or toward building competence. For instance, reassuring anxious employees helps build participation commitment, so the reassure style is commitment oriented. It is helpful to keep in mind the orientation of a style so you will know what the goals of using it are. When a style is commitment oriented, your goal is to build the follower's commitment level as you use this style.

> Each style also has a basic orientation toward the person or toward the task.

Each style also has a basic orientation toward the person or toward the task. People-oriented styles work on goals for your people. They focus on how the person thinks and feels about the work and the situation. As you've seen throughout this book, how your people think and feel is the key to how motivated they are, so this people orientation is just as important as an orientation toward

You need to keep in mind the appropriate orientation and to pursue leadership goals appropriate to that orientation.

the work that needs to be done, and half of the C-Lead styles are focused on people concerns rather than task concerns. Task-oriented styles focus on getting the job done. For instance, directive leadership involves showing and telling someone how to do a job. The direct style of leadership is therefore task oriented, and when you use it, your goal is to get the task done.

In contrast, the guide style is people oriented because the leader is thinking about how best to guide the follower's personal development of task-related skills. The leader's goal when using the guide style is therefore to help the follower learn, grow, and develop to a higher level of performance. The task is just a means toward this end.

In order to use a C-Lead style correctly, you need to keep in mind the appropriate orientation and to pursue leadership goals appropriate to that orientation. In the descriptions of each style that follow, you will find a key to the orientation of each style, as well as examples of appropriate leadership goals for you to adopt as you use that style.

In addition, the write-ups of each leadership style include a text section that gives you detailed descriptions of what the style is like and how it can be used. For a richer, more detailed picture of a style in action, study these detailed descriptions.

Reassure

Help follower cope with the stresses and challenges of work life by being supportive.

Orientations: Commitment (vs. competence). People (vs. task).

Goals: Build commitment to participating in the current situation by reducing anxiety and fear. Help people feel better. Give them a reasonable hope of "winning" in the current situation in spite of the problems they may face.

Detailed description of the reassure style

Your followers are anxious and under too much stress to focus on task learning or productivity goals. They see great risks or danger in the current situation and worry that they will not be able to take care of themselves properly. Perhaps changes have been too swift or big, and their resiliency is used up. Or perhaps things seem to happen randomly so that they no longer trust the situation to reward good or poor performance fairly. Help them gain a sense of self-control to overcome this insecurity they feel. They need to have their fears addressed. They need to be reassured and "secured" before they can refocus on task performance.

Your goal is to reduce their anxiety to a more moderate level. A little anxiety is a good thing–it leads to optimal productivity–but too much is crippling. Start by listening to and addressing their personal concerns. Tell them exactly what is going to happen to them, as best you can predict. An honest sharing of information reduces their uncertainty. Anxiety is lower after we get bad news than while waiting for it!

Also help them "recharge" physically and emotionally by going easy on them for a while, and even by giving them some special perks like time off or a pizza party. The idea is to redirect some of their energy from working to "coping" so that they will recover more rapidly. (And the pizza and other perks give them extra energy.) Encourage them to support each other as they go through this trying time. Help them regain a feeling of "control" over short-term results of importance to them. And make sure you exert a calming influence through your behavior and example. Don't add to the stress and confusion at this critical time.

Anxiety is lower after we get bad news than while waiting for it!

Challenge

Push follower to "wake up" and get more involved in critical issues and concerns.

Orientations: Commitment (vs. competence). Task (vs. people).

Goals: Build participation commitment by making it clear to followers that they have a lot to lose if they don't participate fully. Get people to focus on the tasks at hand by making these tasks important to the people. Reduce the sense of complacency among followers so they will be less focused on their own wants and more concerned about what they need to do in order to succeed.

If your understanding of the situation leads you to believe changes must be made, then you need to share your understanding of the situation with your followers.

Detailed description of the challenge style

Your followers are complacent and set in their ways. They feel entitled to what they have and are no longer willing to work hard for it. They won't take risks. It is hard to get them focused for long on improving performance or learning new tasks. They need to be challenged. They need a wake-up call!

Your goal is to increase their insecurity levels in a positive manner. Create both positive and negative outcomes related to their performance. (For instance, you can link specific performance targets to bonuses.) Share information about the situation, especially the challenges and opportunities right now and how these are likely to affect them personally. If your understanding of the situation leads you to believe changes must be made, then you need to share your understanding of the situation with your followers. Don't shelter them from reality. Offer "tough love." Sometimes it is even advisable to "engineer" a crisis by allowing their apathy to lead to a fall rather than protecting them from such negative consequences.

Empathize

Listen to follower's side, understand how follower feels, and work with follower to choose appealing goals.

Orientations: Commitment (vs. competence). People (vs. task).

Goals: Build commitment to your leadership goals (cause commitment) by aligning these goals with followers' needs and concerns. Appreciate and relate to people's concerns and feelings. Let people know they are important and that you want them to feel good about their situation.

Detailed description of the empathize style

Your followers are not emotionally committed to your leadership and your goals. And they probably doubt your personal commitment to them. Until the cause *feels* right, they will have trouble committing to it and to any specific tasks associated with it. You need to win their hearts before you can win their minds. Do this by being empathetic. Listen to them, carefully and at length. Put yourself in their shoes. Don't dispute their views right now. Let them know you care how they feel. Remember Lao-Tzu's advice, "To lead the people, walk behind them." Spend as much time as you can with your followers, and make sure it's "quality time."

Your vision of the future is important right now. Share the feelings you have that make you enthusiastic about the goal or direction in which you are now trying to go, but don't overwhelm them with your opinions. Reach out to them through kindness, compassion, and a genuine concern for their development and success. This is the time to use those "right brain" interpersonal skills that help build rapport and enthusiasm. Also seek ways to use symbols and gestures that convey your concern for them and your enthusiasm for your cause.

Your vision is important right now–even if you don't have one! If you don't know what the right goal or direction is, then take time out, alone and also with your followers, to seek the right cause. Devote some time to reflection and clear-headed thinking in order to gain a clearer understanding of how events are unfolding and what you and your people need to do as a result. You need to find and communicate an intuitively appealing vision of the future before anyone will want to follow you there. This is a creative act, so prepare yourself and your followers accordingly. And then you need to project your vision, not so much in what you say as in what you do. Now is the time to "walk the walk," not "talk the talk."

> What you would seem to be, be really.
>
> —BENJAMIN FRANKLIN

Inform

Provide the information needed to convince follower of the wisdom of the "big picture" plans that guide follower's work.

Orientations: Commitment (vs. competence). Task (vs. people).

Goals: Build commitment to your leadership goals (cause commitment) by sharing the information and knowledge needed for people to see why these goals are so important. Give people enough background information about their work for them to get excited about the importance of performing that work quickly and well. Make sure people understand what the work is all about and how it fits into the big picture.

Detailed description of the inform style

Your followers are emotionally committed and ready to be lead, but they aren't sure you know which way to go. They are doubtful of or concerned about the direction. Even though they like and respect you, you still need to convince them that your goals and plans make sense. Your followers need to know that the cause is rational and logical, and the plans well designed. They don't want to "go off half cocked" or to engage in some "wild goose chase."

Show them the *evidence* that what you (or your organization) have in mind ought to work.

Their skepticism is justified–they have probably seen many programs and management fads come and go. So your task as a leader is to convince them that this is "for real." Show them the *evidence* that what you (or your organization) have in mind ought to work. Convince them that others within your organization or industry are or will soon be heading in the same direction, too. (Or, perhaps, that going in a different direction will help you outcompete those other firms.)

Encourage your followers to consider the alternatives in order to see that the pros and cons of the chosen one are most favorable. Don't discourage discussion and debate–you need followers to get involved by thinking hard about the issues right now. Just make sure debate is kept on an intellectual rather than emotional level so that irrelevant feelings don't cloud their judgment. Anger has no place in these debates. Information does.

Even if followers don't have any real input into what the goals and plans will be, they still need to come to terms with them, and that requires a clear understanding of what the goals are and why they have been adopted. This starts with an understanding of how they will be affected by any changes, so be sure to translate your vision into detailed information that allows them to analyze it on a personal level.

Now is the time to "talk the talk" and encourage followers to do so, too. That way, everyone will be ready when it comes time to walk the talk.

Explain

Explain clearly what follower must do, why follower must do it, and make sure there is useful feedback about how follower does it.

Orientations: Commitment (vs. competence). Task (vs. people).

Goals: Build commitment to performing specific tasks by showing how these tasks relate to important goals, and by making sure followers can see how well they perform the tasks. Design feedback systems to make sure tasks keep on "explaining themselves" clearly to those performing them, even after you have gone on to other things. Get your people focused clearly on what they need to be doing, why they need to be doing it, and how well they are doing it.

Now your followers accept your leadership and go along with the "big picture" goal or cause—but that doesn't mean they understand their specific tasks or responsibilities.

Detailed description of the explain style

Now your followers accept your leadership and go along with the "big picture" goal or cause–but that doesn't mean they understand their specific tasks or responsibilities. They may be confused about what you expect of them right now. Or perhaps they understand what you are asking, but worry that it is inconsistent with your overall leadership goals or direction. It could even be that they agree the task makes sense, but that the existing systems in your organization make it dangerous or unrewarding for them to actually do it.

As a result of one or more of these problems, they have little enthusiasm for the tasks of most concern to you. They aren't focused on the tasks you need them to do. You need to bring their full attention to the responsibilities of greatest importance right now. Do this by explaining clearly what their tasks are and why they matter. You don't need to spend a lot of time on this–saying the same thing over and over is unproductive–but do be clear and consistent.

They need that line of sight from their tasks to the ultimate goal or cause.

Don't overwhelm them with details of how to perform their tasks right now. All you want is for them to understand what their assignments are and why. They need that line of sight from their tasks to the ultimate goal or cause.

Ask for feedback from them about the task so that you can check their understanding. Did they "hear" you fully and accurately? Are the other messages they hear in the organization consistent with yours? If not, be patient. Go back over what you want them to do and why, this time trying to explain it in a more appropriate and helpful manner. There is no point trying to teach them how to do something until they know what they are supposed to do and why you want them to do it. So make sure to explain their roles and responsibilities clearly up front.

Oh, and one more thing. Be sure the task you have designed for them will make good sense and be motivating as they do it. Once their work starts, after all, the experience of doing the task will be far more important than your description of it. Is it a "whole" or natural unit of work? Will followers get the right sort of feedback–informational, not controlling, and positive as well as negative? If so, then their experiences with this task will reinforce your initial presentation of the task rather than contradict it. You need to make sure they never lose sight of the task or the reason for it. The view to the task and the view to the goal are both important in building and maintaining commitment to the task.

Direct

Oversee follower's work, telling follower exactly what to do and supervising and correcting as follower does it.

Orientations: Competence (vs. commitment). Task (vs. people).

Goals: Make up for a lack of competence by supervising your people carefully so that they do the job well. Help people do challenging work by giving them task-related instructions and support. Make sure your people don't make any serious mistakes as they perform important tasks.

Detailed description of the direct style

Your followers are ready and willing to tackle the tasks you have set for them, but they don't have the knowledge and experience they need to perform those tasks well. If they are already trying, their performance indicates a need for significant improvement. More likely, you are asking them to do something new enough that their abilities are unproved.

Don't push them into a position of responsibility too quickly. Start by supervising their work closely and instructing them in the necessary specifics. Encourage lots of questions and "what-if" speculations. Tell them what to do, when, and how in order to get them involved in the task at a high level.

Then immerse them in the work in such a way that they are (temporarily) protected from the dangers of failure. They need this initial safety zone to experiment and "mess around" in order to do real-world learning about the task. And you need to give them this safety net in order to make sure they don't mess up your important tasks!

It is helpful to show them how to do the work, by your own example or by asking someone skilled at the task to demonstrate and act as mentor. A demonstration is worth a thousand words. But remember that you are directing and judging their work, but not judging them. Give them lots of performance feedback–positive as well

Immerse them in the work in such a way that they are (temporarily) protected from the dangers of failure.

"The game is the best coach."

as negative–about what they do and how they do it. Keep the feedback informational rather than controlling. And keep the feedback about the task and how it is going, not about the people doing it.

Be sure you don't blame them for mistakes or tell them they are stupid. Everyone has to start somewhere. Your ultimate objective in this style of leadership is simply to get them started. As they say in many sports, "The game is the best coach," so just give them enough information about the rules to get them out on the playing field.

And don't worry if they are too dependent upon you at this stage. It's natural for them to look to you for instructions or clarifications, and you should encourage this so that they don't mess up their work while they are gaining skills. Soon they will gain competence, and you will be able to turn more of the responsibilities and thinking over to them (by shifting to a guide and then a delegate leadership style). For now, however, you need to help them walk through whole tasks so that they can get a real feel for how to do them right.

Guide

Guide development by helping follower try new things that improve his or her skills.

Orientations: Competence (vs. commitment). People (vs. task).

Goals: Help people get better and better at what they do by guiding their learning and development. Turn your followers into highly competent people with the potential to be star performers. Identify people's weaknesses and help them develop in their weaker areas. Identify people's strengths and help them capitalize on their strongest areas.

Detailed description of the guide style

Your followers are no longer beginners. They are committed and capable enough to take on increasing responsibilities and

Forging Good Will Through Good Works with Jack Morton Co.

When Pharmacia and Upjohn merged, they faced that classic problem of how to integrate the two cultures and sets of employees into one motivated entity that identified with the newly created corporation. The Jack Morton Company, which specializes in experiential communications for its corporate clients, designed a series of events to bring the people together and forge a new identity and motivation in the work force. One of the most exciting events was a visit by employees to the Boggy Creek Gang Camp for chronically and terminally ill children. Teams of employees cooperated there to do landscaping work—for instance, they laid turf to create a new lawn. According to the Jack Morton Company, "This meaningful task lifted spirits" for the employees involved.

Analysis. I've spoken at one of the Jack Morton Company's events, and I can tell you that when they do something they go all out. I'll bet the employees got a lot of landscaping accomplished, and I know that many of them welcomed the opportunity to work with peers from the "other side" of the merger on a good cause. Cooperating on good works that benefit society is a great team-building exercise. It gives everyone a chance to accomplish something they feel proud of by working together. And since that's exactly what you want them to do at work, you can think of charitable work as a rehearsal for on-the-job motivation.

I recommend this approach highly. And when you start looking around, you'll find there are lots of charitable organizations that need your help. It's a real win–win to devote a day of employee training time to team projects on behalf of a local charity. As the folks at Jack Morton put it, it helps everyone "catch the spirit." Employees will feel good about themselves and what they've done, and that's a great foundation for future job motivation. ▣

develop into skilled performers in their own right. Now you need to stop telling them what to do and encourage them to learn through their own experience. All you need to do is tag along on their journey to keep them out of danger and give them new challenges when appropriate.

The key to their development now is clear, quick, accurate, and frequent feedback, but this should flow naturally from the task if you designed it well, so all you need to do is add your voice if they lose the path. Let the results tell them what to do, not you! And when you do have to step in, use as clear, open, genuine, and honest a communication style as possible. This will encourage them to be honest and open, too–making possible the accurate information flows so important to their development.

They are held back now by their lack of experience and knowledge, so structure their work to give them increasing responsibilities and exposure by shaping "stretch" goals that challenge them as much as their level of competence will comfortably permit.

As a teacher, you are a coach now, not a lecturer. Think like a coach. Design "practices" in which followers have to use key skills repeatedly. "Stretch" and "strengthen" them through on-the-job challenges and perhaps appropriate training as well.

When they ask you for advice, ask them what they would say if they were in charge instead of you. Then add your own ideas if necessary–but often it's not necessary. Also use continuous improvement goals to keep their work engaging and make their journey as challenging as they can handle. Ask them to propose ways to make their work processes flow more smoothly or to produce higher-quality results.

Expose them to multiple perspectives and information sources, for example, by requiring some job sharing or cross-training. If appropriate, expose them to quality data and feedback from their customers. Your goal now is to help them grow and develop through their work, in the hope that they will soon be even less dependent upon you. If you do this well enough, they will eventually be more skilled and knowledgeable about their work than you are!

MOTIVATION IDEA 26

Problem Playgrounds

Create common areas (in halls or lobbies) in which there are play materials or structures. Nerf basketball hoops. A sandbox table with tools for building castles. A dart board. Try to pick games that are not likely to lead to injury, that are fun to do with a small group, and that don't usually occupy people's attention for more than a half hour (no elaborate video games please!). Put a sign above the area saying Problem-Solving Area. See how people end up using it. (Idea: offer a selection of activities on a rotating basis to find out which work best.)

Benefits. Allows people to separate from thinking tasks long enough to gain some creative insight. Encourages interpersonal interactions among employees. Great for idea sharing and development and shows employees that you trust them to make appropriate use of their time. If you don't trust them, don't use this method because you will end up regulating how long people can play, which takes all the fun out of it, and then some.

Delegate

Trust follower to take on full responsibility for meaningful tasks.

Orientations: Competence (vs. commitment). Task (vs. people).

Goals: Minimize your involvement in getting a task done by pushing as much responsibility for it onto followers as possible. Take advantage of and build competencies in your people by giving them increasingly challenging tasks. Get work done quickly and well by giving it to the right people.

Detailed description of the delegate style

Your followers are ready to "fly on their own wings." They are increasingly uncomfortable with close supervision and control because they sense they are capable of guiding and controlling themselves to a high degree. If you overmanage them now, they feel that you are treating them like children and resent it. This can undermine their emotional support for your leadership, so it is important to "let go" and give them the trust they've earned. Recognize that this means taking some risks–things may go wrong when you turn more responsibilities over to your followers. But they are ready for this trust, and will show it by recovering from any problems quickly on their own, and by learning to avoid them in the future.

Many managers fail to understand the relationship between delegation and empowerment–and so don't delegate as fully as employees need them to. Delegating a trivial task does not involve much trust, so it is not empowering. The trick is to delegate gradually increasing responsibilities, for ever-more-difficult tasks. This "grows" the trust between you and your followers, encouraging them to be increasingly trustworthy and capable. At first, then, delegate small tasks. But gradually move to higher-level tasks, trusting followers to figure out what lower-level tasks they need to perform in order to accomplish a higher-level task.

Many managers fail to understand the relationship between delegation and empowerment—and so don't delegate as fully as employees need them to.

Trouble with Toys

This is a cautionary tale. It illustrates the ups and downs of trying to switch gears from managing on the resistance path to managing on the motivation path. It also happens to be a classic in the literature on participation, one of the first proofs that giving people more input and control is good for their motivation and performance. In this case, participation did boost performance, but was rejected anyway when it clashed with a prevailing command-and-control culture.

The setting is a toy factory's production line in the 1950s. It is staffed by women who sit at workbenches and paint dolls. It is a fancy new production line in which a conveyor belt carries dolls by at a carefully calculated "optimal rate" and the women are supposed to keep up with it by taking an unpainted doll off a hook, painting it, then putting it on the next free hook. Modern engineering at its best. Except the women hated the new system and their productivity was very low. The majority of hooks arrived empty at the far end of the conveyor belt and management decided to call in a consultant to find out what was wrong.

The consultant convinced the foreman to talk to the women. The foreman learned that the women felt the room was too hot and wanted fans. Management was sure fans were not going to help, but eventually decided to give the suggestion a try anyway. And production went up.

But it was still sub-optimal, and so the consultant continued to push management toward a dialog with the workers. Out of one of their meetings came the employee suggestion that the workers be allowed to control the speed of the belt. Again, the management was sure the idea was crazy, but with the consultant's encouragement, let them give it a try.

As soon as the women gained control over the speed of their production line, their morale and productivity went through the roof. They ran the belt slow at some times of the day, faster at others, working in a rhythm that suited them best. And soon their productivity was so high that management became upset, complaining that the women were earning higher bonuses than other workers elsewhere in the factory and that they were producing too much output for other departments to handle.

This case started with management's concern that these employees were not sufficiently motivated. By the end of the process, management felt that these employees were *too* motivated. Rather than adopt similar practices throughout the plant, management decided to fix the perceived problem of overproduction by reverting to a fixed-speed belt. But you can't turn back the hands of time. The women on the doll line had tasted something finer, and were no longer willing to put up with the old conditions. Most of them quit within a few months and the department reverted to its earlier poor performance levels.

Analysis. I think the analysis is as obvious to you as to me. You *can* achieve high motivation and performance when you loosen the controls and listen to your people. But once you've given them a chance to walk the motivation path, they will no longer accept the resistance path as passively as they did when they knew nothing better. If you are sincere about building motivation, go for it. But don't change your mind mid-stream or things may be worse than before. Just as a taste of freedom "spoils" the slave, so, too, a taste of control and flow spoils the employee, at least if you want to preserve the option of a coercive style of supervision. You have to stand up and choose. Which may explain why the striking success this case illustrated more than forty years ago has yet to be fully taken advantage of in most workplaces. Many managers have a very hard time letting go of the old ways, even when the evidence of better alternatives is crystal clear.

And always watch your followers from a distance so they know you care and know you know how they are performing. You must trust them to do it on their own—but don't ignore them! They need to be reassured that you value their work and consider the task important.

When you help someone develop sufficient commitment and competency to take on the work in a delegate style, you are free to focus your leadership efforts on others who are not as far along in their development. Whenever you start delegating to someone, stop and ask yourself if there is someone else whom you could now turn your leadership attention toward. That way, you are always "bringing someone up" through the C-Lead development cycle. And you will be rewarded as a leader by ever-higher performance levels on the part of your followers.

Parting Shots

This chapter has introduced you to the commitment-based leadership approach, in which you select an appropriate leadership style based upon your assessment of your employees' state. Do your employees have the multifaceted commitment to their work that is required for high motivation and the development of high competency levels? If not, you work on getting commitment right before you focus on the task and what they did wrong in it.

It is interesting to examine your own behavior as a leader to see whether you use the full range of styles available to you in the quest for motivated, competent employees. Did all those styles seem comfortable and familiar, or were some out of your normal range of behavior as a supervisor?

It is interesting to examine your own behavior as a leader to see whether you use the full range of styles available to you in the quest for motivated, competent employees.

In my studies of leadership style in businesses, I've surveyed many employees to find out which of these styles their managers use the most and the least fully. Interestingly, the most commonly used style is the delegate style, followed by the direct style. That means managers most often tell their people to *go do something*. And next most often, they tell them *how to do something*.

There are times when delegating is appropriate. But only when dealing with highly motivated and competent employees. It takes a

> He is not only idle who does nothing, but he is idle who might be better employed.
>
> —SOCRATES

lot of work to develop your people to the stage where you can safely delegate important tasks to them.

There are times when directing is appropriate, too. But only when employees have high commitment combined with a lack of skill. Too often, managers think employees who perform poorly don't know any better, when in fact they aren't motivated. They lack some form of commitment rather than basic skills. In which case, directing them in how to do the work is disrespectful of their competence and doesn't help raise performance levels significantly. In fact, it often hurts performance, frustrating the supervisor and employees alike.

So both the delegate and direct styles are greatly overused. Be careful not to fall into these two traps that so many other managers do. Think before you delegate to or direct your employees.

The style that is the least used is the empathize style. Employees report that their managers do not seem at all empathetic.

What this suggests is that most managers are not using interpersonal skills and styles appropriate to the motivation path. They aren't taking a genuine interest in their employees. They aren't applying their interpersonal intelligence. And so they have no right to expect anything beyond minimum compliance and mediocre performances from their people.

You've reviewed a great many powerful motivational techniques in this book. You've learned a lot about what creates true motivation. Please keep in mind that much of it requires an empathetic approach and a good ear. You need to motivate people as individuals, reaching out to them one at a time to encourage them to grow and develop. Each one needs to be given opportunities to succeed because success is the greatest motivator of all.

Good luck on your quest for higher motivation. I wish you well, and I believe you are better prepared and more concerned than most managers, and therefore far more likely to succeed in your quest.

Appendix A

Planning, Creativity, and Motivation

This appendix is a useful guide if you are concerned about how to stimulate more independent thinking and creativity in your people. It is also relevant if you are developing a plan or working from a detailed plan of action since there are hidden links between planning, creativity, and motivation.

I bet I just combined three words you've never said in the same breath before. But planning, creativity, and motivation have a lot to do with one another if you think about it. Since people are motivated by development opportunities and the chance to accomplish something significant, you need to think about how planning and creativity both affect those opportunities to have motivating experiences. And it turns out that planning often gets in the way of those motivating opportunities, while opening things up to permit more creative improvisation helps bring about higher states of motivation. So *planning and creativity have significant and opposing effects on motivation.*

When Planning Destroys Motivation

Plans get in the way of high motivation in two serious ways.

Let's start with planning. Managers often resort to planning as an antidote to uncertainty and risk, and as a device for controlling the allocation of people, time, equipment, money, and any other limited resources.

So planning makes good sense. Without at least a little structured anticipation, most businesses would drift onto the nearest shoal in a hurry. That's the good side of planning.

However, plans get in the way of high motivation in two serious ways. First, they can easily overstructure and overcontrol people's work. For example, an annual plan for your department might well include projections for how much work will need to be performed in terms of people, hours, and salaries in order to produce whatever the plan says you must produce. Such projections are helpful for anticipating budget needs and making sure the goals are realistic, to be sure. And you need to do that sort of thinking at least once a year.

But for the rest of the year, that plan becomes a burden. Its projections are based on assumptions that can easily become constraints.

If you try, for example, to improve motivation through vertical job loading, you will end up wanting to change the nature of some of those jobs. But the *plan* says you have so many people doing such-and-such work. Can you really change the job descriptions in midstream?

Or will what's written in the plan keep you from being able to experiment with one of the most powerful levers in your entire motivation toolbox? Probably the latter. In which case, you, like so many managers before you, have become a prisoner of the plan. That plan's projections of the future have now become descriptions of the future, and if you don't fit the description, you are going to get into trouble.

Never mind if you have a better idea that would boost productivity. That's not in the plan!

Avoid "Microplanning"

This folly of overplanning was first pointed out to me by Kitty Axelson, a friend who served as editor-in-chief of a newspaper for many years. She calls the problem "microplanning" and says it takes all the fun out of work by imposing excessive controls. Her opinion is that you need to make the goals very clear and inspiring, then support and keep an eye on employees as *they* figure out how to accomplish those goals. They will probably develop much better ideas than you could have when you were writing that annual plan. And they will be much more excited about executing their own plans than yours.

They will be much more excited about executing their own plans than yours.

In her business, for example, some editors tell reporters exactly what facts and quotes they want to see in a story. That's microplanning, and it is no more motivating than shopping for someone else's grocery list. She found that it worked far better to tell them what the objective was, then let them go out and develop their own approach to the story. Their work was better and more creative, and usually came in more quickly as well. Of course, sometimes somebody tries an idea that is just plain bad, in which case you have to work through the problems with them, and send them back to do it again. But as long as that is a rare occurrence, you should avoid more structured plans.

Most managers are too nervous to loosen up and see what happens.

In fact, I'd recommend *seeing how little planning you can get away with*. Cut back the level of detail in your plans and see what happens. When people ask you how to do something, say you want them to come up with ideas and run them by you or try them out to see what happens. If everything goes well, reduce your planning and control another notch and observe the results. At some point, you will probably run into the limits of their ability to handle tasks. The lack of structure will get to them. Then you can tighten back one notch and know that is the loosest level of planning you can use effectively with the group.

My feeling is that people are most motivated and are developing and achieving at their current limits *when your plans and controls are as loose as possible*. But most managers are too nervous to loosen up and see what happens, so they never find that optimal point. Please try to have more courage and a more experimental attitude toward planning and control than most managers do. If you feel yourself losing your nerve, just remember:

> **People are at their best when they work with the *least* control possible.**

So one way to think about your task as a manager is as continually seeking ways to loosen the controls over your people without hurting performance. If you worry about preventing damage as you loosen, then you can leave it to people's natural self-motivation to take care of the upside. They will feel renewed enthusiasm and engagement, and their motivation and productivity will rise, as if by magic.

But I use the phrase "the least control possible" for a good reason. If you throw people into an "empowered" situation in which they go from high structure to little or none, they will react negatively instead of positively. And motivation and performances will plummet. You can't expect people to create lots of new structure and control their own work all of a sudden. There is safety and comfort in those old plans and controls, even if there isn't much in the way of motivation. So don't make the empowerment mistake and throw them into the water so they can learn how to swim. Ease up gradually, a notch at a time, and wait for your people to become comfortable with their growing roles before pushing them into deeper water.

There is another problem with plans, aside from their tendency to provide the most structure possible instead of the least. That is the tendency for plans to be *wrong*. In this day and age (if not always), you simply can't write a plan that anticipates everything important that will happen. Try planning a single day and you'll see what I mean. If you can't follow a scripted plan exactly for yourself for a single day, then why should an entire department or company be able to follow a detailed plan for an entire year? It's absolute folly to even try, but try we do.

And when plans turn out to be off the mark, it is very frustrating for employees. They find themselves having to do things that don't seem right. And, even worse, they find themselves having to ignore or sidestep opportunities because they weren't in the plan. Boy, that sends a discouraging message to your employees!

Nobody would ever claim that telling people, "Do the wrong thing and don't even think about trying something better" is motivational. But that's what a plan's inaccuracies and failures to anticipate opportunities say, plain and simple. That's another good reason to try to get away with the least possible planning, not the most.

Nobody would ever claim that telling people, "Do the wrong thing and don't even think about trying something better" is motivational. But that's what a plan's inaccuracies and failures to anticipate opportunities say, plain and simple.

Creativity and Motivation

Creativity is in some ways the opposite of planning. You can be creative about what you do and how you do it if you don't have to follow a plan. When you reduce your planning, try to replace it with creativity. If you don't shoot for a more creative work force, by the way, the opposite of planning will be chaos instead of improvisation. Aside from the fact that chaos isn't so good for bottom-line results, it is not in the least bit motivational. You can't feel as though you are accomplishing anything if everything is falling down all around you. On the other hand, *creativity is highly motivational.* People feel great about themselves and their work when they are able to contribute something creative. Even finding a better way to do your own filing is a motivational event for an office employee. Any little acts of creativity are worthwhile, whether they are suitable for a formal suggestion system or not (and most aren't).

To make sure that your people think and act creatively to solve problems and pursue opportunities, you need to reduce the structural barriers to creativity in their workplace.

What are structural barriers to creativity? They are ways of working that put a wet blanket on innovative thinking and fresh ideas. And in my consulting and training work, I find that most organizations put a wet blanket on their people's creativity every day except the one day they bring me in. When I'm with a group of employees in a creativity session, we have a great time. We discover that they are full of creative ideas. I don't really have to teach them how to be creative at all. But the next morning, when they return to their routines and their supervisors, those creative ideas dive for cover. Because there are so many structural barriers that they never stand a chance.

It is true that people are about 2 percent as creative at work as they were when they were going to kindergarten. But it's because of their work, not them.

Who Said People Lose Their Creativity?

A number of leading books and studies on creativity cite an old statistic that says people lose all but 2 percent of their creativity by the time they are forty. I used to accept this statistic, too. But when I looked into it, I found out it came from studies of how people acted on the job, not how they *could* act. It measured current behavior, not future potential. And it is true that people are about 2 percent as creative at work as they were when they were going to kindergarten. But it's because of their work, not them.

You don't just lose creativity, like an appendix you had to have out. It's a basic human behavior, and if you have ever been highly creative in the past, you can easily be highly creative in the future. Furthermore, when you have a chance to tap into your creative potential at work, it is highly motivational.

So what can you do about the fact that your employees' natural creativity is probably being stifled? You can start by recognizing and encouraging creative behavior in yourself and your people. If someone is thinking, encourage them instead of discouraging them.

Creativity is after all a mental activity. And you hired your people for their brains far more than for their hands. So encourage them to think!

"I know that," I can hear you thinking. "I'd never discourage someone from thinking about their work." Well, none of us would on purpose, but in truth we all do. For instance:

- *Do you run meetings with a railroad track agenda?* That's what I call any sort of meeting plan that orders the thinking you'll do in the meeting. It forces everyone down a mental railroad track. First you talk about X, then Y, then Z. And it is considered inappropriate and disruptive to blurt out ideas or suggestions or questions that don't lie along that track. But creative ideas almost always pull you in some new direction. They cannot be scripted in advance. So employees learn to sit on their hands and ignore those creative rumblings in the backs of their brains. They try to make the journey down your railroad track with you even though it isn't usually an interesting journey since everyone knows where the train is going.
- *The alternative is to run meetings using what I call a blue-water agenda.* It invites people to travel wherever they want on a large body of water (or subject area) in order to come up with creative insights and suggestions. Instead of looking like a list of topics by order or time, it usually starts with a description of its purpose. For example, "We will meet this morning to explore the team projects and seek improvements to the process since we are running out of time and some teams are stuck." Note that the use of the word *explore* is important in these statements since it signals a blue-water condition instead of a railroad track to follow. Then the agenda usually substitutes a list of questions for the traditional list of topics and reports.

  The questions in a blue-water agenda represent your brainstorming on the problem, and are intended to jumpstart other people's imaginations. Don't number the questions or put them in any special order. And don't try to make people talk to the specific questions. It's enough to have thought

Employees learn to sit on their hands and ignore those creative rumblings in the backs of their brains.

None of these questions will lead to thoughtful, interesting, or even honest answers. You might as well not bother asking.

about them in advance. If you use this sort of plan for your staff meetings, and leave updating each other to e-mail or interoffice memos, then the meetings will bring out that latent creativity and prevent you from having to write detailed plans that probably wouldn't work anyway.

- *Do you ask closed questions?* A closed question is one that encourages a yes, no, or other highly structured answer. Here are some examples:

  "Do you know what you are doing there?"
  "When do you think you will be done?"
  "Are you having any trouble?"
  "Did you know that you messed up another invoice yesterday?"
  "Can you give us a report on your team's progress to date?"

  None of these questions will lead to thoughtful, interesting, or even honest answers. You might as well not bother asking. The ones that force a yes or no response obviously prevent the employee from opening up and telling you what's really going on. But other questions do, too, for less obvious reasons. When you ask for a report on the team's progress, for instance, the employee gets a pretty clear and structured image of what you want. It should sound like a formal report of what's been done. And it should emphasize progress. If the employee has a nagging fear that the team's basic approach or instructions are flawed, you will not learn about it. Because your question closed off that answer. Nor will you learn about any new and better ideas the team has had unless the employee is especially self-confident and bold. After all, your question didn't ask for creative ideas, did it?
- *Do you (really) listen to people's ideas?* The alternative to closed questions is open questions, ones that invite employees to structure the answer however they think best.

That gets them talking and you really listening. Open questions are ones that probe for or encourage details and ideas. "What do you think?" is the ultimate open question.

It's interesting that many employees find it very uncomfortable when their supervisor says, "So, Fred, what do *you* think?"

Poor Fred starts to sweat when he hears this question, and stammers out something inane like, "Um, ah, um, I mean, well, I guess you're on the right track. Yup." The reason open questions make employees uncomfortable is that they are not used to having their ideas and creativity valued. *They are afraid it's a trap.*

For instance, if you say, "So what do you think, Fred?" and Fred says, "Well, I actually think we're on the wrong track. If we approached the problem a different way . . ." What would the average manager say in return?

How about a curt, "Thanks, Fred, but that's not really very helpful right now. I don't think we can afford to dismiss the work we've done so far. Any other ideas?"

No. Not a one. After seeing poor Fred get slammed, nobody else is going to say a thing unless they think the manager already agrees with it. In practice, most managers ask false open questions–I call them *open/closed questions*. They open doors that lead to dead ends. They are insincere invitations.

Open/closed questions are avoided by savvy employees. And because most employees have learned to avoid them, they are fearful of any question that looks like an open question. It could be an open/closed question instead, and they might get another door slammed in their face.

So you have to be patient when you try to introduce open questions with your people. It will take a while for them to learn they can trust you. And you better be trustworthy. Don't ever close the door once you have opened it. You have to listen to their ideas respectfully, whether they seem useful or not.

It will take a while for them to learn they can trust you. And you better be trustworthy. Don't ever close the door once you have opened it.

When you rethink the way you organize and supervise your people, you find it is fairly easy to loosen some of the controls, stop microplanning, and give them many more opportunities to engage their creative intelligence at work. And these opportunities are highly motivational for employees. It's a classic win–win. You get more motivation and better ideas. They get opportunities to do challenging, interesting things in their work, instead of having to wait until the clock strikes five and they can escape to do something meaningful!

They get opportunities to do challenging, interesting things in their work.

Appendix B

Is It True?

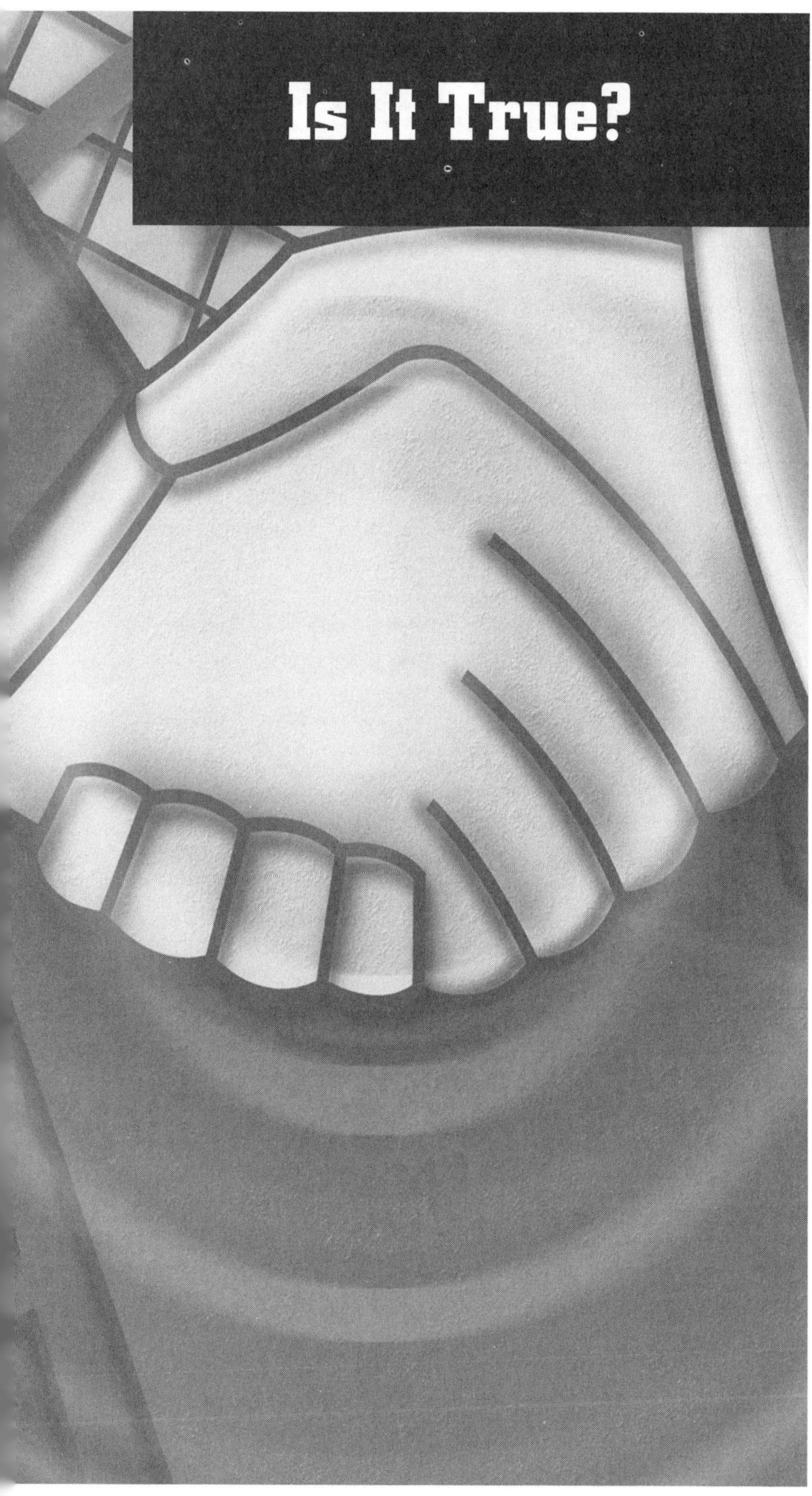

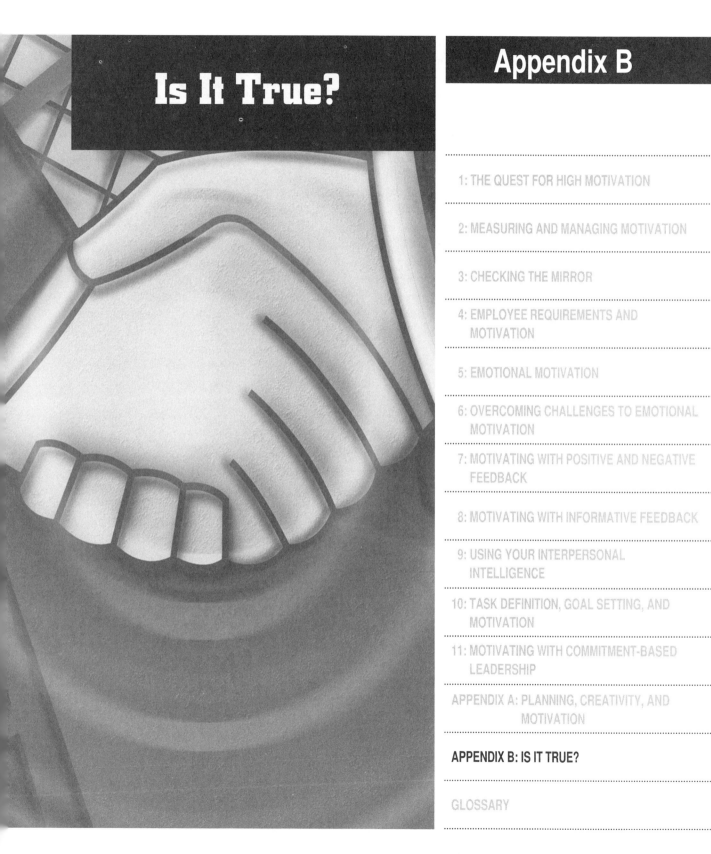

You've gotten an earful of my opinions about how to motivate and reward employees. But is it all true? Do I know what I'm talking about?

The question is a pressing one because most people are operating on a very different system than the one I describe. They are focusing predominantly on the resistance path, not the motivation path. They are coercing their people. They are getting tough with them, or they are—most often—simply ignoring them. Let's face it, most supervisors do not exhibit much concern for their employees. They certainly are not taking responsibility for how their employees feel, which is in my view the essential foundation of real motivation.

What I've presented you with is a contrary view of the workplace. A view that holds that the majority of managers are doing it wrong, so you should break ranks with them in order to achieve exceptional results for yourself and your people.

I expect you want to be absolutely *sure* I'm right before committing to a whole new approach. Once the excitement of reading about a new approach wears off, you will probably want to spend at least a few days thinking through the implications and deciding whether you will actually follow my advice. And I admire this caution. Management should always be approached with thoughtful concern. And I have to admit it's taken me many years of developing and testing these ideas before I was willing to put them in print, let alone use them wholeheartedly in my own work. I had to be sure, too. There is a lot at stake for both of us.

> Will the theory stand up to rigorous, formal testing in the real world of business management?

One approach to certainty is the one I have used repeatedly in the book—grounding the theory in common sense, in our daily experiences of life, in findings from psychology, and in studies of those who have truly achieved exceptional results. That's a pretty good way to develop and refine theory. But there is another way, too, another approach that I will share with you in this appendix. That is to actually *test the theory* in real-world business organizations in order to see if there are valid, statistical results to back it up. In other words, will the theory stand up to rigorous, formal testing in the real world of business management?

I've conducted one large-scale statistical study of my own, and I will share the findings of that work with you here. But I regard my study, for all the effort it entailed, as a fairly crude test. I worked with a little over a hundred companies. The results are striking, but I don't feel they provide the final word by any means. In addition, I focused on one particular group of companies–those engaged in adopting quality improvement methods.

So I am also going to share another set of studies with you, studies derived from a far larger and richer database compiled by the consulting and research firm Surcon International of Chicago. Richard Petronio, the president of Surcon, kindly agreed to share some findings from the company's experience surveying more than a million employees, compiled from studies of organizations in a dozen industries. I asked him if his data supported my theories before I began writing this book, and his initial input proved very helpful as I developed my thinking. Furthermore, while I was writing, he was performing some interesting statistical analyses using his large internal database. His findings form the second part of the scientific approach to proving the theory, and they, too, are covered in this appendix.

Let's have a look at the evidence.

Let's have a look at the evidence.

My Findings from Company Surveys

I became interested in the total quality management (TQM) initiatives of the 1980s and wrote a book of case studies of U.S. companies adopting the then-new TQM practices (it's called *Closing the Quality Gap: Lessons form America's Leading Companies*). I followed up this effort with survey-based studies of larger samples of companies to learn more about why some of these quality programs really worked and others didn't seem to make much difference. To make a long story very short, I tracked a bunch of variables (including those of importance to the Malcolm Baldrige National

I assumed that the major technical investments were at the root of any successes achieved.

Quality Award) and created a statistical model to describe the path from new quality methods to bottom-line results. I wanted to examine the impact of statistical process controls, quality teams, participatory management practices, benchmarking, process reengineering, and the many other innovations sweeping through businesses at the time.

The emphasis of total quality management practices is generally a technical one, and in fact the field tends to be dominated by quality engineers and statisticians. I, like most people, assumed that

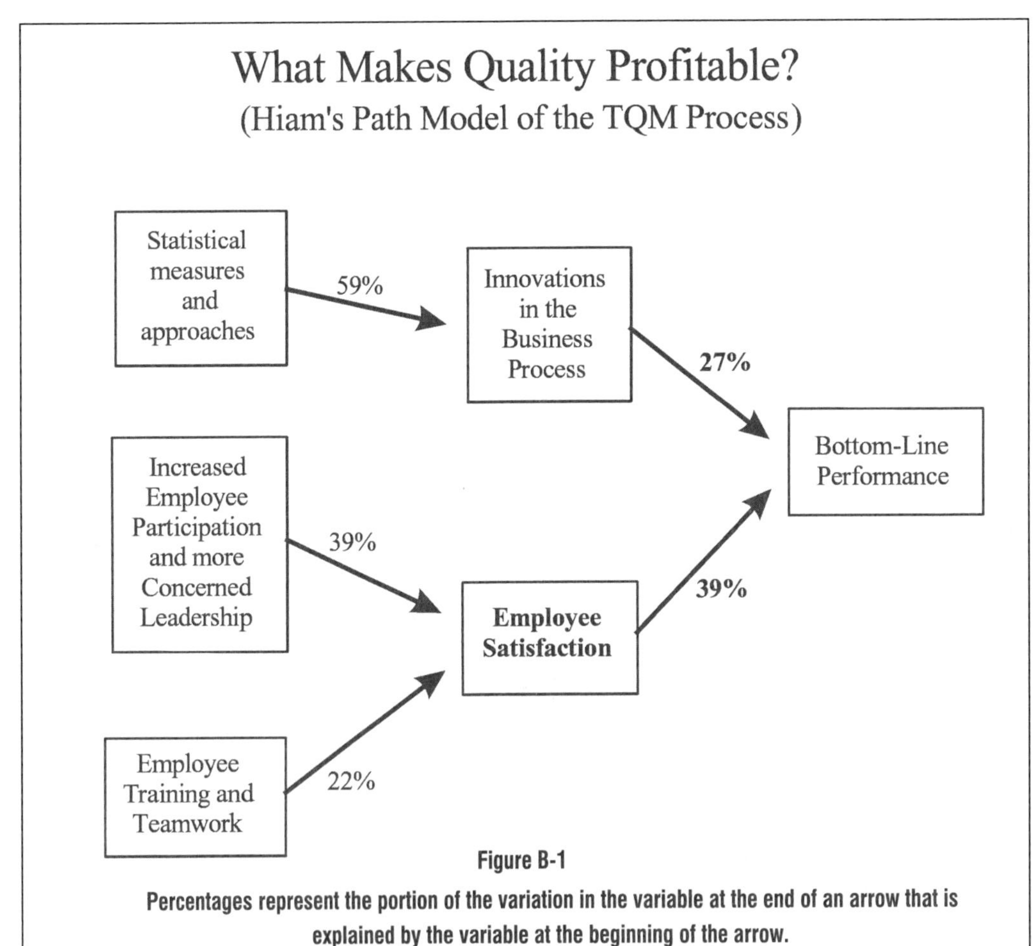

Figure B-1

Percentages represent the portion of the variation in the variable at the end of an arrow that is explained by the variable at the beginning of the arrow.

the major technical investments in new or improved business processes were at the root of any successes achieved. Well, I was wrong. Yes, the use of fancy statistics and new processes was important, but it was by no means the most important factor.

The classic technical components of total quality management explained about 27 percent of the variation in performance. (I measured business performance in terms of profitability, shareholder value, competitiveness, customer satisfaction, and market shares.) A 27 percent impact is not bad—these process factors obviously do have an impact on the performance of the business. But the surprising result was that *employee satisfaction had a far bigger impact.* It accounted for 39 percent of the variation in business performance. (That makes it 44 percent more important.) How employees felt about their work was the most important factor in whether TQM really profited the company or not. Figure B-1 summarizes my findings.

But in most of the companies I studied, employee feelings were treated as a minor or secondary consideration. As a result, many companies failed to reap significant benefits from the quality movement. In fact, I came to believe that the engineering mentality had blinded us to the key issues in making TQM work, contributing to the failure or minimization of TQM in many organizations.

In every company there is a formula relating management practices directly to bottom-line results.

I was interested to learn, some years after performing my study, that Sears had developed a similar statistical model of its own performance and was using it to effect a successful turnaround. In their experience, five-unit improvements in employee attitude could be linked directly to 1.3-unit increases in customer satisfaction, which in turn produced 0.5 percent increases in revenue growth. (If you want to see how their model works, look up the following article: Anthony J. Rucci, Steven P. Kirn, and Richard T. Quinn, "The Employee-Customer-Profit Chain at Sears," *Harvard Business Review,* Jan.–Feb. 1998.) My data from more than a hundred companies leads me to believe that every company has a formula similar to this one, but that most managers don't realize it. However, it wasn't until I learned about Surcon's findings that I realized many of these formulas had actually been worked out in detail already.

Surcon International's Results

Surcon International, Inc., is an organizational research consulting practice based in Chicago. It specializes in developing custom employee, management, and customer surveys to help improve performance or bring about positive change. The company is considered a leader in linking employee opinions to business performance, and I was especially pleased that Richard J. Petronio, Ph.D., president and CEO of Surcon, agreed to contribute some of his firm's findings to this book.

From 40 to 50 percent of profit margin fluctuations at companies are predictable based on employee feelings and opinions.

Petronio explains that Surcon's database includes data on employee attitudes and business performance from many companies, and that the statistical results indicate each company has a unique formula. Key variables have unique impacts on bottom-line success in each company his firm has studied. However, there are certain similarities between different companies (and similarities are more pronounced within industry groups). Working with a cross-company and cross-industry database, it is possible to make certain generalizations that hold for all companies.

The first generalization is that *from 40 to 50 percent of profit margin fluctuations at companies are predictable based on employee feelings and opinions*. The other 50 to 60 percent of profit fluctuations are explained by changes in the company's market, the economy, the political environment, and a host of other factors. In sum, positive attitudes alone don't ensure success, but they certainly have a large impact.

Petronio reports that most managers are greatly surprised by this powerful link from employee attitudes to company profits. In general, managers believe that the link between how employees feel and how much profit the company makes is a small one. It would not surprise the average manager to learn that employee attitudes explain a few percent of profits. But as much as half? No way. Most managers find that incredible.

Managers tend to view (and treat) employees as just another controllable expense. The idea that how employees *feel* might be critical to bottom-line results is a bit of a shocker. It certainly requires a major shift in approach for many managers (as we've seen in this book). But Surcon's statistics are clear on this point. How employees feel is the biggest controllable contributor to bottom-line profitability in many organizations. (And why not? Who does the work of the organization, after all?)

The second broadly applicable finding from Surcon's database is that survey-based measures of employee motivation are strong predictors of profit margins in the typical organization. At Surcon, employee motivation is measured by several variables: job satisfaction, desire to work, and organizational commitment. These tend to be interrelated, and for our purposes, we can consider them equivalent to the employee motivation construct this book has described and explored. If you measure how satisfied people are with their jobs, how motivated they feel to perform their jobs, and how committed they say they are to their work, you are doing a pretty good job of measuring their job motivation. (Note that the job motivation level inventory in Chapter 2 should produce results that track fairly closely to Surcon's measures.) According to Petronio, "We find about a .53 correlation between the three motivation-related categories and profit." Which means that a significant portion of the variation in profits is explained by changes in these motivation-related measures in Surcon's studies.

Some people look at a number like that and reason that the causation may flow the other way. Could it be that employees are more happy and motivated at companies with high profits than low? Surcon has performed extensive statistical analyses to find out what causes what. Petronio explains that, "It is not changes in profit margin that produce employee attitudes, but rather the other direction. Management concern, work group cohesiveness, and other primary results drive profits via the attitudinal results. In our analyses, profit margins don't predict attitudinal results."

Two factors pop up in every organization.

The third finding of importance to us is that Surcon's database gives us clear indicators of *which factors drive employee motivation*. Petronio finds that two factors pop up in every organization. They are both concerned with how supervisors relate to employees. So supervision can and does drive motivation, which can and does drive profits. The intricacies of how you relate to employees on a daily basis do trickle down to the bottom-line results in a very real and tangible way according to the analysis. And what are these two key supervision factors? They are:

- *Initiation of job structure.* When supervisors are good at organizing and structuring work, identifying who does what, managing and teaching the technical aspects of the work, and generally providing appropriate structure and roles for each employee, employee motivation is higher. A concern with task structure and definition is key. Surcon's findings support the recommendation in this book that you focus on creating and managing opportunities for your employees. And it suggests that the task-oriented aspects of commitment-based leadership are especially important as you define employee opportunities. Chapters 10 and 11 cover practical techniques for providing appropriate job structure, and Surcon's findings prove that use of such techniques is relevant to the motivation–profit equation. (Also note that your use of feedback has a great deal to do with job structure. You can use feedback to create appropriate structure for employees based on the techniques in Chapters 7 and 8 of this book.)
- *Consideration.* When supervisors are considerate of employees, when they are good at listening, communicate well, make themselves available, and are considerate of employees' feelings, employee motivation is higher. An empathetic concern for how employees are feeling and doing is key. Surcon's findings support the recommendation in this book that you focus on how your employees feel, and make sure they have the kind of environment and the kind of emotional foundations necessary for high motivation. Chapters 3 through 5 are clearly about this consideration dimension, and Surcon's findings demonstrate the power of this approach to build motivation and boost profits. In addition, the other chapters of the book explore related issues and also have much to do with this consideration factor. And note that Surcon's findings point to the central importance

An empathetic concern for how employees are feeling and doing is key.

> of the empathize style in commitment-based leadership (see Chapter 11).
>
> It may interest you to learn that I've found in independent studies of leadership style that employees rate their supervisors and managers the lowest on the empathize style. At most companies, employees don't feel their managers are empathetic or considerate. Evidently, we all have considerable room for progress on the consideration dimension!

Initiation of job structure and *consideration* are the two key variables that cross company and industry boundaries in their power to drive motivation and profits in the Surcon database. No matter what company or industry you are in, these are important to your management style and have considerable power over your bottom line. And it is interesting to see that they correspond to the two classic variables in the literature on leadership and management. Initiation of job structure requires you to focus on the *task*, and consideration for employees requires you to focus on the *people*. And task and people are the two dimensions of the commitment-based leadership model covered in this book. The findings lend additional support to this approach to leadership.

It is also interesting to think about the many factors that *aren't* critical to results in the Surcon database. The company measures many variables, such as working conditions and job security, that one might think would be key. However, they have a negligible impact compared to initiation of structure and consideration for employees.

There is also a fourth conclusion from Petronio's study that is relevant to this book. It is the finding that a motivational approach based on high consideration and careful job structure wins out over more conventional approaches *in the long term*. If you track these variables for two or three years, you generally find that motivation and profits rise with them. But you don't find as strong an impact in the short term. You may have to wait more than a month or two to see profits actually rise. And this makes intuitive sense because people do have long memories. It takes a while to redefine your relationship with your people. If you just show up one morning acting

A motivational approach based on high consideration and careful job structure wins out over more conventional approaches *in the long term.*

completely differently, people will not take the change at face value. They will remember the old you. They will not embrace the new you until they are sure it is the *real* you. So the motivation path is going to take a little while to travel. The methods in this book are not guaranteed to transform your bottom line overnight.

> The initial bottom-line feedback from the Chainsaw Al style of management is often positive. So it is easy to be seduced by the resistance path.

What can you do if you care only about the short term? Is there a fast way to produce results? Yes, according to the Surcon studies. If you take a strict, task-oriented approach, ignoring employee feelings and needs, you will poison the well and damage your long-term results. But you may see a short-term boost in results. In Surcon's studies, an autocratic management style, when combined with high structure, may increase results in the short term. It will also create stress, resentment, and turnover, and so hurt long-term results. But it may pay off in the short term. Which explains why many managers continue to walk the resistance path. The initial bottom-line feedback from the Chainsaw Al style of management is often positive. So it is easy to be seduced by the resistance path. When the house of cards collapses, you can jump to another job and leave it to someone else to rebuild.

But you don't really want to do that. Not when it is possible to build a solid foundation and create durable motivation and long-term profitability! In Surcon's studies, a participative management style based on what Petronio calls considerate leadership will increase commitment and create sustainable results.

For example, take the case of two plants within the same company. This is a good example because the company, product, and other possible contributors to results were the same in each plant. Their main difference was a difference in management style. The results are summarized in Figure B-2.

Surcon surveyed the employees in each plant and found that one plant fit the profile of participative management, the other of autocratic management. In the first plant, fairness, concern, and consideration scores were about 20 to 50 percent higher than in the second plant. As a result, in the first plant, employee motivation scores were 35 to 40 percent higher than in the second plant. And as a further result, the first plant's performance (in terms of quality,

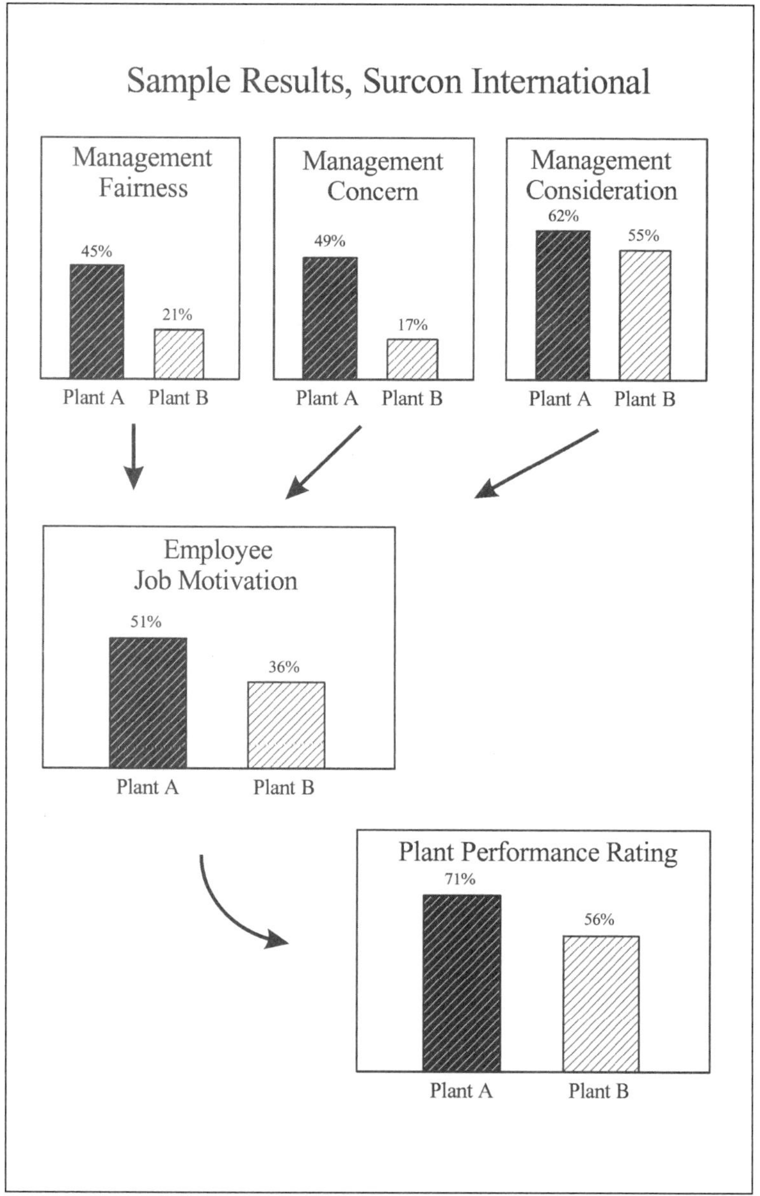
Sample Results, Surcon International
Management Fairness
45%
21%
Plant A
Plant B
Management Concern
49%
17%
Plant A
Plant B
Management Consideration
62%
55%
Plant A
Plant B
Employee Job Motivation
51%
36%
Plant A
Plant B
Plant Performance Rating
71%
56%
Plant A
Plant B

Figure B-2

efficiency, and productivity) was rated about 25 percent higher than the second plant's performance.

In addition, the two plants were both engaged in implementing significant companywide changes, and the first plant's change results were more than 50 percent higher than the second plant's results.

In this case, as in many others, employee consideration and job structure drive motivation and produce a more productive and flexible organization. Any short-term benefits of the more traditional, top-down style of management prove unsustainable. The bottom-line differences between the two methods are striking.

The bottom-line differences between the two methods are striking.

Is it true that a considerate, individual approach to employees motivates them to produce exceptional results? According to the available evidence, the answer is a loud yes.

If you wish to contact Surcon directly, their phone number is 773-883-1229 and their Web site is: **www.Surcon.com**.

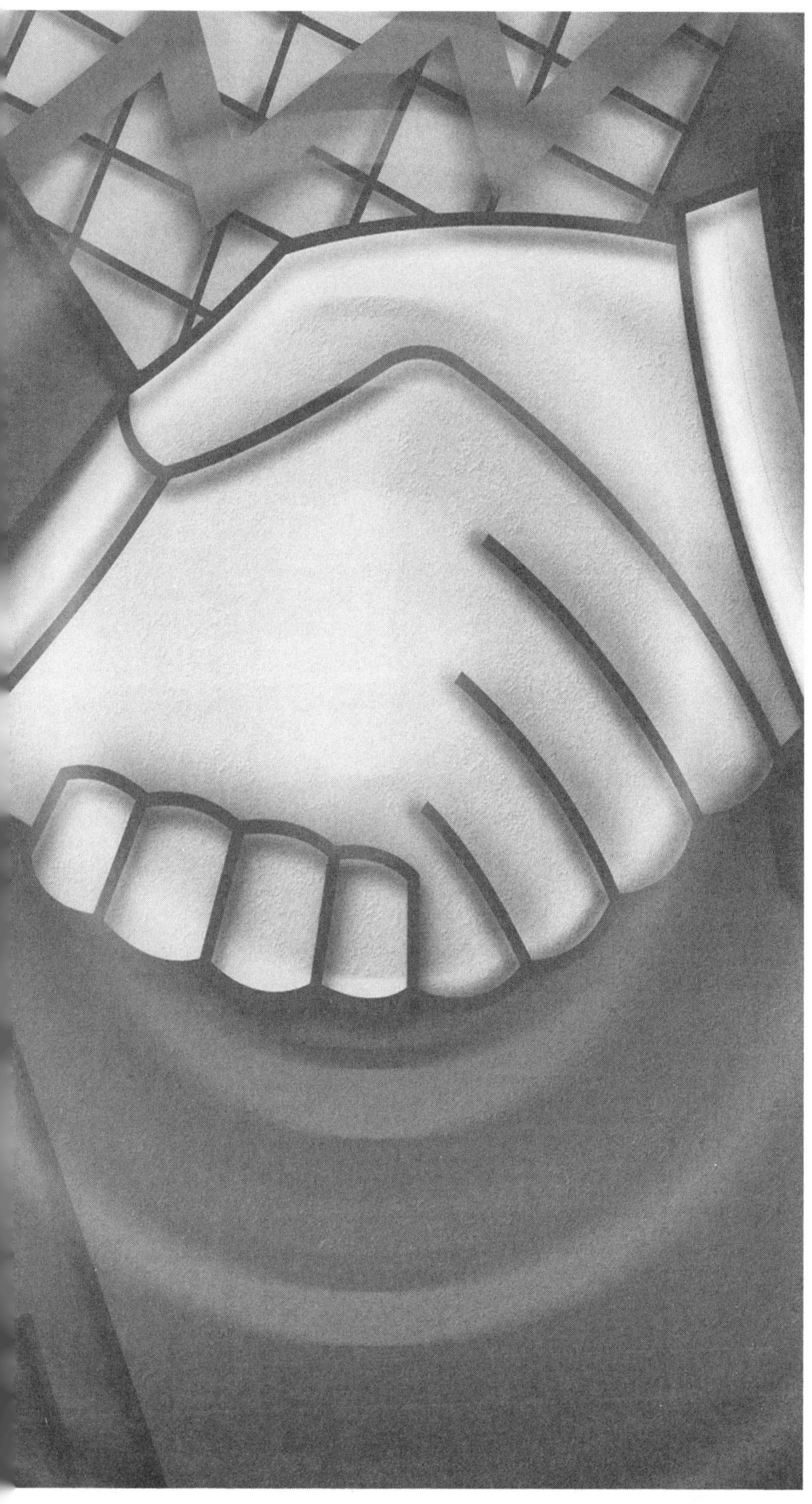

Glossary

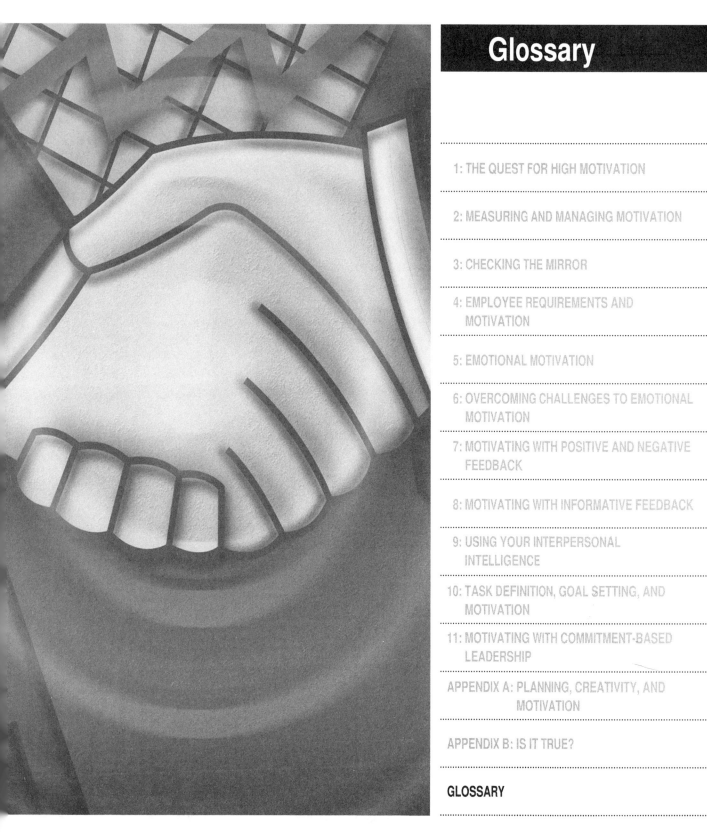

Achievement. The accomplishment of worthwhile goals or endeavors. *Highly* motivational to employees. When managers design work environments, tasks, and feedback systems such that it is feasible for employees to achieve high success levels, then the employees are optimally motivated and engaged in their work.

Closed question. Any question that limits the possible answers, such as a yes/no question or a question imposing a structure to the answer. Managers usually use closed questions with their employees, preventing the employees from expressing their honest opinions and feelings as a result. See *open question* and *open/closed question.*

Commitment. When used by employees, commitment refers to their concerns that management be consistently behind whatever new direction it asks employees to go. When used by managers in commitment-based leadership, it refers to employees having the foundation of being emotionally compelled to pursue managers' job goals or objectives for them. It is built up out of commitment to performing in the workplace situation, commitment to pursuing a goal or cause through the work, and commitment to performing specific tasks because they relate to the cause.

Creativity. The natural engagement of your imagination to solve problems and develop new ideas and opportunities. Often thought of as making novel combinations of things or ideas. In the business context, creativity is important to motivation because employees who are encouraged to take a creative approach to their work feel a greater sense of responsibility, control, challenge, and accomplishment, all of which can contribute significantly to motivation.

Development opportunities. Chances to try something new and challenging or interesting. Employees thrive on development opportunities, which may be provided in the form of new "stretch" performance goals, opportunities to do creative problem solving, enriched job definitions, and other task-oriented challenges. A job promotion is a form of development opportunity, but since supervisors rarely have the chance to promote someone, they need to think of many smaller opportunities to offer employees on a more regular basis.

Emotional motivation. An approach to motivating employees in which you first make sure the employees feel good about themselves and optimistic and hopeful about the work they have to perform. This creates the emotional foundations for high intrinsic motivation.

Fairness. An important employee concern is that they be treated fairly compared to other employees, other similar workplaces, and general concepts of worker and human rights. Yet the fairness requirement is often violated, damaging employee motivation as a result.

Fear. Employees often feel some fear of their managers because the managers don't appear fully trustworthy and because the managers have considerable power over the employees. Fear gets in the way of motivating employees.

Feedback. Visible results arising from one's behavior. Employees need plenty of feedback to know how they are doing and to make it interesting and challenging to improve their performances. Feedback can be negative or positive, informative or controlling, clear or unclear, so managers need to think long and hard about their employees' feedback. In general, feedback is the key to ongoing motivation and performance improvement. The essential reward for doing a good job is to receive positive feedback about the performance. All other rewards are secondary.

Flow. A term coined by psychologist Mihaly Csikzentmihalyi to describe the feeling of total absorption and pleasure experienced by people when they are doing a challenging, engaging task well.

Incentives. Extrinsic, or external, prizes or benefits of any form when used to reward employee performance. Incentives tend to be controlling and not to increase the intrinsic motivation to perform the job itself, so they are incompatible with the motivation path and fit better on the resistance path.

Informative feedback. Feedback that gives the employee useful information about his or her performance. The opposite of informative feedback is controlling feedback, which tells the employee how the manager or organization feels about the performance instead of how the performance itself is. Informative feedback makes employees less dependent upon their supervisors and encourages the development of high intrinsic motivation.

Interpersonal intelligence. Understanding of and ability to use a wide range of interpersonal skills, along with sufficient empathy and genuineness to be able to know when they are appropriate. Interpersonal intelligence is key to success in supervision and management and is the basis of successful leadership.

Intrinsic motivation. Motivation that wells up from within. The urge to succeed is an internal motivation. See *extrinsic motivation*.

Job enrichment. Redesigning work to create more opportunities for achievement and recognition. Opposite of job loading, which adds more work without making the work inherently more important, interesting, or challenging. One simple way to enrich a job is to loosen management control over it so that the employee has more autonomy. Another way is to encourage the employee to develop and apply special expertise.

Job motivation level (JML). A general indicator of how motivated to perform an employee is; measured by the JML inventory (see Chapter 2).

Motivation. The urge to do something because of either external or internal factors. The urge to avoid a danger is an externally stimulated motivation. The urge to accomplish something important is an internally stimulated motivation. Managers or supervisors wishing to optimize their employees' performance need to focus on creating the circumstances for strong, internally generated motivation to succeed.

Motivation curve. The range of motivation, from high to low and from motivation to survive to motivation to succeed. Motivation is generally high in survival situations, and also in situations where there is high opportunity to succeed. In the middle, the curve falls to a low because motivation is lowest when neither state is present. Yet that is the case for many people in their daily work routines, which explains why employees often appear not to be motivated.

Motivation path. A developmental path in which employees pursue challenging workplace opportunities and develop increasing levels of intrinsic motivation in order to achieve high levels of commitment and competence in their work. Makes work more meaningful and intrinsically rewarding for employees, and produces higher and more sustainable performance levels than the resistance path. See *resistance path*.

Motivator. There is no such thing as a simple external factor that creates motivation in others. Managers often use the word *motivator* in the mistaken belief that there are programs or rewards that will create high internal motivation in their people as if by magic.

Open/closed question. Any question that invites employees to voice opinions and ideas, but then cuts them off with a curt dismissal or a criticism of their ideas. Such question styles are commonly used by managers, and they discourage employees from saying what they think.

Open communications. A condition in which employees feel they have ready access to the information they need to understand their situation and pursue performance improvements and other opportunities for success. To most employees, open communications is the number-one issue, and they feel that managers are not open to them.

Open question. Any question that invites employees to voice opinions or ideas. Supervisors generally need to practice asking open questions instead of closed questions. Open questions encourage a thoughtful, informative answer that requires thinking on the part of the employee. Opposite of closed questions, which generally require a yes, no, or other short answer. Managers often ask closed questions, which discourage employees from voicing their thoughts or sharing full information. Open questions stimulate open communication and also encourage employees to think about their work and to take a creative problem-solving approach. Therefore, managers should use open questions as much as possible if they want to maximize employee motivation. See *closed question* and *open/closed question*.

Opportunity. Any situation that is recognized by the employees as providing the potential for them to achieve their personal goals, such as opportunities to succeed in a new or challenging task or to achieve higher levels of competence and performance quality in current tasks.

Optimal experience. The absorption in an engaging, challenging activity that leads a person to experience flow. Managers can optimize employee motivation and performance by seeking situations in which employees can have optimal experiences at work. See *flow*.

Performance puzzle. The dilemma many managers experience in which their incentive and reward programs fail to produce lasting change or progress. The performance puzzle is the result of reliance on extrinsic motivation instead of intrinsic motivation, and is a characteristic result of the resistance-path approach to management. See *resistance path*.

Performance review. A periodic, formal review of the employee's performance that generally serves administrative goals, such as providing data with which to make decisions about how to allocate funds earmarked for raises. Because the performance review serves organizational purposes and becomes part of the employee's formal record, it is regarded with just suspicion by many employees. It is no substitute for one-on-one, individual feedback and will not produce motivation or performance improvement. Also, the performance review's infrequent and often arbitrary nature makes it very low in task clarity, which further reduces its motivational power. If your organization uses performance reviews, minimize their damage by giving your employees as favorable reviews as you can. And develop other forms of feedback so that you don't count on the performance review to help you motivate your people.

Recognition. Notice of achievement by peers, supervisors, or the organization as a whole. Because achievement is such a strong motivator, recognition of that achievement is also important to employee motivation. Praise is the simplest form of recognition, but tangible and symbolic rewards of many kinds also provide valuable recognition.

Resistance. Feelings that interfere with the employee's efforts to comply with job requirements or supervisor requests. Resistance to change and resistance to increased productivity or quality are all common forms of workplace resistance. When employees feel they are being told or forced to do something that they worry might be detrimental to them, they naturally feel resistance. They also feel resistance when they sense a lack of respect, fairness, security, or other basic needs in the workplace.

Resistance path. A developmental path in which employees are pushed through controlling feedback and threats or rewards to achieve higher performance. Produces temporary performance peaks based on raised extrinsic motivation, but fails to produce sustainable high levels of motivation. Characteristic of the majority of workplaces. See *motivation path.*

Respect. A general requirement of employees is that they be treated with respect by their employers, yet this requirement is often violated, and employee motivation is damaged as a result.

Rewards. Good things that happen for the employee as a direct result of good performances. The basic reward every employee needs is positive feedback when performances are good. Additional rewards can be used to add variety to this foundation of performance feedback or to make note of exceptional performances. The best of these exceptional employee rewards are development opportunities and recognition for special achievement. Praise from supervisors is a potent form of employee reward. And there is an incredible range of tangible and symbolic rewards, such as certificates, plaques, honorary titles, gifts, gift certificates, and trips. Warning! Rewards should always be for performances, not people. If you reward people for what they've done, then you are providing useful performance-oriented feedback.

Security. A feeling of being safe from threats or risks in one's work, at least for long enough to be able to concentrate on the work at hand.

Task clarity. A condition in which employees receive accurate, rapid feedback about aspects of their performance that they can control. Task clarity stimulates intrinsic motivation. Employees often lack task clarity, so supervisors should work on increasing the quality of feedback in order to boost motivation.

Threats. Any stated or implied negative consequences used by the organization or the supervisor to compel employees to comply. Threats are destructive to employee motivation.

Verbal abuse. Inappropriate, rude, or angry verbal behavior that puts employees down and hurts their self-image. Many managers are abusive without realizing it, and their behavior dampens their employees' motivation.

Index

INDEX

About the Author

Alexander Watson Hiam (High-am) acquired his understanding of employee motivation through a series of research projects in the areas of leadership, change, motivation, total quality management, teamwork, sales management and related areas, as well as through his active consulting and training practice. He received his undergraduate degree in anthropology from Harvard and his MBA in strategy from U.C. Berkeley, and currently runs a consulting and training firm in Amherst, Massachusetts. Hiam has consulted for a wide range of organizations, including General Motors, The Coca-Cola Company, Kellogg's, The Vermont Country Store, Mass Mutual, Spalding Sports Worldwide, JIAN, and American International College. He also served as a visiting lecturer at several business schools, most recently at U. Mass Amherst.

His books and works include *The Vest-Pocket CEO, The Vest-Pocket Marketer, The Entrepreneur's Complete Sourcebook, Closing The Quality Gap: Lessons from America's Leading Companies, The Manager's Pocket Guide to Creativity, The Portable Conference on Change Management, The Portable MBA in Marketing, Adventure Careers, Marketing for Dummies, Think Before You Speak,* and *The Fast-Forward MBA in Negotiating and Deal-Making* (with Roy Lewicki). His training programs include Flex Style Negotiating, The Personal Creativity Assessment, and Quality Function Deployment. Hiam also co-authored *Exploring the World of Business* with Ken Blanchard, Bob Nelson and Charles Schewe.

He welcomes professional inquiries at his business address or at **hiam@javanet.com**. And for specific inquires about employee motivation or additional information and motivation tools, please visit the **streetwisemotivation.com** Web site.

Related Products and Services

General. Alexander Hiam & Associates provides a full range of executive-level consultations. It's mission is to help individuals and their organizations develop and perform better. Its emphasis is on developing and sharing insights of value to employees, supervisors and executives. Services include consulting, training, decision-making support, diagnostics, and facilitation. Specific consultation and training practices exist in the areas of innovation, leadership, marketing and business development, and employee motivation.

Motivation. The Job Motivation Level Inventory and related assessment and training products are available from Alexander Hiam & Associates, 69 South Pleasant Street, Suite 204, Amherst, MA 01002 (or call 413-253-3658 for details). Trainings and presentations are available on the subject of motivation as well–please visit our Web site at **streetwisemotivation.com** for the latest events and offerings.

Questions? Please feel free to visit **streetwisemotivation.com** or **infoworth.com** to ask Alex for an opinion on your motivation or other management questions. Or if you prefer the telephone, call his office at 413-253-3658.